C000116899

Cafés and Bars is part of a seri[es] historical, theoretical and prac[tical] It looks at the architectural sig[...] history and how their materia[...] possibly facilitated, the social [...] renowned. Contemporary café [...] of significant designers and ar[chitects whose concepts are informed] by a precise yet highly intuitive understanding of the role of interior design in visual strategy and branding.

The book begins with a collection of essays tracing the development of cafés, coffee houses and bars from the mid-seventeenth century until the present day. These are followed by a series 21 case studies that are drawn in time and place from 1826 to 1999 and from the Parisian boulevard café to the Viennese Kaffeehaus and the English pub, and which show the vast range of form taken by the café over the centuries.

Illustrated throughout with a wealth of photographs and line drawings, this book is an innovative and important contribution to the literature of architectural and interior design theory.

Christoph Grafe is an architect based in Amsterdam and London, and Associate Professor of Architectural Design/Interiors at Delft University of Technology. An editor of the architectural journal *OASE* and the *Journal of Architecture*, he has published widely on post-war European and contemporary Dutch architecture and the modern public interior.

Franziska Bollerey is Professor of History of Architecture and Town Planning at Delft University of Technology and director of the Institute of History of Art, Architecture and Urbanism (IHAAU) at Delft. She has published widely on utopian urban and architectural models, architecture and town planning of the early twentieth century and the emergence of the modern metropolis.

Cafés and Bars

Interior Architecture series

Christoph Grafe, series editor

Interiors play a significant role in the patterns of changing use and meaning in contemporary cities. Often designed as short-term proposals in existing (and often former industrial or commercial) buildings, their designers are able to respond flexibly to larger developments on an urban and global scale, both following fashions and trends and establishing them. In the design discipline, there is high level of awareness of new developments in the wider cultural field, including the visual arts, popular visual culture, advertising and media, that other disciplines within the architectural profession sometimes lack.

At the same time, the study of interiors is a largely untheorized field, operating largely outside the traditional territory of academic thought. This series aims at an investigation of the historical, theoretical and practical aspects of interiors by subjecting the results of current design activity and historical precedents to academic examination, discussing them at the level of technical solutions (light, materials and services), and against a wider cultural and historic background. All volumes contain a series of critical articles, texts by practitioners and documentation of key projects which have been selected to illustrate both their place in the history of design and the architectural solutions employed by their designers. The volumes in the Interior Architecture series can be used as handbooks for the practitioner and as critical introductions to the history of material culture and architecture.

Forthcoming titles
Boutiques and Other Retail Spaces
The architecture of seduction
Edited by David Vernet and Leontine de Wit

Routledge
Taylor & Francis Group
NEW YORK AND LONDON

Cafés and Bars

The Architecture of Public Display

Edited by Christoph Grafe
and Franziska Bollerey

Additional research by Charlotte van Wijk

INTERIOR ARCHITECTURE

First published 2007 by Routledge
2 Park Square, Milton Park, Abingdon, Oxon, OX14 4RN

Simultaneously published in the USA and Canada by Routledge
270 Madison Avenue, New York, NY 10016

Routledge is an imprint of the Taylor & Francis Group, an informa
business

Design concept by Claudia Schenk
Typeset in Akkurat and Chaparral by Florence Production Limited
Printed and bound in Great Britain by The Cromwell Press, Trowbridge,
Wiltshire

The authors and publishers would like to thank the individuals and
institutions credited on pages vi–vii for giving permission to reproduce
illustrations. We have made every effort to contact copyright holders,
but if any errors have been made we would be happy to correct them
at a later printing.

British Library Cataloguing in Publication Data
A catalogue record for this book is available from the British Library

Library of Congress Cataloging-in-Publication Data
A catalog record for this book has been requested

ISBN10 0-415-36327-6 (hbk)
ISBN10 0-415- 36328-4 (pbk)

ISBN13 978-0-415-36327-3 (hbk)
ISBN13 978-0-415-36328-0 (pbk)
ISBN13 978-0-203-01363-2 (ebk)

Contents

Illustration credits

Franziska Bollerey is Professor of History of Architecture and Town Planning at Delft University of Technology and Director of the Institute of History of Art, Architecture and Urbanism (IHAAU) at Delft. Her research centres on social, economic and cultural aspects of architecture and urbanism. She has published widely on utopian urban and architectural models, architecture and town planning of the early twentieth century and the emergence of the modern metropolis. Her most recent publication, *Mythos Metropolis: The City as a Motif for Writers, Painters and Film Directors*, appeared in 2006.

Hermann Czech is an architect in Vienna. After his studies with Ernst Plischke and Konrad Wachsmann, he set up his own practice, which has been responsible for a large variety of projects, including a series of public interiors. He has published widely on architectural culture in Vienna and modern architecture and was the winner of the Vienna Architecture Prize in 1985. He has taught as a guest professor in Vienna, at Harvard and Zurich.

Christoph Grafe is an architect and writer based in Amsterdam and London, and Associate Professor of Architectural Design/Interior at Delft University of Technology. An editor of the architectural journal *OASE* and the *Journal of Architecture*, he has published widely on post-war European and contemporary Dutch architecture and the modern public interior.

Acknowledgements

We would like to thank all the contributors to this book: the case studies contributors, Irene Cieraad, Udo Garritzmann, Filip Geerts, Otakar Macel, Eireen Schreurs, Cor Wagenaar, Willemijn Wilms Floet and Jurjen Zeinstra, all at TU Delft; Christopher Woodward for both his advice and his contribution; Holger Pump-Uhlmann of TU Braunschweig, whose research in archives and libraries in Germany, Austria and Italy was essential and who contributed two case studies; Axel Föhl for advice and translating one of the two introductory essays; Michael Lucas, who provided the beautiful drawings of all the case study projects; Wendy van Os-Thompson and Robyn Dalziel-de Jong for translating and Dlaine Camp for editing; Susan Dunsmore for polishing the manuscript further; Katherine Morton for keeping the production on the road; Claudia Schenk for her graphic design; and, finally, Caroline Mallinder for having faith in the project and her invaluable advice at every stage.

The ideas for this publication were developed in extensive discussions at the Institute of the History of Art, Architecture and Urbanism and the Interiors Research Group and we would like to thank all our colleagues, and particularly Professor Tony Fretton for his unfailing support.

In the various archives and institutions we contacted for the material in this book we would like to thank all who have helped us, including James Lafferty-Furphy, Ingrid Kastel, Eva Farnberger, Francesca Velardita, Adrian Reginald Allen, Dion Neutra, Simon Elliot, Sandro Bisa, Shoko Hara, Paul Suijker, Hervé Degand, Anne-Françoise Jumeau , Audrey Magnan, Cecilia Rueda Ruiz, Dianella Gobbato, Peter Elze, Ursula Köhler, Jindřich Chatrný, Jürgen Uhlmann, Markus Holmer, Christine Hoh-Slodczyk, the Bezirksamt Charlottenburg-Wilmersdorf der Stadt Berlin, Luc Boegly, Mihail Moldoveanu, Philippe Ruault, Mitsumasa Fujitsuka, Charlotte Huisman, Gustav Lohrmann and Letje Lips.

Foreword

Cafes and Bars: The Architecture of Public Display is the second book in the 'Interior Architecture' series, edited by the Chair of Interiors at TU Delft, which aims to disseminate the research and teaching on public interiors to the wider world.

In our view, the field of public interiors encompasses everything from the largest public spaces to the smallest places of social transaction. Our investigation is into how they are made and how members of society come together in them, as well as understanding them and their times.

Unlike paintings, plays or films, interiors and buildings are a part of the everyday material world and are always around us. Yet within this ubiquity and apparent inflexibility the things designers create are sensually and socially charged, applying distinct approaches and techniques that have developed in the practices of Architecture and Interior Design for this purpose.

With intuitive means similar to those that all human beings use in their daily lives, a designer will take common cultural knowledge and manners, buildings and objects that have acquired social meaning and modify them to suit the job in hand.

A well-designed café or bar will accommodate a client's feelings as they enter, wait at the bar or sit down alone or in a group. Issues such as physical and emotional comfort, status, privacy, display, rituals of use and behaviour will be at play and embodied directly in the building's fabric and fittings. Almost inevitably, and probably obliquely, the design of such a place will touch on the social, political and economic events that continue to shape the modern world.

Tony Fretton
Professor, Chair of Interiors
Faculty of Architecture
Technical University of Delft
The Netherlands

Introduction
Cafés and bars –
places for sociability
Christoph Grafe and
Franziska Bollerey

Caffé Canova, Crespano
del Grappa (2005).

Of all the institutions that have appeared and still have a place in the modern metropolis, the café may well be the one that has attracted the most attention from authors and artists, scholars and journalists. Cafés are at the heart of urban myths, they are celebrated as physical places and as somehow intangible sacred halls where works of art have been produced, revolutions plotted, lives made and hearts broken. This book presents cafés and bars as a type of space, of architecture as well as urban form, and as a background to public display and sociability, exploring in what way the material construction of these spaces has reflected, and possibly facilitated, the social and cultural practices for which cafés have provided a venue.

The existing literature on cafés and bars can be divided into several categories. There are richly illustrated compendiums of contemporary projects addressing professional designers and showing spectacular images of public interiors in which the hand of the designer is patently discernible. These are advertised by titles that invariably contain qualifications such as 'contemporary' or even 'hip', but these publications do not present cafés and bars as they can be experienced by their customers. Rather, they present images of carefully styled and framed interiors, often without a human being in sight, empty stage sets illuminated to great effect by halogen fireworks and studiously hidden light sources. Like most design publications, these books focus on exceptional and visually powerful projects that lend themselves to be reproduced and consumed as images. The presentation of cafés as *designed* interiors, not encumbered by traces of use and functional or decorative adjustments, has its precedent in the design encyclopaedias and manuals that appeared in the nineteenth century and were developed as a format by architectural publishers in the 1920s and 1930s and the post-war period. Aimed at professionals, these publications treat cafés and bars as part of architectural culture and as examples of how this culture might have an improving effect on the everyday environment by applying educated taste and rationality to commercial design.

Another type of literature will emphasize the role of cafés as meeting places of artists, writers or celebrities, with hardly any reference to the architectural form. Rich in anecdotal detail, these books are essentially exercises in local historiography and appear in the form of essayistic or literary studies of cafés in Paris, Vienna or other cities. This emphasis on the role of cafés in particular cities is not unexpected. The form given to places of sociability, after all, is closely related to the social codes and assumptions of specific local cultures. Yet, cafés are also places that show an almost endless variety of innovations and fashions; the vitality of nineteenth-century café culture is essentially a product of migration, of people and of ideals and cultural patterns. The development of the café is therefore also a history of cultural and economic exchange, from the Levantine merchants introducing coffee or chocolate as new exotic commodities and with them new forms of sociability, via the *patissiers* and *cafetiers* migrating from rural regions in Switzerland to Germany, or Alsations setting up brasseries in nineteenth-century Paris to today's migrant entrepreneurs populating large cities in Europe and North America. In the innumerable cafés that have emerged in the large and small cities of Europe and the Americas, from Montevideo to Odessa, Helsinki to Casablanca, this demand for a place of civilized, yet convivial sociability has materialized in sophisticated interiors emulating the models of Paris and Vienna. The types and styles invented for cafés are part of the pattern book of nineteenth-century urbanism and architecture, providing a template for the decorum for the public life of the various strata of the middle classes and the working man. Types of cafés and bars such as the Grand Café, the *Konditorei*, the English public house or the American bar were established across cultural boundaries as accepted concepts for commercial spaces and forms of public behaviour.

This is not merely a historical phenomenon. In contemporary cities, diversifying lifestyles have found their expression in reworkings of the established models for bars and cafés. These developments have attracted the attention of designers and architects whose sophisticated concepts for new bars are often informed by a precise, yet highly intuitive understanding of the role of interior spaces as part of the visual strategies aimed at diverse groups of urban consumers. At the same time, these designs also contribute to the refashioning of the image of entire cities such as Barcelona, Paris or London, addressing the need for flexible public environments for leisure and work.

This book aims to combine the study of material everyday culture with an examination of the development of a building type and the wealth of spatial, programmatic and decorative solutions invented for cafés. It presents the café as a material construction as well as a social construct. In two introductory chapters, the cultural history of the café and its typology are discussed. In Chapter 3, the reader finds a selection of texts about the people who populate coffee houses and Chapter 4 presents a statement by the Viennese architect Hermann Czech, who discusses the requirements and considerations that inform his designs of cafés.

The core of the book is a series of case studies, including the fully developed types of the Parisian boulevard café, the Viennese *Kaffeehaus* and the English pub of the late nineteenth century, twentieth-century experiments with these established models, as well as a variety of contemporary projects. All these examples are discussed in detail, showing the wide variety of forms that cafés have taken in the past three centuries and introducing the context, the main architectural and commercial patterns and management concepts that have emerged since the first coffee houses were introduced in Western Europe.

The café is many things: an object of nostalgia, a stage for inventing oneself, a place for creating relationships and a home, in the words of the Austrian critic, Alfred Polgar, 'for all who wish to be alone, but need sociability for this'. Café life represents one aspect of the ways in which people from different backgrounds have come to terms with transitory existence in the modern metropolis. For many, they were one of the few places in which these experiences could be negotiated in a space situated between private and public life spheres and between work and leisure. The longing for privacy, the staging of public display and the organization of a rational machinery at the service of hospitality, all these aspects and their effect on the physical arrangement of cafés and bars are presented in this book. Addressing the design intelligence, professional expertise and the contingencies of appropriation or fashion, we hope to contribute to the understanding of the phenomenon of the café and the role it has played in our culture, throughout the modern period and in the cities we inhabit today.

The architecture of cafés, coffee houses and public bars
Christoph Grafe

1.1
Café Sperl, Vienna (2008)

This chapter explores the architectural forms that cafés and bars have assumed in the modern metropolis as it has emerged since the seventeenth century. This may seem a straightforward proposal; after all, cafés are an essential part of everyday life, at least in cities in Europe and North America, and have played a pivotal role in urban cultures for centuries. We have learnt to take their existence for granted, as well as their general layout. Yet, as the most superficial glance will show, there are substantial differences between all establishments that are identified as cafés, and both the tourist and the entertainment industries exploit these differences in their efforts to attract custom. This survey of café typology describes the development of cafés in Europe and, to some degree, North America in the modern era since the seventeenth century. This period coincides with the introduction of coffee as a commodity and it might seem appropriate to define the café as an urban institution selling coffee. Such a definition would, however, be too limiting. While coffee obviously played a decisive role in the emergence of certain café types, no particular beverage should be taken as the *raison d'être* for these institutions. Rather, as the contributors of this book argue, it is the provision of places for sociability that defines the social function of cafés. It is this definition of the café that allows an extension of the range of types covered in this discussion. In many places in Europe, cafés serve coffee as well as other beverages, with or without alcohol, and have been doing so for three hundred years. The sharp distinction between cafés or coffee houses and taverns or pubs in England and North America, against this background, is an exception that disguises the fact that all these types are essentially places for different types of sociability.

This broad definition excludes restaurants which are distinguished by the emphasis on food preparation and consumption. The café may also serve food, but eating is neither a condition for use nor has it had a fundamental effect on the planning and arrangement of the establishment. Even so, the variety of individual solutions for the programme of the café is vast, indeed, so large that attempts at a systematic categorization are difficult. This survey departs from the observation that the great majority of cafés can be described either as a shop or as a public environment evoking a domestic atmosphere, a 'home away from home'. This relatively simple – and like all categorizations, simplifying – point of departure provides a framework for a discussion of cafés as types: evolving, mutating and influencing each other over a period of roughly three centuries and in very different cities.

Cafés may be quintessentially urban institutions possessing recognizable, to some degree universal, spatial characteristics, but as objects of architectural study they are generally ignored. Books on cafés tend to deal with their role in local cultural histories or the history of literary movements, or more generally the cultural history of drinking. Other publications will present mainly contemporary projects as material expressions of fashion. A history, informed by a typological analysis, as for other types of buildings and spaces (theatres, museums, or prisons) since the eighteenth century, does not exist for cafés. There is one exception to this lack of an academic treatment of café typology: in the professional attempt to include every aspect of the city in an encyclopaedia of all phenomena associated with building, nineteenth-century handbooks, particularly in Germany, included detailed information of the types of places for sociability that existed in the fully developed capitalist metropolis of this period. It is from publications like the *Handbuch der Architektur* (published in a series of editions between the 1880s and 1906)[1] and various more specialized surveys of café architecture that much of the material used here is derived.

1
Eduard Schmitt (ed.) with Josef Durm and Hermann Ende, *Handbuch der Architektur*, Stuttgart: Arnold Bergsträsser Verlagsbuchhandlung/A. Kröner, 1904, vol 4/1

If cafés and bars have not been subject to the kind of systematic study devoted to other types of buildings and interiors, this may also be explained by the fact that they were often the result of improvisation and intuitive decisions of their owners. The absence of published evidence seems to be directly related to the anonymity of the designers of many of the early coffee houses. Yet there are also examples of the involvement of professional architects, even if these remained exceptional well into the nineteenth century. Friedrich Schinkel, Claude Nicolas Ledoux or Robert Adam, for instance, are known to have contributed projects for coffee houses and by the 1870s the planning of metropolitan cafés and bars had become one of the types of commissions used by architects to launch their professional careers. Towards the end of the century, the 'artistic' café, tea room or bar made its appearance, the interior design employed as a form of propagating and demonstrating particular social and cultural agendas. These functions of the café as a place of sociability, public display and advertising form the recurrent motifs in this brief history of typology and interior design from the seventeenth to the twenty-first century.

The emergence of new forms of sociability

Public places where people gathered to be in the company of others have existed for as long as there have been records of urban settlements. Mediaeval European cities housed a large variety of institutions offering hospitality and sociability in exchange for payment. Wine cellars in German town halls or inns managed by religious congregations catered to travelling artisans and the members of guilds and other civic associations. Often located in or around civic or religious buildings, many of the inns and taverns derived their status from these host institutions and, at the same time, provided a venue for a large variety of social practices, ranging from ceremonial meetings to commercial transactions. This semi-official character was reflected in the hierarchical arrangement of rooms around a main hall invested with architectural and artistic representations of civic pride. The café-bar is related to a longer genealogy of places of sociability. The scale, however, on which venues for drinking and talking appeared in

European cities at the end of the seventeenth century and the invention of types still existing today suggest that the café-bar in most of its forms is essentially a phenomenon of the modern city, the type of city which is itself the product and the site of a market of goods and ideas.

The relation between the development of new economic and social arrangements and the emergence of new types of places of sociability is poignantly visible in the history of the London coffee house in the seventeenth and eighteenth centuries and it has remained one of the constant factors in the development of ever new types of cafés, bars or pubs ever since. In the developed capitalist metropolis of the nineteenth century, the rise of a sizable urban middle class offered the conditions for an extraordinary diversification and the almost infinite inventive energy of café entrepreneurs and brewers. The emergence of coffee houses, cafés and bars in eighteenth-century Paris or nineteenth-century Vienna, but also the development of the English pub into a place designed to provide a spark of glamour in the lives of the industrial working class, reflect the social and functional differentiation, newly established distinctions between spheres of production and leisure, the everyday and the ceremonial and the crystallization of a bourgeois public sphere.

Pre-modern forms of drinking in public, the consumption of beer, ale or wine in guild halls or wine cellars, tended to be associated with rituals of establishing a sense of commonality, many of which are retained to the present day.[2] In the café and coffee house, but also in public bars serving brandy and gin, these patterns of formalized collectivity were replaced by something more ambiguous. Rather than acting as a venue for corporate gatherings, the coffee house, and the nineteenth-century café or bar, operated as a commercial enterprise offering a place for forms of informal contact, newsgathering, social exchange and business transactions. This did not mean that the coffee house eliminated experiences of sociability. The interaction of its visitors, however, acquired a different nature; the explicit demonstration of collectivity was replaced by the act of entering an environment for private persons coming together in a publicly accessible space. It is exactly this function as a type of place where one could meet people from a large range of social backgrounds and the suspension of hierarchical relationships that allowed sociologists and political thinkers to identify the coffee house as one of the birthplaces of the modern public sphere.[3]

Selling coffee and more – differentiation and diversification

How is the character of the coffee house as a venue of informal sociability reflected in the architectural form of the spaces and their decoration? The popularization of coffee in the seventeenth and eighteenth centuries introduced new forms of sociability. At a time when cities like London or Amsterdam were establishing themselves as financial and commercial centres, the coffee house offered a venue

2
W. Schivelbusch, *Das Paradies, der Geschmack und die Vernunft – eine Geschichte der Genußmittel*, Munich: Hanser, 1980, p. 201

3
J. Habermas, *Strukturwandel der Öffentlichkeit*, Frankfurt: Luchterhand, 1961. An English translation, by T. Burger, was published only in 1989 as *The Structural Transformation of the Public Sphere: An Inquiry into a Category of Bourgeois Society*, Cambridge, MA: MIT Press, 1989

where transactions could be made, and where information that was potentially crucial could be obtained. Visiting the coffee house was a necessity in the daily struggle of establishing a position in the new economic system. The dynamic nature of an urban culture based on venture capitalism and colonial expansion, as well as small-scale manufacturing, is reflected in the rudimentary arrangements of the first coffee houses in the 1660s. A mere fifty years later, however, the design of the coffee house, its relative comfort or the display of a more or less educated taste had become part of the strategy of the owners to attract their clientele.

Amid the social and cultural changes that have affected coffee houses and cafés since the eighteenth century, there has been one constant factor: once the beverage had lost the appeal of an exotic novelty, serving coffee allowed little space for distinction, while the profit inevitably relied on a large turnover. Venues serving alcohol had the advantage that they could present their offerings as specialities but there, too, what was sold was seldom specific enough to fight competition. However wide the range of speciality beverages or however much sophistication was invested in the preparation of coffee, the main commodity a café could offer was sociability, in a venue where visitors were invited and able not only to meet other people but also present themselves as public personae. The range of additional services invented for cafés – newspaper tables, reading facilities, writing and typewriter rooms and, more recently, computer terminals and Wi-Fi networks – illustrates the constant need to diversify and to establish the enterprise as a venue for activities other than drinking coffee.

The introduction of coffee as a socially acceptable beverage, which stimulated its consumers rather than making them unfit for business, coincided with a profound change in public manners. Sober and keenly aware of the opportunities offered by the café, its visitors took up the invitation to use the institution as a place where they could improve themselves and their social standing. The design of the premises, then, became an essential ingredient in establishing the café as a micro-stage where the visitors could enact their chosen personalities.

Perhaps unsurprisingly, the development of specific café cultures is an indicator of the waves of modernization that have affected cities across Europe and the Americas in the past three centuries, from London in the seventeenth and eighteenth centuries, via pre-revolutionary and Haussmann Paris or 1920s Berlin to contemporary coffee lounges. The history of the forms, the spatial arrangements and the decorative patterns used for cafés are never very far removed from the economic and cultural developments associated with every major wave of modernization. New inventions, new types of cafés and gastronomic proposals tend to reflect these changes accurately, whether in celebrating technological innovations or in the expression of unease and nostalgia. Cafés develop within the existing building fabrics of cities, which are the products of local climate, social arrangements and particular urban cultures. New inventions or

1.2
Caffè Nero, Old Compton
Street/Frith Street, Soho,
London, 2006

fashions, generated by the desire of entrepreneurs and landlords to attract a larger clientele, found their limitations in these material and immaterial realities of ownership patterns, functional zoning, land values, rents and social mores, establishing the café as an institution and architectural type, both rooted in traditions and accommodating, even ushering in, broader cultural changes.

Shops: places for selling drinks

Before describing the development of cafés as shops or *boutiques* selling coffee or other beverages, it will be useful to define these terms. In most cases a space referred to as a shop can be described as the smallest type of commercial unit, a room usually directly accessible from the street and presenting itself to the outside world either through a window allowing a view of the inside or, less often, completely open to the pavement during the opening hours. The owners of the first coffee establishments could be said to have inherited the shop model as one of the possible forms of organizing their trade, especially since it had also been used for selling beer and wine over the counter for private use, and it is perhaps hardly surprising that many of the seventeenth-century coffee houses started their existence in this form which was well established and understood.

Although its oriental, exotic origin was one of the attractive aspects of coffee – in fact, the first example of Orientalism affecting everyday culture in the West – and despite the fact that many of the first coffee sellers shared this provenance, there is little evidence that the tradition of urban coffee houses existing in the major cities of the Ottoman Empire had any direct influence on the first places serving the drink in Western Europe in the seventeenth century. Travellers and merchants trading in the Levant had brought with them descriptions of the coffee houses of Constantinople, Smyrna (Izmir) or Damascus. Sometimes lavishly decorated and highly popular with men sipping coffee and smoking tobacco from water pipes, these houses attracted the curiosity of Europeans, but when the first beans arrived in the West, coffee was initially consumed in private circumstances.

The enterprise that a certain Pasqua Rosée, a man probably of Greek or Turkish origin, established in 1652/1653 in St Michael's Alley in London, in what has been described as 'an integrated retail and business space', was no more than a simple stall.[4] It featured decorated shutters providing rudimentary shelter for the customers when opened and a sign showing an image of the owner dressed in Oriental fashion. Coffee was roasted and brewed in the shed and sold over the counter. How the hot liquid was consumed is not clear, but it appears that patrons had a choice of either drinking it on the spot, standing at the counter, or taking their cup to the adjacent cloister.[5]

The coffee shops in other European cities were similar to Pasqua Rosée's enterprise in London. In Paris, for example, Armenian and Greek street vendors had started selling coffee from stalls, when in 1670 Francesco Procopio dei Coltelli set up a first coffee shop near the fair of St Germain. In contrast to the itinerant coffee sellers, Procope, as he called himself in Paris, explicitly targeted a respectable clientele by setting up his *boutique de café* in a fashionable neighbourhood.[6] In Venice, a reference to the origin of the coffee house as a shop was retained in the colloquial term for the numerous coffee houses occupying small commercial spaces in and around the Procuratie Nuove in the Piazza San Marco; the Caffè Florian and the Quadri (both of which still exist) started out as simple *botteghe da caffè*. In all of these cases, the alterations made for preparing and serving coffee were very small and in illustrations the shops invariably appear as sparse semi-interiors opening directly onto the arcade or the street.

In Vienna, the first commercial public coffee shop was opened after the Ottoman siege of 1683. Managed by an Armenian tradesman, it operated in the basement of a house and was referred to as a 'coffee vault', a name that was widely used in the eighteenth century in German-speaking countries.[7] Numerous coffee stalls set up by other Armenians, baptized Turks and former Ottoman soldiers followed, sometimes in other vaults, in other cases in small temporary booths or sheds, or occasionally in kiosks in a vaguely Oriental style positioned near bridges or gardens. In 1766, the Emperor Joseph II opened the largest of these green areas, the Prater, for public enjoyment, and

4
Markman Ellis, *Coffee House: A Cultural History*, London: Weidenfeld and Nicolson, 2004, p. 31

5
Ibid., p. 32

6
Yves-Marie Bercé, 'Le Procope', in Delphine Christophe and Georgina Letourmy (eds) *Paris et ses Cafés*, Paris: Marie de Paris, 2004, p. 39

7
Karl Teply, 'Die Anfänge des Wiener Kaffeehauses – Legenden und Fakten', in Reingard Witzmann and Hans Bisanz (eds), *Das Wiener Kaffeehaus, von den Anfängen bis zur Zwischenkriegszeit*, Vienna: Historisches Museum der Stadt Wien, 1980, p. 19

1.3
Street vendor, Torrington
Place, London, 2005

8
Ulla Heise, *Kaffee und Kaffeehaus – eine Bohne macht Kulturgeschichte*, Cologne: Kiepenheuer, 1997, p. 143

permitted the establishment of coffee houses and similar establishments. Here the temporary and mobile coffee stalls gave way to more permanent enterprises in houses and modest neoclassical villas like the first *Praterkaffeehaus*. The pattern of the shop, however, prevailed until the late eighteenth century; in 1781, a travelling correspondent observed that in the Imperial capital 'the coffee houses are arranged on the ground floor in the Italian manner and one enters them like a shop from the street'[8] – even the free-standing villa in the Prater presented itself to its visitors with a glass shop front.

The consolidation of coffee houses and their development from improvised stalls into urban institutions coincide with a steady increase in the size of newly founded establishments addressing the middle classes. During the eighteenth century, the half-open sheds disappeared as the coffee house became absorbed into the patterns of everyday life of the middle class. Emulating luxurious domestic rooms and salons, the design of cafés reflected and followed the fashions of architectural design from elegant classicism and rococo, via archaeological and fictional historicisms in the nineteenth century to the attempts at reform in the early twentieth century and the various stylistic proposals, futuristic or nostalgic, available to contemporary designers.

Most of these establishments were inaccessible to the working classes. Both in Paris and in Vienna, the working class continued to patronize the ambulant street sellers, who offered the drink from belly shops held by strings around the neck, which held a simple device for brewing coffee or a surrogate, as well as a few cups. The tradition of presenting prepared food and drinks in the form of an urban shop resurfaced, however, in new types of enterprises catering for the increasing working-class and artisan population. While the coffee houses turned themselves from shops into 'homes away from home', in the taverns and *guinguettes*, collective forms of drinking and bonding and of domestic appropriation disappeared as the organizational arrangements of guilds and workshops gave way to the anonymity of industrial production. Manual workers, whose everyday routines had been governed by highly local and integrated patterns of life and work, were the first to encounter the fragmentation of the early industrial metropolis, their lives increasingly divided between the spheres of work and reproduction. Often located halfway between the workplace and the overpopulated slum tenements or cottages, the tavern offered momentary relief from constraining realities.

Gin shops for the working man

The effect of these changes in the life of the urban working class is directly tangible in the development of the metropolitan gin shop in London. Whereas the traditional English taverns tended to present themselves as houses and consisted of a series of rooms of varying degrees of comfort and accessibility depending on the class of

9
Mark Girouard, *Victorian Pubs*,
New Haven, CT: Yale, 1984, p. 23

10
Schivelbusch, op. cit., p. 165

11
Girouard, op. cit., p. 20–1

customer, the gin and dram stores appearing in the course of the eighteenth century started to sell cheap alcohol, wine and beer across a counter either to be taken away or drunk on the spot.[9] This coincided with the popularization of strong alcoholic beverages such as brandy and gin.[10] In the early nineteenth century, this arrangement of drinks served at a counter was probably also introduced in existing taverns, while gin shops turned themselves into what the writer George Cruikshank described as 'gaudy, gold-beplastered temples' where gin was 'served by young women dressed up like the "belles Limonadières" of a Paris Coffee House'.[11] Glass shop fronts, richly carved mahogany woodwork and brass fittings were employed to advertise the shop in which drinks were now proudly displayed in decorative barrels or coloured bottles arranged behind a counter. The middle classes registered this transformation of the tavern as a public house into an urban shop with considerable amazement and concern. A Westminster grocer described how a tavern in his street was turned into a small drinks emporium with

> [a] splendid edifice, the front ornamented with pilasters, supporting a handsome cornice and entablature, and balustrades . . . the doorways were increased in number from one . . . to three . . . the floor was sunk as to be level with the street; and the doors and windows glazed with very large single squares of plate glass, and the gas fittings of the most costly description.[12]

12
Quoted in Girouard, op. cit., p. 22

Located along the major streets, the gin shops in early Victorian London and elsewhere served the needs of a rapidly expanding city, allowing continuous and quick service and producing a significantly higher turnover than any traditional tavern could have realized. As working people were forced to walk increasing distances between work and home, the gin shop found along the way attracted passers-by with cheap drink and some warmth. As Maurice Gorham wrote in 1949, in one of the first serious attempts to write the history of the Victorian pub: 'The gin-palaces were to the Victorian slum what the super-cinemas are to the drab districts today.'[13] At the same time, the transformation of the tavern into a shop for quick, anonymous drinking reinforced the resentment of the middle classes, and the urban pub became seen as an essentially working-class environment not to be entered by a gentleman, let alone a respectable lady: 'Visiting a pub in Victorian England is almost as scandalous as visiting a brothel'.[14]

13
Maurice Gorham, 'The Pub and the People', *The Architectural Review*, October 1949, p. 213

14
Schivelbusch, op. cit., p. 165

In Paris, both the working and the middle classes retained their use of the café, which occasionally operated as one of the few places where both social groups interacted. Yet, here too, social differences found their expression in different service and spatial arrangements. While the fashionable cafés on the boulevards appeared as festive rooms, often extending onto the first floors of the *immeuble* and featuring large street terraces, the typical Parisian working-class café

1.4
Parisian corner café, Avenue
Ledru Rollin/Rue de Charonne,
2005

15
W. Scott Haine, *The World of the Paris Café: Sociability among the French Working Classes*, Baltimore, MD: Johns Hopkins, 1996, p. 157

16
Handbuch der Architektur, op. cit., p. xx.

17
Ibid., p. 155

18
Haine, op. cit., p. 169

19
Ibid., p. 130

20
See the image of an early nineteenth-century Boston tavern in Perry R. Duis, *The Saloon: Public Drinking in Chicago and Boston 1880–1920*, Urbana, IL: The University of Illinois Press, 1983, page not numbered.

was described as 'a shop with no gas, few chairs and a lot of smoke'.[15] Situated on a street corner, allowing customers to walk in and out and catering to a mixed clientele, these cafés operated as neighbourhood shops, often combining the service of drinks with the sale of tobacco.[16] A degree of subtle social differentiation can still be observed in many Parisian cafés: while the terrace facing the street invites a mixed public ready to pay an extra charge for table service, the bar counter is the territory of the – mostly male – habitués, usually from the neighbourhood. Often the difference between standing and sitting customers reflects social distinctions; working-class camaraderie and middle-class private respectability both have their respective territories within the same space (Fig. 1.4).

The *Handbuch der Architektur* offers a characteristic example of a large café following the model of the shop facing a boulevard and extending deep into the urban block (Fig. 1.5). Situated on the Boulevard de Strasbourg, the Café du Globe is arranged as a series of distinct areas. Guests could observe the boulevard from a terrace, or retreat to the front salon subdivided by high banquettes into two sections. Behind this salon, the drawing shows a large beer hall, and at the rear two very large billiard rooms with 123 tables in total.[17] Also visible on the plan is the pattern of banquettes and tables positioned along the walls of the café, which is shown on numerous illustrations from the eighteenth century onwards.

In Paris, the counter, often covered in zinc, became a standard feature of bars and cafés after 1830. Its introduction had a dual effect: on the one hand, it allowed a higher degree of social mixing, allowing strangers to meet and interact, on the other, it emphasized the authority of the landlord or the couple owning the café.[18] The landlord acquired a new social role, as an arbiter of the affairs of the neighbourhood, while the 'zinc' itself became the notional centre of working-class sociability, compensating for the decreased influence of religious organization. In Scott Haine's description, the counter 'truly made the café and its owner analogous to the church and its priest'.[19] The display of coloured bottles, mirrors and other forms of decoration supported this symbolic function of the counter and its pivotal role in the social organization of the café and its neighbourhood.

Urban bars – territories for male bonding

In North America, the typological development of the bar is largely indebted to the English example. If one looks at images of older taverns, the interior looks not very different from older inns in England, featuring varnished wooden wainscoting and bar, simple colonial chairs and shelves for glasses and tin mugs on the back wall.[20] The display of gaudily coloured liquor bottles, which became the standard ingredient of most American bars and English public houses in the Victorian period, was still absent, as were the brass rails which were later noted with conspicuous interest by continental European travellers.

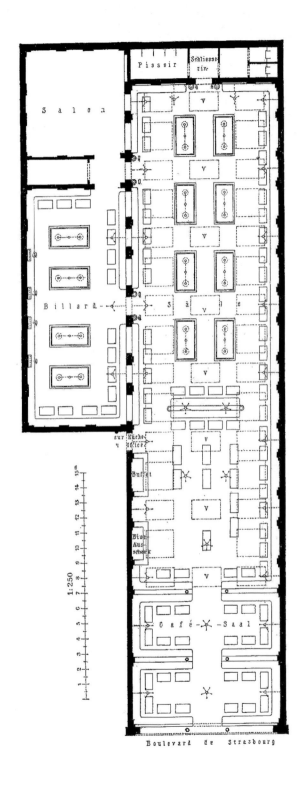

1.5
Boulevard Café: Café du
Globe, Paris

In the second half of the nineteenth century, the arrangement of bars and saloons in the quickly expanding industrial cities on the East Coast shows a tendency towards standardization, which was the result of the concentration of the drinks trade, as most bars were taken over by the large brewing companies. Anti-drinking campaigns and serious limits to the number of licensed bars contributed further to this concentration.[21] Brewers also provided fixtures in return for monthly repayment and agreements to serve their products exclusively, including the conventional back bar with mirror, furniture, swinging doors and kitchen equipment. Particularly in Chicago, this seems to have generated a need for saloonkeepers to distinguish themselves, trying to avoid the standardized appearance of many bars in the city. One, called 'Hester's Fish Camp', had a large live fish pond, another sported a bar made out of 480-year-old oak and yet another attracted potential customers with a bar 100 feet (30 m) long, advertised as the longest in the city.[22]

The arrangement of the urban bar as a shop designed to achieve maximum turnover in combination with a degree of anonymity unknown in continental cafés or taverns intrigued European commentators as much as they were taken aback by it (Fig. 1.6). In 1904, the authors of the *Handbuch* observed:

> In America, too (as well as in England), it is the custom to enjoy drinks standing. The guest has the barkeeper or his staff pour the desired drink and, if he wishes to make himself comfortable, drinks half-seated at the bar itself or at a table nearby. Mostly, however, the guest will consume his drink quickly standing, and pay in order to resume his business. There is an astonishing display of variety in the open shelves behind the bar, which are furnished with rows of exquisitely cut glass bottles, which are filled with a choice of contents and have often striking labels. These bottles serve for the mixing of drinks which are produced by mixing some of these liquors and other suitable ingredients and which are popular in America and are generally preferred to simple liquors.[23]

When the American bar was introduced into Europe in the 1890s, its character of a working- and lower middle-class venue was abandoned, as was the arrangement of the liquor shop itself. The *Handbuch* mentions the example of a hotel bar in Frankfurt, 'where the comfort of German guests is provided for by placing tables and chairs in the room'.[24] European 'American' bars such as Harry's New-York Bar in Paris (1911) adopted the arrangement with a long counter and the exuberant display of bottles from the transatlantic original, but the cultural associations had changed profoundly; while the American saloon bar had been designed to allow uncommitted social contact and camaraderie for clerks, artisans or salesmen, the European bars, which were often part of a large hotel, were decidedly more exclusive in character.

21
Ibid., p. 31

22
Ibid., p. 68

23
Schmitt, op. cit., p. 16

24
Ibid., p. 17

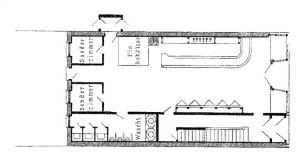

Sometimes bar owners went astonishingly far in their desire for Americana as symbols of modern sophistication: in Harry's Bar the full equipment of a New York bar was shipped to Europe, including the wooden panelling and the 10 m-long mahogany counter. Adolf Loos' American Bar ('Kärntnerbar', case study on p. 140) in Vienna of 1907/1908 is an example of a free, utterly Central European interpretation of this model.

Cake shops for the ladies

While the American bar, especially in the form of the Western saloon that entered popular imagination, would figure as one extreme example of a male-dominated, rough drinking venue, the *Konditorei*, which emerged in the early nineteenth century in German-speaking countries, represents one of the rare examples of a place designed for the social needs of an audience of both sexes. The *Konditorei* had its origins in cake and pastry shops, of which the coffee room was initially an extension. These shops were usually managed by immigrant *cafetier* dynasties from Eastern and Southern Switzerland setting up cafés in a variety of large cities; the Stehely and Josty families, for example, operated in Berlin, Hamburg, Bremen, Leipzig, Breslau (Wroclaw), Königsberg (Kaliningrad) and elsewhere. Unlike the plebeian taverns and cafés that were associated with critical debate and political activity, these establishments could rely on the implicit support of the authorities and launched themselves as institutions in the social life of respectable women.[25] Salons for playing cards and billiards, an essential element in most cafés, were absent and smoking was only allowed in special rooms, partly because a shop was expected to be free of smoke, partly to suit the female clientele that this type of enterprise particularly attracted and addressed. Like the Glasgow tea rooms (case study on p. 133), which emerged towards the end of the century and also catered to middle-class women (as well as men), the *Konditorei* relied on the display of bakery products, and selling cakes to take away remained an important commercial motive. The style of the outlet itself – light, 'feminine' pastel colours, refined elegant ornaments and direct access to the street – allowed the produce of the *Zuckerbäcker* (literally, sugar baker) to become absorbed in the decorative scheme of the shop. The layout of *Konditorei* Schilling, one of Berlin's cake-and-coffee institutions published in the *Handbuch*, is representative of this pattern;

25
Petra Sieling-Biehusen, 'Kaffee statt Schnaps – Die Bremer werden ordentlicher', in Christian Marzahn, *Genuß und Mäßigkeit*, Bremen: Temmen, 1995, p. 156

15 The architecture of cafés, coffee houses and public bars

the shop is situated on a corner, allowing daylight to enter into an enfilade of rooms along the façade. The first of these is the shop proper, dominated by a long counter for displaying cakes and sweets and leading into three smaller back rooms with up to four chairs each (Fig. 1.7).[26] From the 1870s, most of the old *Konditoreien* transformed themselves into large cafés and the shop function became less and less prominently visible, without, however, disappearing altogether, as the example of the Berlin Café Kranzler (case study on p. 172), rebuilt in the Western part of the city after the Second World War, illustrates.

Immediately before the Second World War, a technological innovation brought about a type of café that seemed to return to the old pattern of the *bottega da caffè*. In 1938, a new system of forcing hot water and steam through ground coffee was invented in Italy and after the war Giovanni Achille Gaggia, a bar owner in Milan, integrated these elements into the first modern espresso machine. Espresso bars had existed in the city in the 1930s, but the availability of a well-designed and functional element with which to prepare individual cups of coffee allowed the pattern of selling coffee over the counter to become popular. In Italy, espresso bars became symbols of the transformation of the country into a modern industrial nation, a message which was immediately taken up by café entrepreneurs and designers. They spared no effort to demonstrate the modernity then associated with stainless steel surfaces, glass and mirror walls and the use of teak veneers, marble or Formica, a material that had been invented in 1912 but was popularized in Europe during the 1950s. Persuaded by the stylish environment, young middle-class visitors were invited to accept that drinking a cup of espresso standing at a counter and chatting to the bar man was not only modern, but also deeply fashionable. In the following decade the espresso bar spread across Europe, and arrived also in London, where coffee shops managed by Italian families appeared in Soho, Knightsbridge and Chelsea (Fig. 1.9). Used by a mixture of tourists, businessmen and young intellectuals, the espresso bars were, according to the *Architectural Review*, among 'the first everyday environments to adopt and popularize the cheerful modernism of the Festival of Britain, allowing their customers to associate themselves with continental European style'.[27] Almost three hundred years after the first shop selling coffee opened its doors, London experienced what the author John Pearson described as an 'espresso revolution', the shops providing not only a beverage but signifying a cultural innovation.[28]

26
Schmitt, op. cit., p. 135

27
Marghanita Laski, *Architectural Review* 1118, March 1955, p. 166–7

28
John Pearson, 'Revolution Espresso', *The Listener*, 55(1401) (5 January 1956), p. 10

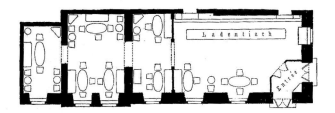

1.7
Konditorei: Café Schilling, Berlin

1.8
Konditorei: Dresden, 2005

1.9
Espresso bar: Bar Italia,
Soho, London, 2005

1.10
Café Américain, Leidseplein,
Amsterdam, 2006

17 The architecture of cafés, coffee houses and public bars

A home away from home

The emergence of the café in the seventeenth and eighteenth centuries not only introduced new forms of sociability. It also coincided with the emergence of quite another cultural concept, that of domesticity and 'home' as a place, a space and a mode of behaviour. The home of the middle classes was required to provide physical and mental comfort and warmth. Establishments selling coffee often managed to meet these requirements for a domestic environment, where private houses or apartments failed. The coffee 'house' offered what a new urban middle class was gradually learning to expect from the home and in its various forms this proposal of selling not only a beverage but also a warm, cosy and convivial environment became the common model for places of sociability, from the London coffee house of the eighteenth century via the mirror salons of Paris to the Viennese *Kaffeehaus* of the late 1800s.

The tendency of establishments selling coffee to remodel themselves as domestic arrangements became almost immediately visible after the beverage was introduce for consumption in public: when Pasqua Rosée's humble stall was made into a permanent institution and moved into a building opposite the first location, the simple shed became a house, establishing the precedent for the arrangement that would become the standard type for serving coffee to the middle classes, not only in London, but across Europe and the North American colonies in the eighteenth and nineteenth centuries. No images or plans of this second venue, a real coffee 'house', survive, but it appears that it was a large building possibly with four floors and allowing a view into the adjacent courtyard and the alley.[29] Offering a range of rooms and fitted with fires and stoves, the coffee house provided an environment that was more spacious, refined and warmer than most homes of the time and that emulated the domestic arrangements its visitor may have aspired to, but would not have been able to afford.

Following Rosée's example, a large number of London coffee houses established themselves as venues where a large variety of business and what we might now call leisure activities could take place. Coffee houses seem to have acted as postal centres, employment agencies, auction rooms, lost property offices, business addresses, gambling dens and Masonic lodges.[30] This extension beyond the prime purpose of the coffee house established a pattern of spatial and functional differentiation both inside the building and distinguishing different enterprises from each other. Besides the main coffee room, private rooms appeared, to which customers could retreat and which could be used for special events. The coffee house of Mr Garraway, situated near the Royal Exchange, for example, contained a sale room with a small rostrum for the auctioneer and seats for buyers. These events were advertised in the main coffee room of the house that

29
Markman Ellis, op. cit., p. 38

30
Antony Clayton, *London's Coffee Houses: A Stimulating Story*, London: Historical Publications, 2003, p. 43

31
Ellis, op. cit., p. 168

32
Aytoun Ellis, *The Penny Universities: A History of the Coffee Houses*, London: Secker and Warburg, 1956, p. 112

33
Advertisement, published in 1698 and held in the British Library

34
Markman Ellis, op. cit., pp. 169–70

35
Heise, op. cit., p. 142. Sometimes they reverted to being a tavern. The site of Pasqua Rosée's coffee house, for example, has been occupied by a wine bar since the nineteenth century

occupied the prominent corner site, allowing visitors to observe the surroundings. Garraway's, which existed until 1866, was tastefully decorated with 'panelled walls, gilded ornamentation, moulded ceilings, heavily craved chairs and tables' and the furnishings 'were of a rather better quality than those found in many private houses'.[31] The activities by which the coffee house distinguished itself from other establishments took place outside the main coffee room. In 1711, an emerging insurance company, the Sun Fire Office, for instance, took two rooms on the first floor of Garraway's before moving into a building of their own some ten years later.[32] Some coffee houses were stages for the presentation and publication of scientific demonstrations and popular lectures. In 1698, Moncreff's coffee house advertised an exhibition of 'a monster, that lately died, being human upwards, and bruit downwards' to be viewed at sixpence a visit, plus 'a very fine civet cat, spotted like a leopard'.[33] In other coffee houses auctions would have been held 'by the candle', using the period of a candle burning down as the interval during which customers could bid.[34] The coffee house became, as it were, a multifunctional institution in the network of commercial activities of the London financial and cultural market.

Although in London existing taverns and inns often reopened as coffee houses,[35] most of these venues were built as ordinary town houses and their domestic appearance can be explained by the modest scale of the existing buildings. Generally, the coffee house occupied rooms that were designed as domestic rooms and often the owner of the venue would live in other parts of the same building. Even where coffee houses were established in purpose-built venues, the character of a fashionable town house open to the public prevailed. The British coffee house designed by Robert Adam in 1770 (Fig. 1.11) was a four-storey building with three bays, each floor featuring a large tri-partite window divided by columns. Inside, the plans follow the conventional layout of the Georgian London house, albeit on a grander scale. On the ground floor and directly accessible from the street there was a 'Coffee Room' and the 'Bar' with the 'Chamber of the Master of the House' at the back. A second entrance gave access to a corridor connecting to a staircase leading to the two 'Chambers for Company' on the first or 'Principal' floor. There are no records of the interior decoration or furnishings, suggesting that these might have been rather simpler than the rather elaborate façade with its Spalatro, Ionic and Corinthian columns and classical urns would have suggested. The detailed drawing made for Sir John Soane in 1812, however, shows that the coffee room and the main room for company had a highly differentiated rectangular shape with an apse towards the back of the salon.[36]

In other cases, the domestic aspect was even more prominent. In the fashionable suburb of Chelsea, Don Saltero's coffee house occupied an entire building that was furnished, in what might today

36
David King, *The Complete Works of Robert and James Adam*, Oxford: Butterworth, 1991, pp. 42–3

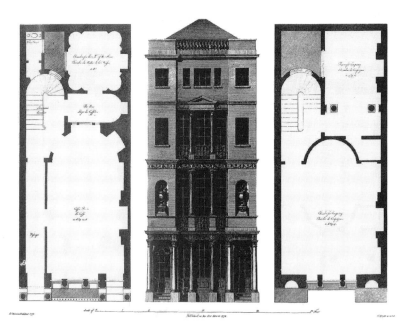

1.11
Robert Adam, British Coffee
House, London, 1770

be called a theme-café, as a chamber of rarities. Its owner, a certain James Salter who had been a member of the household of Sir Hans Sloane, president of the Royal Society and one of England's most important collectors of books, prints and other objects, had furnished his house with objects cast off by his former employer.[37] The business did not limit itself to selling coffee; catalogues of the 'Rarities to be seen at Don Saltero's Coffee House' were published over a period of almost 70 years.[38]

These London coffee houses were strictly the domain of men. By contrast, they seem to have been surprisingly open to various social strata, including the lower ranks of nobility and merchants, but also craftsmen. The display of social openness astonished foreigners like the Abbé Prévost, observing 'a lord, or two, a baronet, a shoemaker, a tailor, a wine merchant, and a few others of the same stamp poring over the same newspapers'.[39] All these would have been seated around a large table in the middle of the main room, where newspapers and writing utensils were available. This seating arrangement, which is illustrated in numerous contemporary engravings (Fig. 1.12), facilitated and enforced the repression of social differences, but it also allowed for a certain amount of male bonding. In 1764, an English correspondent described the coffee room in the merchant guild hall in Bremen established in 1673, the first recorded institution following the London model in Germany, as a rectangular and not very spacious room, in the middle of which:

there was an egg-shaped table and a large quantity of chairs. On the table there was a large coffee pot with three taps on its sides, from which everyone could serve himself, as the necessary cups and sugar were amply provided for.

37
Clayton, op. cit., p. 83

38
A Catalogue of the Rarities to Be Seen at Don Saltero's Coffee House in Chelsea, London, published between 1729 and 1795.

39
Abbé Prévost, *Adventures of a Man of Quality in England*, 1930, 119, quoted from: Porter, *Enlightenment*, p.20.

40
Th. Lediard, *Der Deutsche Kundschafter in Briefen eines durch Westfalen und Niedersachsen reisenden Engländers*, Lemgo, 1764, quoted in Sieling-Biehusen, op. cit., p. 145

41
Clayton, op. cit., p. 24

42
Otto Friedlaender, 'Kaffeehaus', in Petra Neumann (ed.), *Wien und seine Kaffeehäuser*, Munich: Heyne, 1997, p. 34

43
François Fosca, *Histoire des cafés de Paris*, Paris: Firmin-Didot, 1934

Customers would sit down or remain standing in small groups, walk about to join in conversations around the table, get up to refill their cups (not only with coffee but also spirits, as the correspondent finds out), leave the premises and return a little later.[40] As the coffee houses evolved and diversified, the central table gradually disappeared and was replaced by a series of smaller ones devoted to specific topics.[41] Elsewhere, booths or boxes resembling church pews appeared, with high backs allowing a greater degree of privacy. In eighteenth-century engravings, these are shown as executed in oak or soft wood, succeeded by more comfortable, upholstered banquettes covered in leather and velvet during the nineteenth century.

Illustrations of London coffee houses invariably show a counter where customers paid their penny, giving them access to services of the house. Slightly raised from the floor and occasionally defined by posts and a canopy, this counter gave an air of authority to the person seated behind it, supervising the coffee room. From her raised position the woman – it was nearly always a woman – could overlook the entire café and keep control over waiting staff, usually young handsome boys, and customers (Fig. 1.13). This was an arrangement that would appear and reappear in cafés in the 1700s and 1800s. Parisian establishments had their 'Belle Limonadière', advertised as part of the attraction of the establishment and paid handsomely for her presence. In Vienna, the counter was usually located near the entrance and occupied by the cashier:

> surrounded by the sugar cups and rum bottles, the *Gnädigste* (the benevolent lady) ruling with her charm, that never goes old, with her heaving bosom, diamonds in the ears and a high blonde coiffure of freshly burnt hair. In most cases it is not the landlady herself, but a so-called *Sitzkassiererin* (a seated cashier), but always she is a voluptuous lady with a friendly smile, who has to unite *coquetterie*, virtue and conscientiousness.[42]

The café as a fashionable salon

In Paris as well as in London, cafés underwent a similar development, moving from simple stalls and shops into buildings. When the Café Procope moved to a permanent venue in rue Fossés-Saint-Germain, it occupied several floors of an existing house. In contrast to the London coffee houses, the furnishings of the Procope suggested something substantially grander than a respectable bourgeois home. 'Furnishing the interior of the simple shop with tapestries, mirrors, paintings, marble tables and chandeliers, [and] investing his café with an atmosphere of comfort and luxury',[43] the *cafetier* positioned his enterprise as a decidedly upmarket institution, and as a public salon for Paris society. Among these features, the large mirrors, a remnant from the Turkish baths that had been located in the building, were most notable, if only because Procope established a precedent followed by hundreds of cafés in Paris and elsewhere.

1.12
Constantinople, London, Paris, Amsterdam: men sitting, standing, crouching

21 The architecture of cafés, coffee houses and public bars

Responding to the aspirations of an increasingly influential bourgeoisie, the café adopted the interior effects known from aristocratic palaces, the mirror salons of Versailles supplying a particularly powerful image, and made them available for the sociability of those outside the court. The efforts of Procope were not without success: in the eighteenth century, his house established itself as one of the centres of Parisian cultural life, attracting Voltaire, Diderot, Rousseau and other writers and philosophers. In the nineteenth century, the Procope, which by this time had lost its status as the main meeting place of the Paris elite of writers and philosophers, illustrates how the arrangement of a café on several floors invited social differentiation. As Scott Haine writes: 'On its first floor "serious types" played dominoes and booksellers discussed their business; on the second floor, students smoked and played billiards.'[44]

Compared with the London coffee houses of the eighteenth century, the distinction between (bourgeois) 'cafés' and the older established (plebeian or working-class) wine taverns in Paris was essentially 'metaphorical', as both continued to serve alcoholic beverages, and probably referred to a difference in the social setting of both types.[45] In any case, its exuberant interiors and its organization as a series of mirror salons made the French café of the eighteenth century appear significantly more exclusive than its London equivalent, something that was observed by English travellers.[46] An example of the sumptuous decoration that became the hallmark of the Parisian café was the main room of the Café Militaire (now in the Musée Carnavalet), one of the first designs by the architect Claude Nicolas Ledoux, realized in 1762. The room which was situated on the ground floor measured 6 x 10 m and was decorated with 12 *faisceaux de piques* ('beams in the shape of card spades') holding panels decorated with courts of arms and large mirrors extending from floor to ceiling. Evoking the image of a military camp after a victorious battle, the Café Militaire was reserved for soldiers.[47] The effect of the decoration must have been startling. In 1762, Élie Fréron reports in the *Année littéraire*: 'Everyone goes there to admire . . . [the ornaments]. . . . Everything there is rich, grand and simple and smells of antiquity. . . . It is extraordinary that a café shows the imprint of real taste and offers us a model for this.'[48]

In the course of the nineteenth century, the Parisian middle-class café underwent significant changes as many enterprises chose the boulevards as their natural location. In an article reviewing the renovation of the Café Riche in 1894, the journal *Construction moderne* described this process as 'democratization', and observed that the former white and gold panelling had been increasingly replaced by mosaics and stained glass.[49] In that year the Café Riche, which had existed since 1791 and was located on the Boulevard des Italiens, was transformed into a *café-brasserie*, a series of public living rooms arranged on two floors. On the ground floor the salons called 'Vin', 'Bière', 'Café', 'Thé' and 'Absinthe' were arranged as an enfilade of

22 Christoph Grafe

44
Haine, op. cit., p. 158

45
Markman Ellis, op. cit., p. 81

46
Ibid., p. 204

47
Michel Gallet, *Claude Nicolas Ledoux, 1736–1806*, Paris: Picard, year, pp. 47–8

48
Ellie Fréron. *L'année Littéraire*, 1762, vol. 6, p. 262, quoted from: Daniel Rabreau. 'Le Café Miltaire', in Christophe/Letourmy, op. cit., p.46

49
'Le Café Riche, à Paris', *La Construction Moderne*, 27 October 1894

50
Donald Olsen, *The City as a Work of Art*, New Haven, CT: Yale University Press, 1986, p. 65

separate rooms, three of which opened onto a street terrace covered by an elaborate glass canopy. The first floor consisted of a series of more intimate 'Salons', presumably dedicated to dining, arranged along a long corridor, much like a standard Parisian middle-class apartment. While following the domestic arrangements its clientele would have aspired to, the café added to these an atmosphere of festive elegance and brightness, subtly articulating the difference between the boulevard and the interior.

Comfort and respectability: the Viennese *Kaffeehaus*

From the street, the Café Riche offered the image of a range of salons decorated with mirrors that reflected the movement of visitors and those passing the café as an incident that was part of the afternoon or evening promenade. With its series of doors open to the pavement, the café provided a choice of modes of public presence; its visitors could occupy a table on the terrace, in full view and as stationary participants of the moving tableau of the boulevard, or they could retreat indoors, sheltered during the day by the lower light level inside, or in the even more private spaces upstairs. This gradual transition was not available to the users of the Viennese *Kaffeehäuser*; first of all, because the climate of the Austrian capital with its cold winters did not allow the degree of openness customary in Paris. There were other factors beyond the different climates in the two cities which caused the *Kaffeehaus* to develop into a type of café that, unlike the shops described in the 1780s, presented itself as a highly differentiated, comfortable interior, well protected by the firm walls of houses or palaces in the mediaeval inner city or its suburbs. One of these factors, as Donald Olsen suggests in his comparative study of urban cultures in London, Paris and Vienna in the nineteenth century, stems from the conservatism of Viennese society when it came to the status of areas or spaces in the city and the stable socio-economic geography that characterized the Austrian capital.[50] The daily promenade constituted a movement between well-established fixed points, initially concentrated around the Graben and the Hofburg (the main open space in the old town and the Imperial Palace). After the construction of the Ringstrasse in the 1870s on the site of the former fortifications, the socially accepted route led along the inner side of this boulevard around the old town.

The choice of locations of possible venues for the more respectable or privileged echelons of Viennese society seems, therefore, to have been limited from the outset by these conventions. The fact that the term *Ringstraßencafé* was introduced to describe the *Kaffeehaus* of the late nineteenth century and the observation that many of the most important establishments are located along the boulevard, seem to support this thesis. On the other hand, the cafés of Vienna, where coffee in all its possible varieties was the main beverage sold and which served *Bäckerei* (cakes and rolls) was explicitly a venue for all times of the day. Open from 8 in the morning to midnight (and beyond), the

51
Handbuch der Architektur,
op. cit., p. 87

Kaffeehaus provided a public breakfast room, a place for morning and afternoon coffee and for sociability in the evening. From the 1820s, the *Kaffeehäuser* were allowed to serve light meals, but these hardly extended beyond sausages. In the *Handbuch*, the Viennese cafés are described as 'a venue for comfortable pleasure, a *Stelldichein* [rendezvous], an informal gathering venue for social and private conversation',[51] allowing the promenade through the city, as it were, to be relocated inside. Comparing the *Kaffeehaus* with its French equivalent, the author of the *Handbuch* continues:

> the Parisian café is desolate and empty in the morning. Nobody is found in there, except for the yawning *garçon* who has only started sweeping the floor with a broom and sawdust, while the Viennese are already happily having their breakfasts, and may already have left the *Kaffeehaus* to resume their businesses.[52]

52
Ibid., p. 86

The central role that the *Kaffeehaus* played in the organization of the day and the economic life of the city is also stressed in the numerous anecdotes about habitués using the café as their offices and workspaces, supplied with telephone connections and various other services. This pattern of use is reflected in the arrangement of the café rooms and the requirements for access of daylight; the spacious and often high rooms of the Viennese cafés were clearly designed for their use during the day, while more intimate and darker rooms were provided for playing cards and billiards.

The *Handbuch* presents three examples of the Viennese *Kaffeehaus*, two of which were located on the Ringstraße. All three consist of a differentiated set of double-height rooms of considerable size, a layout that was reminiscent of London's gentlemen's clubs of the same period. The larger of these establishments are described as containing one or more coffee rooms, a reading room, a ladies room, rooms for playing cards, domino, chess or billiards and, occasionally, a bowling room.[53] The coffee rooms are located on the ground floor and along the street, allowing a direct view of the street (Fig. 1.14). The spaces are shown as relatively sparsely furnished; there are banquettes along walls or piers and small, round tables. Another customary arrangement, used for example by Café Griensteidl, Café Sperl and Adolf Loos' Café Museum, was that of occupying an L-shaped venue on the corner of two streets. Entering the café, visitors would face the counter positioned on the opposite corner, overlooking two long rectangular rooms, one dedicated to playing billiards, the other functioning as the coffee room proper.

53
Ibid., p. 88

One particular feature of the Viennese *Kaffeehaus* was the window niche into which a banquette was built, allowing its user to hide comfortably, while at the same time overlooking the street and visitors entering the establishment (Fig. 1.15). This solution, which Adolf Loos employed with great elegance in his design for the Café Museum, was revived by Hermann Czech in the MAK café (case study

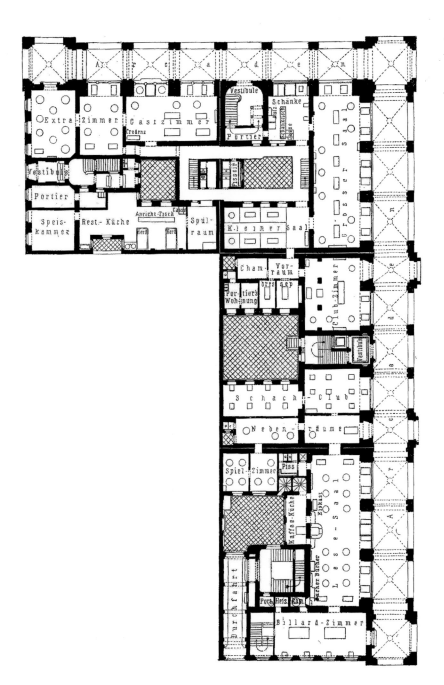

1.14
Viennese Kaffeehaus:
Reichsrat, Vienna

25 The architecture of cafés, coffee houses and public bars

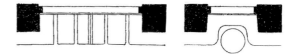

on p. 196). While intensifying the use of the façade zone, the area with most daylight, it also introduced another element that essentially marked the boundary between the interior of the café and the outside world.

One of the cafés that has acquired particular fame or notoriety as the focus of Viennese artistic life in the 1890s and the early twentieth century is the Café Central (case study on p. 112). The Central occupied one part of a palace designed for the Vienna stock exchange by the architect Heinrich von Ferstel in 1863 (Fig. 1.16). When the exchange moved to a new building two decades later, the café was extended into one of the grand interiors of von Ferstel's palace, the so-called arcade courtyard. The effect of these arrangements is illustrated by the description of the Café Central by Helga Malmberg (partner of the poet Peter Altenberg, one of the most notorious habitués of the Central):

> The arrangement of the spaces in themselves was peculiar. One entered in a sombre front room with deep window niches. There was a constant cool dusk, the ideal illumination for *Stubenhocker* ('stay-at-homes') and eccentrics. Then one passed through a narrow corridor and arrived in a kind of courtyard with a skylight, which could be reached via a small flight of stairs with wide steps. The large salon was really a vault without a ceiling. The smoke was distributed until it reached the high glass roof. In contrast to the front room this courtyard was bright and airy. Here we had the customary tables of the individual artists, who were absolutely taboo, the island of the chess players, the oasis of the lovers of domino, the corner where billiard was played. All these departments with onlookers and spies were separated from each other by enough space.[54]

54
Neumann, op. cit., p. 113

The clearly defined boundaries between the interior and the outside world meant that cafés in Vienna hardly exploited the type of street terrace which had become popular in Paris. Instead, some cafés installed mobile 'gardens', the so-called *Schanigärten*, consisting of chairs and tables laid out on the pavement so as to leave a passage along the façade and surrounded by lightweight fences adorned with plants and flowers.

In the 1870s, the the Viennese *Kaffeehaus* was introduced as a model for adaptation outside the Austrian capital. From Budapest to

Paris, Stockholm to Milan, coffee houses following the Viennese example appeared, featuring

> the same tall rooms decorated as ballrooms and located on the ground floor, the same marble tables and the same 'throne' of the female cashier . . . the same intimate arrangements, pressed into the niches of the windows, the same huge mirrors allowing the visitors to lean back leisurely and observe, address and partake in the street life outside, the same elegant, upholstered furniture, the same quieter, dark back rooms for playing cards, the same elegance and ease of this most secret place of recreation – in short, a true imitation of the Viennese *Kaffeehaus* in all its comfort, that has settled here through the years like a mildly shining patina.[55]

55
Alfred Klaar, 'Das Kaffeehaus zu allen Stunden', in *Wienerstadt – Lebensbilder der Gegenwart*, Vienna, 1895, p. 252

At the same time, the grander of the Vienna establishments, like the Café Central, demonstrated that the original proposal of the *Kaffeehaus* as an enclosed public living room had been abandoned or at least adjusted to the increasingly anonymous and dynamic everyday patterns of their visitors in the metropolis at the end of the nineteenth century. Compared to the quaintly modest Griensteidl, the focus of the Viennese literary avant-garde before its demolition in 1899 (commemorated in Karl Kraus' essay 'Die demolirte Literatur'/ 'Literature demolished'), the Café Central with its pressed English wallpaper and exuberant historicist decoration hardly appeared to be a 'home away from home' – even if Peter Altenberg did famously use it as his postal address. Instead, the Central was like a palace, where its visitors – ministerial civil servants as well as the penniless bohemians – associated themselves with high-bourgeois grandeur that was well beyond their station. The idea of a café that would provide a venue that could be inhabited, albeit temporarily, that was grander, more comfortable and luxurious than the private home, was by no means new. It had also been at work in the gradual development of the London coffee houses from simple rooms with dark wooden wainscoting into the refined classical interiors of, for example, Robert Adam's British coffee house, and it was even more visible in the Parisian cafés with their mirrored walls and gilded ornaments. In London, the desire to render the coffee house into an exclusive venue catering to a defined circle of customers, eventually led to the demise of the institution as a place open to everyone; from the mid-eighteenth century, coffee houses started to re-open as exclusive gentlemen's clubs and by the mid-Victorian period, the coffee house had more or less ceased to exist as a middle-class institution. It was from these clubs, furnished in the style of aristocratic manor houses, that middle-class commentators expressed their indignation at the brash glamour of the urban pubs catering for the working man.

In the Austrian capital, many cafés retained their cosy and calm *Biedermeier* character much longer than in other European cities.

56
Claudio Magris, *Il mito absburgico nella letteratura austriaca moderna*, Turin: Einaudi, [1963] 1996, pp. 206–7

57
Ludwig Hirschfeld, 'Kaffeehauskultur', in *Das Buch von Wien. Was nicht im Baedecker steht*, Munich: Piper, 1927; Neumann, op. cit., p. 23

58
Heise, op. cit., p. 144

Claudio Magris described the café as 'one of the most characteristic environments of the old *Mitteleuropa*, of whose culture it seems to enclose the slow, refined and a little indolent rhythm, its comfortable style of life and above all a tranquil and distinguished pace'.[56] Yet also in Vienna, the pressure to keep the *Kaffeehaus* commercially viable eventually had an effect. Early twentieth-century cafés such as Herrenhof, for example, looked suspiciously like a high-style Parisian *brasserie* with neon lights, brightly lit interiors and Art Deco furniture. This change was not appreciated by everyone; in 1927, the author Ludwig Hirschfeld complained about the 'Americanization and Berlinization' of the *Kaffeehaus*, suggesting that this might be the end of traditional Viennese urban culture, and possibly of civilization altogether.[57] Hirschfeld overlooked that the domestic arrangement of the café survived in the less glamorous plebeian establishments in the outer areas of the city, as it did in the working-class coffee houses of English cities, and its post-1945 successor the neighbourhood café ('caff') serving tea, coffee and substantial breakfasts.

This discussion of cafés offering a substitute for the private home by becoming a home in itself would not be complete without mentioning a phenomenon that had its roots in the temporary suspension of the domestic. Inspired by the occasional visits of Ottoman envoys and a taste for the exotic, princely courts adopted the custom of setting up tents in the Oriental style in the parks of castles or summer residences. Following these precedents, coffee tents appeared also in entertainment parks such as Vauxhall Pleasure Garden in London and, as we have seen, the Prater in Vienna. Unlike the urban coffee house, these temporary establishments were open to, and indeed popular among, women.[58]

In the nineteenth century the summer tents became established, reappearing as neo-classical and later historicist pavilions. The Sunday afternoon of a German or Austrian middle-class family would have been incomplete without an excursion to such an establishment and display of relaxed respectability accompanied by *Kaffee und Kuchen* (coffee and cake).

Palaces of consumption

If the middle-class café had almost from its beginnings been a place that affirmed the social and cultural aspirations of its users by providing them with a luxurious entourage, the second half of the nineteenth century added another altogether different dimension to this phenomenon. The metropolitan establishments of this period introduced an increase in scale and effort that constituted a comprehensive departure from the model of the 'home away from home'. Rather than resembling refined houses, cafés now developed into veritable purpose-built palaces combining entertainment and the consumption of beverages and food. The efforts invested in the construction and the décor of these venues, their management requirements and the largely extended range of their offerings required

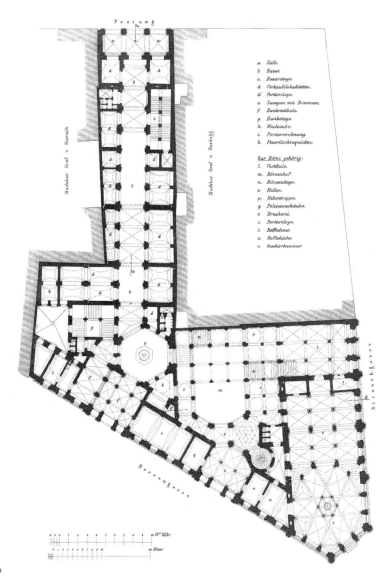

1.16
Heinrich von Ferstel, Palais
Ferstel, Vienna, 1850–60

a considerable financial commitment, which was often beyond the possibilities of individual entrepreneurs. At the same time, the population growth of most European and North American cities, and the gradual increase in leisure time and spending capacity of the lower middle and working classes meant that new types of large entertainment and drinking venues could find their clientele.

The combination of the improvement of the economic situation of urban populations, the concentration of the brewing trade and the development of tourism, first as a middle-class phenomenon, later also for the working class, found its expression in large-scale developments. Railway hotels comprising truly Grand Cafés, large *brasseries* and beer halls, music halls and vaudevilles, café-concerts and the large metropolitan English pubs of the late Victorian period (Fig. 1.17), all these establishments can be seen as the results of these processes of economic concentration and the emergence of a mass market. Describing the emergence of beer halls styled as mediaeval spaces in Berlin towards the end of the nineteenth century, the authors of the *Handbuch* state that these establishments 'have, as it were, become a necessity against the background of the enormous growth of the cities and their population'.[59] Despite the nostalgic, pre-industrial

59
Schmitt, op. cit., p. 21

1.17
The Salisbury, St Martin's Lane, London, 2006

60
Pim Reinders and Thera
Wijsenbeek, *Koffie in Nederland*,
Zutphen: Walburg Pers, 1994,
p. 134

styling of the décor, these halls were utterly modern enterprises, rationally planned in order to serve a wide social range of customers and realize a large turnover. Their atmosphere was seen as 'democratic' and free of the complicated class distinctions associated with clubs and coffee houses.[60] With their highly precise spatial differentiation, served by one core from which various types of food and drinks could be distributed, the large establishments reflected the increase in scale in the organization of retail enterprises in the same period and their development from individual boutiques to department stores. Like these, they offered 'thematic' departments: mediaeval halls, coffee saloons emulating the mirror galleries of Versailles, theatres and ball rooms, winter gardens, romantic caves and grottoes, ranging from highly exclusive to popular and accessible (Fig. 1.18). Styles of buildings which had been invented for the great exhibitions of the mid-nineteenth century were applied freely; entrepreneurs like the Amsterdam café and hotel owner Adolph Wilhelm Krasnapolsky commissioned miniature versions of the Crystal Palace for their establishments in the Dutch capital and London, offering food and drink as well as organizing flower shows (Fig. 1.19).[61]

61
Ibid., p. 135

The development of the Victorian pub in London and other British cities, from the small gin shops of the 1830s and 1840s to the exuberantly decorated and spatially differentiated establishments at the end of the century, is a particularly illustrative example of the successful attempt at realizing a rational organization of distribution disguised by the spectacle of brass fittings, wooden screens and ornamented glass partitions that evoke the image of an interior wonderland. By the mid-nineteenth century, the middle-class customers who had abandoned both the traditional coffee houses and the taverns in favour of private clubs and pubs, found themselves in a constant struggle against the negative reputation of the urban drinking holes as they became the target of increasingly vociferous temperance movements. At the same time, as Marc Girouard showed in his study of the Victorian pub, pub owners and brewers discovered that money could be made out of the poor if the turnover was high enough and that these new customers could therefore be offered an environment that evoked wealth and even respectability.

Efficiency and exuberance – the metropolitan pub

As the old taverns and the more recent gin shops gave way to large public houses, property developers and brewers assumed a prominent role in the drinks business. In the new suburbs of the 1840s and 1850s, pubs became a standard ingredient, often built well before the houses, operating as site huts and paying offices, to be sold on with a profit once the development was complete. In more prominent locations, pubs could literally take the form of palaces. The Eagle Tavern, re-opened on the edge of the City of London in 1839–40, presented itself as a three-storey, neo-classical palazzo with a giant order of Corinthian columns above a rusticated ground floor and four

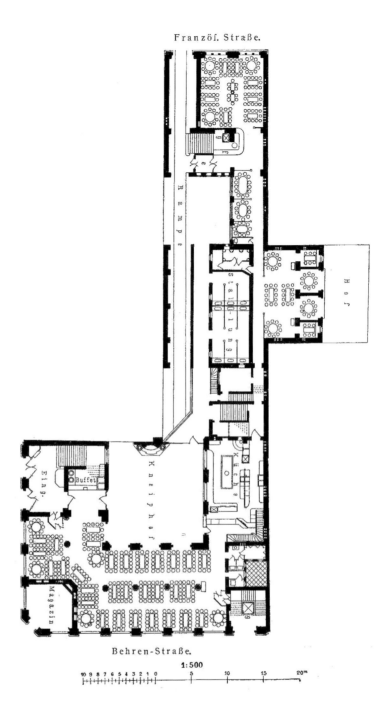

Franzöſ. Straße.

Rampe

Hof

staiglung

Küche

Kneiphof

Eing.

Buffet

Magazin

Behren-Straße.

1:500

10 9 8 7 6 5 4 3 2 1 0   5   10   15   20ᵐ

1.18
Metropolitan beer hall:
Pschorr, Berlin

62
Girouard, op. cit., pp. 35–6

eagles proudly hovering above the parapet. Customers entered the
building via a *faux marbre* hall, with a coffee room and a bar on
the sides.[62] With its grand ballroom on the first floor, accessed by
an equally impressive staircase, the Eagle was a palace not only in its
appearance, but also in the arrangement of its rooms and functions.
In this respect it resembled the Italianate or classical gentlemen's club
operating for the upper middle classes and located in a more
prestigious part of the city.

Although well planned, the organization of this grandest pub in 1840s London still relied on waiter service. It was with the introduction of bar service, combined with the 'perpendicular drinking' pattern (drinks being consumed by standing customers), which so astonished continental correspondents, that the metropolitan London pub acquired its characteristic layout after 1850. The hundreds of pubs which were remodelled or built, especially in the last two decades of the century, responded to two apparently contradictory requirements, combining social differentiation with a rationalized distribution of drinks. The solution, which allowed serving a range of different clienteles from one continuous service area, was a bar counter in the shape of a U, a sort of island from which a large area could be reached. The island counter with a so-called bar 'wagon' displaying bottles and drinks at its centre – a solution that had been invented by the engineer Isambard Kingdom Brunel for a railway refreshment room – allowed for convenient serving arrangements.[63] Yet pubs also needed to find a solution for the differentiation required by a society as madly class-conscious as late Victorian England. This was achieved by subdividing the bar (Fig. 1.20); screens demarcating socially distinct areas such as the public bar for blue-collar workers and artisans, the saloon bar for clerks and lower-ranking civil servants and private bars occasionally used even by middle-class women. The desire, especially of the more respectable part of the clientele, to retain their privacy, resulted in the installation of so-called snob screens with frosted glass panels preventing visual contact between bar staff and customers. According to Girouard, the introduction of the saloon bar, furnished with a fireplace, comfortable upholstered seats and tables and fitted with carpet, can be seen as a deliberate attempt to address a 'better' class of public, who generally still viewed the pub with caution, aware as they were of their social status.[64]

63
Ibid., p. 65

64
Ibid., pp. 74–5

33 The architecture of cafés, coffee houses and public bars

This layout, in fact an efficient machine serving a series of distinct spaces, provided the background for the invention of an extensive catalogue of decorative elements and trimmings, of mahogany woodwork, frosted and engraved glass, brass fittings and ceiling ornaments. Specialist architects, who like their peers designing shops, music halls or popular theatres, operated as skilled commercial designers, could rely on this catalogue of mass-produced parts which only needed to be assembled to achieve the desired effect. For the light fittings they could choose from cast iron or brass elements produced by specialist firms catering for an increasingly lucrative market. In all their brashness, these decorations were not free of artistic ambition. The catalogue of one producer, for example, reads like a veritable study of mannerist and baroque ornament, listing 'Candelabra of the Italian Renaissance' and 'Magnificent reproduction of the finest models of the Louis XIV, XV. and XVI. Periods'.[65] Another firm, specializing in wrought iron, had started as a furnisher of churches before re-launching itself as a provider of metal grills and sign boards for pubs.[66]

Possibly the most important feature of the Victorian pub, however, was glass, in a variety of forms. Given the obsession with privacy, techniques for rendering glass translucent were obviously of the greatest importance and the inventiveness of manufacturers in achieving this aim was almost infinite; glass could be frosted, embossed

65
Perry and Co, Lanterns and Pendants for Halls and Corridors: Chandeliers and Suspensions for Saloons, Catalogue, London, probably 1895

66
Girouard, op. cit., pp. 156–7

34 Christoph Grafe

or cut, and when after 1850 new technologies allowed sheets to be produced and decorated at a much reduced cost, every limitation to the use of the material disappeared. As Girouard put it, 'pubs all over London glittered, glowed, and sparkled as ornamental glass of every description crept over their walls and partitions, lined the shelves of their back fittings, flashed from their snob-screens and . . . splashed far further up the outside windows'.[67]

67
Ibid., p. 174

Standardized experiences

As the example of the late Victorian pub illustrates, the rapid development of industrial technology providing mass-produced ornaments and furniture was fully exploited in creating an atmosphere of unprecedented, but also highly standardized luxury. The French manufacturers of mirrors at Saint Gobain, for example, realized a significant increase in their output when new chemical and mechanic methods allowed them to produce large sheets of mirror glass at a fraction of the previous price.[68] Mirrors, which had been an element of distinction that only the most prestigious cafés could afford, became one of the quintessential and ubiquitous ingredients of the Parisian café of the Second Empire, even in its humblest form. Other elements, such as 'mediaeval' wooden panelling or neo-baroque buffets were standard items in bars and cafés in Germany, from the celebrated Café Bauer (see case study on page 118) on Berlin's Unter den Linden to the more modest beer halls emerging in industrial cities across the newly unified country. Brewers and landlords specifically sought to associate their establishments with specific national or regional identities that were carefully and consciously constructed, depending on the general political circumstances or expressing cultural affiliations. The mediaeval references in Germany (Fig. 1.21) were instrumental in establishing a continuity with the *Gemütlichkeit*, the cosy comfort of the golden age of a well-ordered pre-industrial society, and were understood as such by the clientele. In Paris, by contrast, the oak panelling introduced in Alsatian *brasseries* in the mid-nineteenth century was abandoned in favour of gilded mirror ornament associated with French elegance and conviviality after the Franco-Prussian War and the loss of Alsace-Lorraine to Germany in 1871.

68
Cafés de Paris, p. 139

One element, however, could be found in cafés virtually everywhere in continental Europe. This was the bent wood chair invented by Michael Thonet and produced by a variety of firms in Austria, Germany and France. In 1850, this Viennese cabinetmaker had designed a lightweight chair for Café Daum, then the establishment of choice for government and military officials, and shortly afterwards he supplied Budapest's grandest hotel with 400 chairs.[69] Constant and systematic experiments with methods for bending wood in order to produce a chair that could be made even more simply eventually led to the design of the chair known as model No. 14, which could be mass-produced in a factory rather than made in a traditional workshop. Thonet's chair was shown at the 1855 World Exhibition in Paris and the

69
Allessandro Alvera, 'Michael Thonet and the Development of Bent-Wood Furniture: From Workshop to Factory Production', in Derek Ostergaard (ed.), *Bent Wood and Metal Furniture*, New York: AFA, Catalogue, p. 40

35 The architecture of cafés, coffee houses and public bars

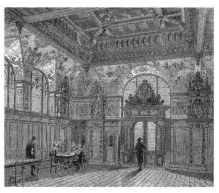

1.21
Industrial medievalism:
a beer hall in Frankfurt

70
Ibid., p. 44

71
Heise, op. cit., p. 158

success of his presentation ushered in the world-wide distribution of what was to become the generic café chair. By 1891, 7.3 million chairs of this type had been sold, the number increasing to 40 million in 1914.[70] Mass-produced and easy to transport and assemble, the Thonet chair was also one of the few 'classless' designs; it could be found in Grand Hotels, prestigious *brasseries*, station tea rooms and humble working-class cafés. Its combination of functionality and simplicity allowed it to be exceptional in another sense, too: it is the only nineteenth-century design object valued and used by modern architects. Its qualities seemed compatible with the design ideas of architectural reform movements around 1900. For his debut in Vienna, the Café Museum (1898), Adolf Loos provided a design based on Thonet's chair, stating that 'there has been nothing more classical since Aeschylus',[71] not so much to improve it but rather to celebrate a functional tradition.

Modern architecture and the café

With the Grand Cafés and *café-brasseries* of the last two decades of the nineteenth century, the design of cafés had reached a climax, both in sheer number and in terms of the diversification of types and decorative proposals. At the same time, the two decades before the First World War were also the first period that the design of cafés appeared in the working field of architects with a decidedly artistic profile. The designs by Paul Hankar in Brussels, Loos' café and his American Bar in Vienna, Mackintosh's Tea Rooms in Glasgow or the projects designed by various Werkbund architects in Germany were examples of the attempts of architects to purge cafés of the mass-produced ornament and brash theatricality of commercial historicist architecture. The changes introduced by these designers, however, did not so much constitute a departure from the established typological models of the nineteenth century. Rather they involved a restyling of these standard types; Loos' Café Museum, for example, closely followed the corner solution for a Viennese café, Mackintosh's Willow Tea Rooms was innovative in its artistic appearance while retaining the layout of the tea shop that had been established for several decades.

It was only after the war, in the dramatically changed cultural circumstances of the 1920s, that new functional and organizational models appeared. Even so, the influence of modern architects remained small; presumably both because other building tasks – housing, education and sports facilities – were given more priority by the architects and because café entrepreneurs were reluctant to accept a design approach that demanded functional and structural 'honesty' for a type of space which for them was essentially about creating comfort, spectacle and festive conviviality. Functionalist cafés and restaurants emerging in newly independent Czechoslovakia (for example, the Café Avion, Brno, of 1926, case study on p. 150) remained, on the whole, exceptions. In Oud's Café de Unie in Rotterdam, which featured in publications as a rare iconic example of functionalist architecture in the setting of an inner city, the design approach was in reality limited to a graphic proposal for the façade, leaving the interior to retain a conventional layout behind a modern billboard.

Cultural change had an effect, however, on the atmosphere of the new large metropolitan cafés offering new types of beverages as well as popular entertainment. New establishments like the Montparnasse café-brasserie La Coupole (founded in 1927), and the string of extensive 'bars de luxe' along the Champs Élysées, illustrated the powerful attraction of brightly lit, large, coherently designed bars with restaurant and dancing areas. Their style was recognizably modern without being puritanically functionalist, using aluminium or stainless steel instead of wood, new synthetic materials instead of leather, neon and fluorescent lighting in the place of the dimmed light of traditional fittings – all of these elements shown in their naked form rather than being covered in ornament.[72]

72
Michèle Lefrançois, 'Cafés des années 1930', Cafés de Paris, p. 158.

The architect Charles Siclis, known for his 'architecture de la joie' was responsible for some of the most remarkable of these glamorous establishments, including the Maison du Café (case study on p. 159) that anticipated the style and arrangement of the post-war espresso bars, using a row of percolators proudly displayed on the curved counter, and the Colisée and the Triomphe, both on the Champs Élysées. Located near the new film theatre palaces concentrated along the avenue, these cafés borrowed cinematic effects; in the Colisée, seats were arranged on what resembled a grandstand, allowing a full view of the street; the Triomphe was designed like a film décor, complete with an illuminated fountain.[73]

73
Ibid., Cafés de Paris, p. 159

Similar establishments appeared in other large cities towards the end of the 1920s and even during the economic crisis of the subsequent decade. In Berlin, for example, entertainment palaces emerged out of existing cafés, offering an astonishing range of attractions and facilities such as evening performances and tea dances, but also a conventional Konditorei, serving hundreds or customers each afternoon. The service offered by these enterprises extended much beyond hospitality in the strict sense. The café Moka Efti on Friedrichstrasse, for example, presented itself not only as 'Europe's largest coffee bar', complete with Egyptian salon and two ballrooms, but also advertised its telephone service, hairdresser's, tobacco kiosks, 16 billiard tables and typewriter rooms at 'cheap prices'.[74] On the roof terrace of the Konditorei Café Berlin, guests were invited to enjoy blossoming pear, almond and peach trees while listening to music performances in the open air, or under a glass roof that could be moved with effortless spectacle to cover the terrace. The largest of these establishments, sarcastically referred to as 'pleasure barracks' for clerks and shop girls by Siegfried Kracauer, was the Haus Vaterland, which advertised 'a cheap recreational world tour' from the Italian 'Piazzetta', via the 'South American Wild-West Bar', a 'Bodega', the 'Rhine terrace' (with a diorama of the Rhine Valley) to the 'Palm Salon'. The café room of this establishment provided seats for 2,500 customers and on the 10th anniversary of the Vaterland in 1938, its management claimed

74
Knud Wolffram, Tanzdielen und Vergnügungspaläste, Berlin: Hentrich, 1992, p. 83

75
Peter Lummel,
'Erlebnisgastronomie um 1900 –
Das "Haus Vaterland" in Berlin', in
Herbert May and Andrea Schilz
(eds), *Gasthäuser, Geschichte und
Kultur*, Petersberg: Michael Imhof,
2004, p. 195

that 10 million cups of coffee, 5 million litres of beer and 1.5 million pieces of cake had been sold.[75] Interior effects such as illuminated columns and skylights, streamline or Art Deco mouldings, ethnic themes – Moorish and Bavarian among the more popular ones – and Americana created an atmosphere of modern glamour and turned the interior into a three-dimensional film décor, allowing the customers to experience and participate in the carefully constructed spectacle.

A survey of contemporary bars and restaurants published in 1928 and 1929 presented contemporary cafés where, as the editor noted, 'one goes to solve problems, not to chat'. It is in these cafés, located near the main concentrations of large cinemas or even including a film theatre, that changing fashions could have an immediate impact:

> This is where the architect has the greatest scope, for they are always modern and being newly opened: happy, extravagant colours, daring room solutions with balconies and hidden corners for intimate conversations, particular, often mysteriously concealed lighting. They do not have particularly comfortable or soft seating and the tables are small, as the space available for the public must be used to a maximum. . . . The architect should not design these interiors as he would a home: comfortable, tasteful, bourgeois, but quite the opposite, extravagant and fashionable with an overwhelmingly brilliant effect.[76]

76
*Moderne Ladenbauten und Moderne
Cafés, Restaurants und
Vergnügungsstätten*, Berlin: Ernst
Pollak, 1928, 1929, p. 12

That these requirements did not necessarily lead to modernist styling could be seen in projects like the sumptuous baroque eclecticism of the Café am Zoo in Berlin by the architects Kaufmann und Wolffenstein, which had walls, columns and balustrades treated with ivory lacquer, bronze ceiling ornaments and light fittings in polished silver or the strange mixture of Art Deco mouldings and French chateau-style curtains employed by the same architects in another of their projects, the Kakadu-Bar on Kurfürstendamm.

The exuberance of the style of the large entertainment cafés of the 1930s disguised their fragile commercial basis and most advertisements kept mentioning the fact that the experiences of luxury could be obtained at modest prices. As the economic crisis deepened, the sophisticated, but also unreal glamour of the cafés looked increasingly out of place in the everyday realities of mass unemployment and the rise of authoritarian political movements. In Germany, the cosmopolitan character of establishments offering employment to gay, Jewish and East European ('Gypsy') artists and musicians abruptly disappeared when the National Socialists seized power in 1933.[77] Elsewhere, too, the fabulously fashionable entertainment palaces saw their clienteles impoverished and worried, leaving them as vestiges of a recent prosperous past stranded in the grim environment of the years before the Second World War. In Berlin, as in other cities, cafés barely survived under these circumstances, only to be wiped out altogether in the war.

77
Wolffram, op. cit., p. 191

Nostalgia, social experiment and global marketing

To the inhabitants of Europe's war-torn cities, cafés and bars reopening amidst the ruins offered the first signs of a return to normality, and establishments made great efforts to return to business as quickly as possible. The desire to forget the austerity of everyday life afforded cafés with the status of enclaves of colour and light surrounded by greyness and hardship. As economic circumstances improved, however, many cafés, particularly the grander establishments catering for the middle classes, found that the general recovery had disadvantageous consequences for their business. Across Western Europe, in Vienna as well as Brussels, Paris or London, many a café that had survived for decades was affected by gradual, but eventually sweeping changes in the ways that the urban middle and working classes arranged their lives. Whether cafés lost their traditional clienteles due to a general tendency towards a privatization of everyday life or the erosion of cultural affiliations that had afforded them a specific identity, the consequences were the same, resulting in a notable decrease in the numbers of cafés, pubs and bars in the 1960s and 1970s. It was in the context of corporate environments, the business hotels introduced by transatlantic chains, that the American hotel bar in its most standardized, non-specific form replaced the Viennese or Parisian café as a model to be applied universally. Otherwise cafés and bars shared the fate of traditional shops, the inner cities abandoned by their middle-class and (former) working-class constituencies.

If café culture has re-established itself in the past two or three decades, this is largely due to the remarkable revitalization of inner cities, both in Europe and parts of North America over the same period. Indeed, cafés and bars have become institutions indicating a social change, this time coinciding with the transition from an economic system based on industrial production to one dominated by service industries. Changes in the organization of work and demographic developments have allowed them to acquire, or reacquire, functions that they had mostly lost since the nineteenth century. The contemporary café, like its seventeenth- and eighteenth-century predecessor, has once again become a place for arranging business meetings, discussing contracts or working on laptop computers. Old-established institutions that had closed down in the post-war period, like the Café Central in Vienna, have reappeared; others that barely survived after the war have been revived. The 'discovery' of former proletarian districts like Berlin's Prenzlauer Berg, Amsterdam's Pijp, Oberkampf in Paris or the East End of London by 'les Bobos' (Bourgeois Bohémiens) is measured by the number of cafés, and the availability of a decent cappuccino within walking distance has become an index factor of valuing urban districts and property.

In the 1980s, new Grand Cafés like Café Costes distinguished themselves through a decidedly modern appearance, involving the use of designer furniture and minimalist light fittings. As we enter the twenty-first century, it seems that enterprises seek an explicit continuity with the café culture of the late nineteenth century, exploiting existing decorative or typological features. Specialist café designers have become versatile in creating interiors that offer perfect illusions of age and patina. Nineteenth-century techniques of treating woodwork and glass have been revived, entire rural regions are being ransacked for 'authentic' furniture and transported to Amsterdam, Paris or Berlin. Traces of decades are created, and nicotine stain applied from bottles suggests a history of smoke-filled nights of intense café life imagined by a clientele happy to believe the fiction. In cities deprived of their traditional function as centres of production, references to artisanal or small industrial activities are exploited in the creation of a sense of authenticity presenting new cafés and bars as former workers's canteens. Where these references are made with a sense of knowing irony, like the Parisian Café Delaville designed by Périphérique (Fig. 1.22), the remnants of a former use are consciously shown as props, contrasting with the contemporary stylistic elements derived from the repertoire of academic 'deconstructivist' architecture. While the traditional cafés of the surrounding neighbourhood present themselves as products of the incremental and inconsequential adding of elements, the Delaville, which was set up by one of Paris's more successful café-impresarios, exploits the fragments of the past and the contemporary additions, each displayed as anecdotal evidence of the various episodes that the premises have gone through.[78] Its users, working in the media, art schools and information technology, recognize the presentation of the café as a 'work in progress', much in the same way that they have learned to appreciate the aesthetics of improvisation and incompleteness in their own homes and workplaces. The interior of the café, with its rusty Cor-Ten steel window frames, its late nineteenth-century ceiling (meticulously restored), layers of render and brickwork and the 'beige and white grotto'[79] of the lounge at the rear draws on established

78
Monique Eleb and Jean-Charles Depaule, *Paris – Société des Cafés*, Paris: Éditions de l'Imprimeur, 2005, pp. 216–9

79
Ibid., p. 217

1.22
Café Delaville, Paris,
Périphérique Architects

1.23
Starbucks, Luton Airport
(2006)

advertising images of the artfully unfinished spaces populated by artists, which have become adopted as signifiers of the 'creative industries' or even the 'creative class'.

Other café typologies have their roots in the counter-cultures of the 1950s and 1960s. The coffee lounge, possibly the one genuinely new café type invented since the Second World War, has changed from a venue attracting Bohemians and artists in New York's Greenwich Village or London's Soho to a model for chains like Starbucks and its imitations. Absorbing some of the qualities of the traditional European coffee house and introducing them in generic commercial environments, the coffee lounge effectively combines the features of the shop with those of the 'home away from home'. The spatial arrangements of the lounge allow this ambiguity to be visible; comfortable furniture, leather sofas and fauteuils, low tables or long ones resembling those in seventeenth-century coffee houses or family dinner tables find themselves next to a large glass counter. The entire arrangement relies on the thorough acceptance of self-service by a young urban clientele and the fact that items such as laptops and related equipment are tolerated and often supported.

Offering a standard product, coffee of predictable quality, served with frothed milk in various forms, and places of sociability where none had existed, the character of the coffee lounge could be described as an act of taking the urban café to the suburbs and into generic indoor spaces. Framed by large shop windows facing the street or entirely open to the air-conditioned environment, the lounge appears to signify or pictorialize the culture of urbane, sophisticated conversation modern consumers associate with the café. These images are reworked into concepts that can be marketed and applied in any environment, from suburban shopping malls via stations and hospitals to airport terminals (Fig. 1.23). The relocation into these types of surroundings goes along with explicitly dispensing with some of the cultural associations of the traditional café, in favour of the healthy and optimistic worldview that has its proper home in the suburbs. The customers of the lounge no longer perceive the stylistic references to comfortable domesticity and the espresso machine, the emblem of a sanitized version of 'traditional' urbanity, as out of place in environments designed to be unspecific. Rather, it could be argued, the phenomenon of the coffee lounge as a global brand and as another type of generic spatial condition entirely fits a culture that has repressed many forms of public display and a society of atomized individuals whose common denominator is the demand for a *large* caffè latte.

Setting the stage for modernity
The cosmos of the coffee house
Franziska Bollerey

Coffee and coffee house: luxury item and location. Both, productively complementing each other, have promoted civic emancipation. English authors consider coffee houses to be the 'cradles of public opinion'. Pubs and inns as places to meet away from home have existed since antiquity. Consumption of alcoholic beverages acts on people's social behaviour in a specific way. Induced by the stimulating effects of coffee, the meeting of people in a coffee house is of an entirely different character.

Encyclopaedic articles describe it thus:

> Consumed hot, coffee acts stimulating on the central nervous system … accordingly coffee furthers mental activity making reflection and work easier … the perception of external impressions and their assimilation is facilitated … a certain urge towards procreation is generated, a drifting of thoughts and conceptions, a mobility and ardour in wishes and ideals.[1]

The coffee house becomes a shelter for the genius loci of critical and creative protagonists.

In the following, our topic will be coffee as an agent from its global spread and its capitalization as economic plant to its global marketing as an everyday mass product. In parallel, we will consider the development and facets of coffee house culture.[2]

'Java jargon'

'Our aim is to see more people drinking coffee than eating hamburgers',[3] is Starbucks' stated intention. Here we are talking of sales, of market shares. Here the multitude of world-wide corporate design-levellers is augmented by one more brand, furthering even more the replaceable character of individual urban scenes. This definitely is not coffee or coffee house culture. It does not help that Starbucks takes refuge in a literary figure, namely that of the first mate in Herman Melville's Moby Dick.[4] The vague trace of a formerly highly differentiated culture may be detected in the number of coffee varieties that the Starbucks chain offers. It was the Italians and the Viennese who created innumerable variants. Among the Viennese variants are: 'very light, medium light, dark, black coffee with or without "Schlagobers" (whipped cream)'; coffee prepared in the espresso machine or in the Turkish way (the latter variant called 'nature' or 'passed', which means sieved). Among the generic names that regrettably are increasingly disappearing nowadays, are 'a cup of gold', 'nut-gold', 'nut-brown', 'Kapuziner' (very dark), 'Obers gespritzt' (very light-coloured), 'Einspänner' (black coffee in a glass, an ample amount of whipped cream on top), 'Melange' (not prepared in an espresso machine), a 'stretched' or 'shortened' coffee.[5] 'Espresso' and 'cappuccino' today form part of clients' orders every day and only real connoisseurs still can discern the origin of the coffee beans or the processes to improve them. The customers patronizing chain coffee

1
Meyers Großes Konversations-Lexikon, 6th edn, Leipzig and Vienna, 1905, vol. 10, p. 421

2
At the end of this contribution, under "References" there is a list of general literature.

3
Howard Schultz, 'Business Review', The Independent, 24 May 2000

4
Herman Melville: Moby Dick; or The Whale, New York, 1851

5
Hans Weigel, op. cit., p. 12

6
Anthony Clayton, op. cit., p. 173

7
Quoted in Delphine Christophe
and Georgina Letourny (eds),
Paris et ses cafés, Paris, 2004,
p. 33

8
Louis Sebastien Mercier, Tableau
de Paris, 1781, quoted in Ulla
Heise, op. cit., p. 102

9
W. Scott Haine: The World
of the Paris Café. Sociability
among the French Working
Class 1789–1914, London 1996

10
Delphine Christophe, op. cit.,
p. 165

shops today, however, long ago reduced their connoisseurship to the 'latte language' or 'java jargon'.[6] With studied casualness, they order a 'latte macchiato'.

What most do not know is that the combination of coffee and milk is an age-old recipe. 'Le café au lait,' Madame de Sévigné wrote in 1690, is 'la plus jolie chose du monde'.[7] The addition of cloves or cinnamon or mixing coffee with chocolate – 'Mocchaccino' in java jargon – also goes back to the seventeenth century.

And Sebastien Mercier, who around the middle of the eighteenth century reveals all facets of the everyday life of Parisians, reports that milky coffee, sold by 'women with huge milk cans, made from tinplate, on their backs, conquered a big following amongst the workers'.[8] This serves as proof that the consumption of coffee – already known since the sixteenth century in the Ottoman Empire – was common in all strata of society. Whereas the working class, no matter whether in London, Paris[9] or Berlin, had their coffee in the streets, sold by ambulant vendors or at stalls, the nobility frequented salons or, since the middle of the seventeenth century, the first coffee houses. There were differences, too, in the quality of the raw product as well as in the refinement of preparing it for consumption. From the nineteenth century onwards, surrogates were offered to the working population due to the price of coffee that was speculatively driven upwards by the commodity exchanges. At the same time, the rich consumed refined creations of coffee or confiserie goods.

Chain coffee shops today, such as the Coffee Republic, Caffè Nero or Costa Coffee in Britain, Coffee Company in the Netherlands and Balzac Coffee in Germany, may well promote the revival of the historic public consumption of coffee – but what does this mean for coffee house culture? Unquestionably, places that allow the application of the term 'genius loci' are not created in this way, for 'branding' nowadays for most brands and chain stores means the world-wide interchangeable and uniformly recognizable appearance that, next to the identical logo, includes the standardized set of interior decoration. The Italian-style British Caffè Nero branches try to achieve a certain differentiation. The Dutch Coffee Company uses a trademark central circular table to individualize their shops. A still more striking exception to this are the cafés of the brothers Costes in Paris who, in 1984, opened their first shop in les Halles quarter. Philippe Starck, then in the first stage of his career, gave a certain modernist-minimalist character to the venue. Meanwhile, however, the Costes brothers since the 1990s have subscribed to the retro-styles of Jacques Garcia: Venetian glass chandeliers, leather, plush and velvet. Eclecticism and neo-historicism – in short, modern 'historic neo-authenticity' – are very much in favour. One example from Paris can be mentioned here: Le Fumoir[10] is a mixture of English colonial style, Casablanca-appeal and historical Parisian café elements. Le Fumoir, however, similar to the Berlin restaurant, Theodor Tucher on Pariser Platz in the immediate vicinity of the Brandenburg Gate, merits a mention here for another reason: following the example of so many famous historical cafés, the presence of books in both places attracts immediate attention. Whether the atmospheric effects can thus be recreated, or if this was intended at all, remains, however, an open question.

One thing strikes the reader of all the recent publications that deal with historic coffee houses: in these texts we hear of personalities, literary and political discourses. Books on contemporary coffee houses, by contrast, exclusively give information on the interior design, the number of branches in the different chains or the annual profit the chain makes. No recent publication can omit mentioning 'cybercafés'. Here coffee is poured from automats into plastic or waxed-paper beakers (which you can see mainly younger people carry away drinking while walking) and the screen-conveyed communication necessarily leads to an atomization of any feeling of community of those present. Here the damnable reduction of experience comes to light, a lack of awareness of an all-encompassing sensitivity. Without disputing the usefulness of such places, coffee houses they most definitely are not. The inspiring power of the coffee house as an atmospheric milieu arose from the physical proximity of other customers, from the sounds, smells and delights present, and, last but not least, from an excellent and expertly served cup of coffee.

The global march of a stimulant

Noir comme le diable
Chaud comme l'enfer
Pur comme un ange
Doux comme l'amour.

Presumably this ode of Charles Maurice de Talleyrand's is based on an Arabic text.[11] Indeed, it was the Arabs who cultivated coffee as a luxury good and bestowed on it the nobility of an object of sensual perception. Wrongly – and to this the Swedish naturalist, Carl von Linné has contributed with his specification of the plant as caffea arabicus (Fig. 2.1)[12] – its origin was supposed to be Arabia (Saudi Arabia).

As a matter of fact, however, the plant originated in Abyssinia (Ethiopia) and in the hill region north of Lake Victoria. One centre of its provenance was the 'Kaffa' region in South-east Ethiopia, probably the reason the beverage later was called 'Qawha'[13] in the Turkish and Arabian language areas. Another etymological derivation is the designation 'Bunn' for the present noun for the coffee 'bean'. 'Bunn' was the word for the fruit of the coffee shrub used by the African tribe of Habaschi. Similar to betel nut or coca, the raw beans were, according to the Scottish merchant James Bruce,[14] chewed or eaten pulverized and mixed with butter or tallow and rolled into balls. In Vienna, to the present day, Hof-Conditorei Ch. Demel's Sons sell roasted coffee beans coated in chocolate.

2.1
Coffee plant and grinder with Osman coffee drinker with 'Ibriq' (Sylvestre Dufour, 1671).

11
Quoted in Gerhart Söhn, op. cit., p. 96

12
Carl von Linné, *Systema naturae, per regna tria naturae systematice proposita*, 7 vols, Leiden, 1735

13
In French: Café; in Spanish: Café; in Portuguese: Café; in Italian: Café; in Dutch: Koffie; in English: Coffee; in Danish: Kaffee; in Swedish: Kaffee; in Norwegian: Kaffee; in Czech: kava; in Polish: kawa; in Russian: kophe; in Hungarian: kávé; in Roumanian: cafea; in Greek: kaféo. from: Gerhard Söhn, op. cit., p. 72
14
Wolfgang Jünger, op. cit., p. 13

Probably the Ethiopians had already taken coffee to Yemen as early as the thirteenth or fourteenth century. From here via the ports of Aden and Moccha – Al Mukha (another term that was to become part of coffee lore), it reached Mecca and Suez, from there, Aleppo – Haleb and ultimately Cairo. The latter developed into an important storage and trading post[15] and – next to Mecca – into a centre of public coffee consumption. A great number of historic sources[16] deal with the effects and spread of this luxury commodity and hand down to posterity the long-term controversy about the psycho-physiological advantages and disadvantages of drinking coffee.

Early proof of the anabolic effects of caffeine is given by the Sufis. According to original Moccha information, it is said of them, that they kept themselves awake night by night by intensive consummation of coffee in order to follow their strict religious rites.[17]

There were two points of entry for the colonization of Europe by coffee – it has also been called the crusade of a luxury good. From Alexandria, it was brought as an export commodity by sea to Venice, Marseilles, the Netherlands, England and Germany in the course of the seventeenth century. A second route followed its course from Syria to

15
Ralph S. Hattox, op. cit., p. 72

16
Prosper Alpinus, De plantis Aegypti liber, Venice 1592

17
Ibid., p. 13f.

2.2
Map of the Ottoman Empire 'Turcicum', 1685

Constantinople and from there to Central Europe. Since Osman I, the Ottoman Empire had been expanding: from Anatolia via Asia Minor to Africa and Europe (in both 1529 and 1683, Turkish armies besieged Vienna; Budapest for more than 140 years was under Turkish reign) and thus became the first territory to experience the spread of coffee (Fig. 2.2). Around 1600, coffee as an everyday beverage was common throughout the whole empire. In its economic centre, however, coffee could not be cultivated. This took place in its region of origin, Ethiopia and especially on plantations in Yemen and Arabia, until in the second half of the seventeenth and in the eighteenth century European colonial powers organized cultivation on a larger scale.

It was the Dutch who – experienced in speculation and the creation of an added value gained by the cultivation of tulips – organized global coffee growing across the so-called 'coffee belt'. In 1614, a Dutch delegation of merchants and agrarian experts went to Aden to spy on Arabic methods of coffee growing and processing. In 1616, they succeeded in gaining possession of seeds and plants.

Coffee shoots were then grown in domestic Botanic Gardens in the Netherlands. The East Indian Company, founded in 1602, as well as the West Indian Company of 1621, formed the structural backbone of exporting plants to the Dutch colonies and re-importing coffee harvests. In 1658, coffee growing started in Ceylon (Sri Lanka) that had recently been taken over from the Portuguese.[18] On the same island, the Dutch unscrupulously controlled the growing of cinnamon and secured a world monopoly.[19] In 1699, they succeeded in establishing the coffee plant on the island of Java in the immediate vicinity of their trading post of Batavia (Jakarta), founded in 1595.

From here, the Dutch organized the systematic spread of coffee across their islands of Sumatra, Bali, Timor and later Celebes. Allegedly, it was the shoot of a coffee plant from Java, cultivated in the Amsterdam Botanic Gardens in 1706 that made history as the ancestor of the entire Central American coffee culture. Nicolaas Witsen, the then burgomaster of Amsterdam, donated a (Java) coffee plant to Louis XIV, whom he ardently admired.

Gabriel Mathieu Clieu, a French naval officer, in 1721 was successful in transporting a shoot of this plant, now from the Paris Botanic Gardens to Martinique, from where cultivation spread: in 1727 to Haiti, in 1728 to Jamaica – Jamaica 'Blue Mountain Coffee' today is the most expensive brand of coffee – in 1748 to Cuba, from there to Puerto Rico, Trinidad, Venezuela and so on. It was the Dutch again who took the first step in introducing coffee to Surinam in 1718. From here, the Portuguese merchant, Francisco della Melo Palheta, smuggled a plant into the Brazilian province of Pará. Brazil, at the beginning of the twentieth century, grew 80 per cent of the world production of raw coffee. After an initial period of coffee consumption, only in 1840 did tea-drinking England start large-scale coffee cultivation in India, in 1878 in central Africa and later East Africa. Australia was reached in 1876.[20]

18
Sinnapah Arasaratnam, Dutch Power in Ceylon 1658–1687, New Delhi, 1988

19
Ibid., pp. 181–93

20
Heise, op. cit., pp. 17–21

46 Franziska Bollerey

21
Ibid., p. 16

2.3.1
This coffee house, situated at Tophane square in Constantinople, shows lavish furnishings (Copperplate engraving by Antoine Melling, 1819)

2.3.2
In the eighteenth century, elaborate waiting systems evolved like this pivotable table that served three rooms at the same time

Global migration of this very young luxury – compared to tea, which looks back on a history of more than 1,500 years – is accompanied by the history of its consummation. Knowledge of this beverage, 'black as ink', is brought to Europe by merchants and travellers to the Orient in the sixteenth and seventeenth centuries. Coffee beans as well as the implements needed for their preparation very rarely reach Europe, as in the case of the Frenchman Jean de la Roque, who brought them from Istanbul to Marseilles. One of the first known European consumers of coffee is William Harvey, physician and discoverer of the circulation of blood (1628) – consummation and discovery here are seen to be directly connected.

Coffee popularity is equally furthered by various representatives of the Ottoman Empire itself, who in the European ports and trading centres or in their European military posts, as well as at universities, did not like to do without their habitual beverage. It is a matter of record that in Venice around 1610 coffee was consumed. An example of the multiplying effect was the visit of Ottoman envoys in Vienna in 1665 and in Paris in 1669.[21] A number of coffee cooks were members of the diplomats' entourage and part of the cultural entertainment programme was a coffee-tasting ceremony for the nobility in Paris and Vienna. Remarkably, it is these two cities that lend their names to the popular typology of places of coffee consumption: the 'Wiener Kaffeehaus' and the Parisian 'Café'. Drinking coffee consequently was no longer a novelty when around the mid-seventeenth century the first coffee houses entered the stage of public life in Venice, Oxford or London.

47 Setting the stage for modernity

The fascination with the unknown – the birth of modern cultural transfer

It is the process of becoming familiar with the consumption of luxury goods such as tea, coffee or chocolate that, more than any other previously traded goods, widens the horizon of Europeans. Together with panoramas[22] and intensified by the presentation of non-European cultures during World Exhibitions, they instigate a yearning for the unknown and the exotic and can thus be regarded as initiators of modern mass tourism.

What can be understood as the fashion for eighteenth-century architectural and interior decoration of royalty and nobility (Chinoiseries, Oriental elements, Egyptomania) – a very late example of this is John Nash's Royal Pavilion of 1815–22 – was to soon become part of the knowledge of the enlightened bourgeoisie. Coffee house owners of foreign origin play the important role of mediators here. According to the provenance and early use of coffee, it was Syrian Lebanese, Egyptian, Greek, Armenian and later Dutch, English or Italian citizens who obtained concessions to roast, brew and distribute coffee.

The growing consumption of coffee during the fifteenth and sixteenth centuries led to a 'hitherto unknown social institution', the coffee house.[23] This aspect is completely ignored in American and Europe-centred literature, even in sociological and philosophical works such as those by Jürgen Habermas,[24] to give only one example.

The history of the coffee house begins in Constantinople in 1555. Two Syrians, Hakm and Shams, were running a very successful coffee shop on the Bosporus (Fig. 2.4). In 1645, a coffee house is mentioned in Venice.[25] Coffee, however, had been consumed there earlier. Diplomatic and economic contacts between the Republic of Venice and the Ottoman Empire had led to a transfer of this luxury item as well. Albrecht Dürer's paintings clearly show the important role of Ottoman merchants in the lagoon city.[26] In 1585, the Venetian, Gianfrancesco Morosini reports from Constantinople on the effects of coffee and its public consumption in coffee houses (Fig. 2.5).[27]

How far-reaching the fascination with the foreign was for the Venetians, who loved masquerades at any rate, is shown not only through the adaptation and imitation of oriental coffee tableware but also by the fashionable habit of wearing Turkish costumes to visit the coffee houses (Fig. 2.6).[28]

In England, it was the Greeks who, as representatives of the multi-ethnic Ottoman Empire, indulged in the consumption of coffee. No less a person than the architect John Evelyn, who after the Great Fire of London supplied a competing design to Christopher Wren's reconstruction plan, as early as 1673 noted in his diary, 'there came in my time to the College [Balliol College, Oxford] one Nathanial Canopius, out of Greece … he was the first I ever saw drink coffee.'[29]

22
Sehsucht. Das Panorama als Massenunterhaltung des 19. Jahrhunderts. Exhibition Catalogue, Ausstellungs- und Kunsthalle der Bundesrepublik Deutschland, Bonn 1993

23
Hattox, op. cit., p. 73

24
Jürgen Habermas, Strukturwandel der Öffentlichkeit, Frankfurt am Main, 1961

25
Söhn, op. cit., pp. 48–9

26
Ludwig Grote, Albrecht Dürer, Reisen nach Venedig, Munich, 1998. Dürer visited Venice in 1494/95 and in 1505–1507

27
Danilo Reato, La bottega del caffè: i caffè veneziani tra il '700 e '900, p. 13

28
Wolfgang Schivelbusch, Das Paradies, der Geschmack und die Vernunft, Munich, 1980, pp. 30–1

29
Clayton, op. cit., p. 10

2.4.1 (opposite page)
This view of the terrace of
a simple Constantinople coffee
house (Copperplate engraving
by William Bartlett, 1839)
going on the Valens aquaeduct
and Hagia Sophia, suggests
the appearance of the first
coffee houses.

2.4.2
The interior of this Tatar
coffee house, too (Copperplate
engraving around 1800) shows
typical characteristics:
raised dais, conversation,
playing of games, conveying
of news or the performances
of a storyteller. The garments
convey a whiff of the exotic
and this oriental fashion
spills over to Europe.

2.5.1
Coffee houses also made
possible easy contacts between
artist and impresario and
served as points of sale for
art. Here, Francesco Guardi
(1712-1793) offers for sale
his Venetian veduti in
"Caffè Florian".

2.5.2
Florian (Lithograph by
Giovanni Pividor, first half
of the 19th century) was,
besides Quadri and Lavena
the most fashionable place
in Venice.

Salon pour la lecture des journeaux étrangers.

CAFÉ FLORIAN
a' Venise. Grande Place S¹ Marc.

49 Setting the stage for modernity

2.6
Coffee is served in Batavia, the modern Jakarta (Le Brun, 1718). A flying coffee vendor (Jean Baptiste van Moor, 1714). Venetian in Oriental garments drinking coffee.

30
Ibid., p. 10

31
Ibid., p. 43

2.7.1 (opposite page)
Since the days of Johann Joachim Winckelmann the German cultural elite preferred Caffe del Greco. Since coffee houses frequently served as postal addresses, "Greco" was the "German's Post Box" (Water Colour by Ludwig Johann Passini, 1856).

2.7.2
The English frequented the nearby Caffe degli Inglesi, for which Giovanni Battista Piranesi in 1769 designed the interior in the Egyptian style.

In the same way, the aforementioned physician, William Harvey obtained his knowledge from an oriental fellow student at the University of Padua. The first place for drinking coffee in public, however, was opened by the Syrian Cirques Jobson in Oxford in 1650.

In London, the strange drink was offered, as is recorded, in 1652, by the Greek citizen Pasqua Rosée, who came to England as a member of the British Levant merchant Daniel Edwards' staff. 'His coffee-making abilities were allied with a gift for publicity.'[30] On handbills, he praised 'the virtue of the coffee-drink'. His immense success caused the envy of the beer brewers and led to his unpopularity, eventually even his deportation. The idea, however, had been sown. Numerous coffee houses or renamed taverns or inns offered coffee now. To attract customers, names such as 'Smyrna', 'Sultanness' or 'The Turk's Head' deliberately played on associations with the exotic. The origin of its founder is betrayed by the name 'Grecian' for the coffee house that mainly was patronized by members of the nearby Royal Society such as Isaac Newton, Hans Sloane or Edmond Halley. 'For many years its name was synonymous with intellectual debate.'[31]

On the Continent, in the second half of the seventeenth century, it was also Greeks and Armenians who ran semi-permanent coffee stalls, for example, during the annual trade fairs of Saint Germain in Paris or the Leipzig Fair. Two Armenians dispensed coffee in Vienna from 1666 from a permanent location. Erroneously, the birth date of the Vienna coffee house frequently is attributed to Gregorius Kolscycki, a citizen of the southern Hungarian city of Zombor. In return for his services as scout in 1683 after the defeat of the Turkish army besieging Vienna, he obtained some coffee sacks left behind by the Ottomans, as well as a licence from Emperor Leopold I to brew coffee. There can be no doubt about the Ottoman origins of the highly developed coffee house culture of the Austro-Hungarian Empire. In Brno, again it was a

32
Two drawings survive as part of a collection of fire place mantle pieces, some of them in the Egyptian style. They are plates 45 and 46 from "Diverse maniere d´adornare I camini ed ogni altra parte degli edifizi desunte dall´architettura egizia, etrusca, greca e romana Toscana", Rome 1769

33
Christian Traugott Weinling, Briefe über Rom (Letters on Rome), entry of 26 December 1767, quoted in Heise, op. cit. p. 205

Turk, in Prague, a Syrian, who in 1702 and 1714 respectively established coffee houses. Likewise, it was a Greek who in 1760 founded the famous Caffè Greco in Rome's Via dei Condotti. The illustrious guest list of this coffee house, which still exists, constitutes a veritable encyclopaedia. There was not a single prominent and cultured visitor to the eternal city, who did not go to this establishment. Mainly here a cultural transfer takes place between the representatives of different nations. In the immediate vicinity, the Caffè degli Inglesi was opened in Piazza di Spagna. The architect Giovanni Battista Piranesi was commissioned with the interior decoration. He enjoyed a great reputation as corresponding member of the London Society of Antiquaries. Architects as well as architectural theoreticians including the Adam brothers, John Soane and other influential British connoisseurs of the art were eager to meet Piranesi during their 'Grand Tour'. The 'Inglesi' also became a trade centre for antiquities.

Here Piranesi confronts visitors with Egyptian culture.[32] (Later, in 1838–42, the Caffè Pedrocci in Padua adopts Egyptian décor as part of the canon of its suite of rooms.)

> In its interior, this coffee house is decorated in the Egyptian style after a drawing of the famous Piranesi. A wealth of Egyptian pagan idols, miraculously combined, appear in the different colours of granite and of other dark varieties of stone,[33]

a traveller reports (Fig. 2.7).

By making exotic cultures a topic of their tenue as well as of the interior of their coffee-dispensing places, these foreigners initiated an international process of cultural transfer. European coffee house owners subsequently cultivated this tendency. Around 1780, the Café Turc opened its doors in Paris on the Boulevard du Temple (Fig. 2.8).

34
One of the most visited convivial places at the time of the ancien régime was the Café Caveau. In front of its garden arcades, there was a roomy, well-furnished tent, that offered seats for more than a hundred people.

35
Jünger, op. cit., p. 190

36
Ibid., p. 188

37
This is impressively demonstrated in the pastry maker museum of Coltura in Bergell in Engadine, Switzerland.

Next to the orientalizing architectural language of the entire building, it was the characteristic element of a canopy that spans the space above the pavement, which clearly imitated the appearance of an Ottoman coffee house, anticipating the modern style of today's coffee houses. Likewise the coffee tents and coffee kiosks (from the Turkish, 'kösk'), appearing in Vienna's Prater gardens, in Berlin's Tiergarten or in Paris,[34] can trace their origins to oriental patterns (Fig. 2.9). The beginnings of a coffee house culture in the emerging Prussian metropolis of Berlin date back to a North African by the name of Olivier. Berlin gave asylum to a great number of French Huguenots, who fled their country after the annulment of the Edict of Nantes in 1683. Together with them, Olivier, who obviously was skilled in brewing coffee, came to Berlin and obtained a concession from Friedrich I in 1711. The royal wash-house near the Lustgarten was converted into a 'Café Royal'. Later it moved to Berlin's boulevard of flâneurs, Unter den Linden, where it survived until 1765. Thus, in Berlin, the foundation was laid for a metropolitan coffee house culture that was to fully develop only in the nineteenth century. Berlin, this latecomer among European metropolises, was, when the first pastry-makers from the Engadin region in Switzerland reached the city, still rather small-town in character. The cultural transfer brought by these virtuosi, who already had been successful in Italy and especially in Venice, generated, in contrast to London and Paris, a different type of coffee house: the coffee-cum-pastry shop. Whoever today wants to evoke the image of those early, 'Biedermeier'-style establishments, should visit Budapest's Café Ruszwurm. In Berlin, the senior of all Engadine pastry-makers, Josty, opened his first coffee-cum-pastry shop at Stechbahn 1. In 1865, he transferred it to the Schlossfreiheit, the area around the château, and still later to Potsdamer Platz.

> Until his old age, Adolph von Menzel used to stop at Josty late in the evening. Usually, he appeared around half past eleven after a rich dinner in the nearby restaurant Frederich. He occupied his reserved seat and was known to become rather unpleasant, when something did not go according to his wishes. Until one o'clock he absorbed himself in the laid-out journals, now and then murmuring under his breath, or sometimes taking out his sketch book and a giant carpenter's pencil to commit one of his sudden inspirations to paper.[35]

The real kind of Berlin pastry shop ('Konditorei'), a certain Giovanoli is said to have established in 1818, in Charlottenstraße. This pattern was followed by his compatriots Stehely (Fig. 2.10), Spargnapani and Stoppany, who all came from Engadine between 1820 and 1825 as impoverished refugees[36] and went back to their native country rich men.[37] Regular customers of Stehely's were, among others, the writer E.T.A. Hoffmann, the philosopher Max Stirner and the writer and poet Willibald Alexis (Fig. 2.10).

2.8 (opposite page, top)
In 1780 on the Paris Boulevard du Temple
Café Turc was opened. In the 19th century the
Oriental mode had developed so far, that in
1850 real odalisques were presented in Café
Mauresque.

2.9 (opposite page, bottom)
Summer blinds and tent architectures,
inspired by Turkish pomp tents appeared
in the European metropoles of the eighteenth
century in Paris' Tuilerie around 1800
or in London's Covent Garden.

2.10
Stehely is a typical coffe house of the
Berlin 'Biedermeier' period with its
three-room-enfilade (Oil painting by
Gustav Tanbert, 1832).

The sun goes down, evening is coming. Out of the pastry shops
of Messrs. Stehely, Sparpagnani, Giovanoli, Josty, Courtin and
whatever the names of all these free Swiss citizens may be, who
bring us cakes instead of freedom, the famous Berlin political
correspondents step into the street. Their face is serene, they
have baked exactly such an amount of news, as suffices to
construct an article full of hidden diplomatic attacks.[38] (Fig 2.11)

The Austrian, Johan Georg Kranzler was a pastry-maker, too. His café
likewise became an institution in late Biedermeier Berlin. In the post-
war period of Wirtschaftswunder (the economic miracle), it had a
renaissance on West Berlin's Kurfürstendamm.

In other parts of Germany, the Dutch not only played an important
role as colonial distributors of the coffee plant and coffee merchants, but
also as promoters of the beverage itself. In 1673, the Dutchman Jan
Jantz van Huesden filed an application with the city council of Bremen
for permission to sell coffee, hot chocolate and 'Potasi', a vegetable soup
based on dried herbs.[39] In the course of the next three hundred years,
Bremen became the leading city of coffee for Germany. In the country's
second major trading centre for coffee, another Dutchman, Cornelius
Decker or Bontekoe from Alkmaar, is said to have set up the first coffee
house in town.[40] In the 1670s, Bontekoe became resident doctor at the
Berlin court of Friedrich Wilhelm, the Great Elector.[41] It can be assumed
that these coffee houses were of less oriental character. They probably
can be regarded as a kind of replica of the interiors that were painted by
the seventeenth-century Dutch artists. Jan Luyken, the most prominent

38
Unsterblicher Volkswitz: Adolf
Glasbrenners Werk in Auswahl
(Eternal Popular Witticism: Adolf
Glasbrenner's Selected Works),
Klaus Gysi and Kurt Böttcher
(eds), 2 vols, Berlin, 1954, vol.1,
p. 82, quoted in Heise, op. cit.,
p. 135

39
Süsse muss der Coffee sein,
exhibition catalogue,
Stadtgeschichtliches Museum,
Leipzig, 1994, p. 17

40
Heise, op. cit., p. 106

41
Söhn, op. cit., pp. 43–5

42
Ulla Heise (ed.), Kaffeekultur.
Bilder aus der Geschichte des
Kaffees, Ausstellungskatalog,
Sammlung Eduscho, Bremen
undated, p. 35

43
See Hattox, op. cit., p. 109

2.11
One of the most renowned
coffee houses was Berlin's
Café Josty at its first
address (Lithograph by C.
Schmidt, 1845) and later at
Potsdamer Platz (Oil painting
by Paul Hoeniger, 1880).

exponent of the copperplate engraving after Rembrandt, in 1694, depicts a 'coffy-huys' (Fig. 2.12).[42] In this way, the citizens of Bremen and Hamburg gained knowledge of the solid wealth of the Dutch: heavy curtaining, decorously gilded mirrors, costly carpets on the tables – still today found in the Netherlands – and chandeliers.

Fighting for customers was typical even in the early days of consumer capitalism, as is demonstrated by the handbills of Pasqua Rosée; the coffee house owners tried to outdo each other in the struggle for customers. Where the personality of the landlord or the notoriety of the guests were not the causa movens for a visit, other attractions were required: the interior decoration, later the attraction of gas or electric lighting, leisure distractions (board or card games, later billiards and reading matter, music or cabaret performances) and carefully selected personnel were the weapons used in the fight for customers.

'Many of the Coffeamen [keep] beautiful boys, who serve as stales to procure them customers',[43] George Sandys notes as early as

2.12
Interior of a Dutch
coffee house: Het Coffy-Huys
(Copperplate engraving by
Jan Luyken, 1694).

55 Setting the stage for modernity

2.13
Central figure of this scene
is the waiter boy – garcon –
of the Ancien Régime – 'Café
Procope'. Another one is to be
seen in a Venetian 'bottega
del caffè' in an etching by
Giovanni Volpato (1735-1803).

1644 in Istanbul. Procopio dei Coltelli had boys aged 8–12 serve in his Parisian Café Procope, as was customary in his Italian homeland (Fig. 2.13).[44] He used the original interior of a former Turkish bath house for his establishment. Even today, one calls for a 'garçon' (boy), to ask for service in a French restaurant. Another member of staff, who in apparel and function more and more diversified over time (headwaiter or marqueur, waiter, Piccolo in Vienna, chausseur or limonadier in Paris and so on) was the seated female head cashier. English representations from the beginning of the eighteenth century show her enthroned in a kind of alcove-altar surveying the premises. The Vienna coffee house of the early nineteenth century has her surrounded by admirers.

The Café Procopio had besides its *garçons* a 'belle limonadière' (Fig. 2.14) for one of the Procope's attractions, next to selling coffee, was the offer of refined lemonades and distilled beverages. Famous to the present day is Procope's 'Rosée du soleil', based on fennel, aniseed, coriander, dill and crushed caraway[45] as well as sorbets, sherbets and variations of ice creams. Even today the very concept of quality is embodied by a 'gelato' manufactured by an individual Italian ice cream producer. It was Procopio who in the French capital aroused curiosity for these novel pleasures that in the public sphere of the coffee houses remained the privilege of the male section of the population.[46] Ladies were served in their waiting carriages before they were allowed entry to the coffee houses. Thus, the coffee house served the process of transporting the consumption of luxury goods formerly reserved for the court and nobility into the bourgeois sphere.

For a long time the fascination for things oriental[47] remained a factor in the marketing of coffee houses. Around 1850, the opening of the Café des Mauresques in the Boulevard St Germain in Paris created a revival of the 'oriental mode'. Showing the same arrogance that led to the presentation of non-European tribal people during the World Exhibitions, the 'Mauresques' 'exhibited' four odalisques smoking water pipes on a divan (see Fig. 2.8). More harmless but still mirroring the colonial power of the British Empire is J. Lyons & Company's contribution to the 1887 Newcastle Jubilee Exhibition celebrating Queen Victoria's fifty years jubilee on the throne. In its Indo-Chinese pavilion-café, Lyons impressed the media and the public with its enormous range of coffees, teas, cakes and pastries. In 1894, London's first Lyons teashop opened at 213 Piccadilly. This is not the place to ask why tea influenced the minds, habits of consummation and commerce differently from coffee, although the Venetian Marco Polo in his *Il Millione*[48] and other widespread writings brought the knowledge of Chinese culture to Europe in the early fourteenth century. It is a fact, though, that tea won the upper hand in England after an initial flourishing of coffee and coffee houses in the seventeenth and eighteenth centuries. The term 'teatime' now is, as on the Continent, a synonym for the fifth hour of the afternoon. Although the tea rooms were part of a retail chain and conceived of as a restaurant catering to the busy city dweller, tea at Lyons, whether in a cup or a pot, was always

44
There is an engraving in the
Paris museum of Carnavalet to
prove this. Delphine Christophe,
op. cit., p. 39

45
Paris. Die schönsten Restaurants,
Cologne 1994, pp. 116-7

46
Likewise the English pub was,
as Christoph Grafe shows in
his contribution, an entirely
male domain.

47
Edward Said, Orientalism,
New York 1979

48
Original in 1298/99, rediscovered
in Toledo in 1933. First title
presumably "Le livre de Marco
Polo, Citoyen de Venise, dit
Million, oú l´on conte les
merveilles du monde"

2.14
The lovely lady of the cash
register becomes the magnet
of many coffee houses and is
strategically employed as
such. In the Paris Café du
Bosquet admirers are crowding
behind the window panes.
In Vienna's Silbernem
Kaffeehaus she is surrounded
by followers (Lithograph
by Katzler, ca. 1820). The
proprietress of Café de Mille
Colonne, known as 'la belle
limonadière' (Copperplate
engraving c. 1830).

57 Setting the stage for modernity

49
The corner house closed in 1977. The last Lyons corner shop closed in 1981

50
See Clayton, op. cit., pp. 135–8

51
Peter Lummel, 'Erlebnisgastronomie um 1900. Das "Haus Vaterland" in Berlin', in Herbert May and Andrea Schilz, Gasthäuser. Geschichte und Kultur, Petersberg, 2004, p. 196

52
Sigried Giedion, Mechanization Takes Command: A Contribution to Anonymous History, New York, 1948

53
As early as 1687, the French developed a coffee machine mounted on an alcohol burner. In 1800, the Frenchman de Belloy invented a precursor of the percolator system. The real inventor of this principle is the American Count Rumford, alias Benjamin Thompson (1753–1814). Söhn, op. cit., p. 160–9.

freshly brewed. In the 1920s, there were already more than 260 Lyons shops. In 1922, the Coventry Street Corner House, opened in the Strand in 1909, was enlarged to cater to 4,500 customers. The legendary Corner Houses in the Strand (1915)[49] and in Oxford Street (1928) had room for 2,500 customers.[50] In their functional character, aimed at maximum sales, the marketing of the culture of the main growing regions of tea, India and China, was not part of Lyons' strategy. Other overseas, European or North American references appear in the styling of cafés in Berlin in the 1920s, 1930s and 1940s. In 1911/1912, the renowned Berlin architect, Heinrich Schwechten built a multi-purpose installation (offices, cinema, restaurants) at Potsdamer Platz. The main attraction here was the 2,500-seat Café Piccadilly, Europe's largest.[51] Sigfried Giedion's book *Mechanization Takes Command* made the informed part of the population familiar with the fact that quantities such as these – like many other developments of a mass consumer society – were only possible through strict mechanization of the production process.[52] With reference to 'mechanization' in the brewing of coffee, the earliest was Loysel's 'Percolateur', that provided two thousand cups of coffee per hour during the Paris World Exhibition in 1855.[53] At the outbreak of World War I, the Berlin 'Piccadilly' was renamed 'Café Vaterland' – 'Fatherland Café'. In 1928, Café Vaterland became 'Haus Vaterland', at 4,500 square metres, the largest temple of event gastronomy. As well as attractions such as a Spanish bodega, a Viennese 'Grinzinger Weinstuben' and a Wild West Bar, there was, among others, a Turkish coffee house (Fig. 2.15). A Turkish café in an establishment thus described constitutes a step on the way from an encounter with authentic representatives of the multinational Ottoman Empire and the individual coffee house down to the present-day neo-authentic and mindless consumerism. Inasmuch as culture degenerates into mere merchandise, it loses its emancipating character. Does cultural transfer like this, made possible by a real coffee house culture, still serve the widening of one's horizon, or the relativity of one's point of view, or does it all too often bow to the conditions of the market?

Trade, media, politics and the coffee house

To grasp the innovative role of the coffee house during the seventeenth and eighteenth centuries, it is necessary to reflect on the historical situation. Apart from rather primitive pubs or inns and guesthouses along routes or at halting places for coaches, there were no other sheltered places for the congregation of ordinary people. Social contacts were established in churches – as one can see in the paintings of Dutch church interiors of the seventeenth century – at trade fairs, at exchanges,[54] in the street or in public squares.

In the latter, merchants and buyers mingled with inhabitants, showmen, sutlers, market criers, ambulant vendors, quack doctors, etc. As early as the fourteenth century the intricate and vivacious urban life was depicted by Ambrosio Lorenzetti.[55] But it was only in the

54
There were exchanges in Bruges and Antwerp (1531), Lyon and Toulouse (1549), Hamburg (1558), London (1566, founded by Thomas Gresham, banker to the court) and Amsterdam (1603)

55
'Il buon e il cattivo governo', from 1338, fresco in the Palazzo Pubblico, Siena.

2.15
Turkish coffee house as part
of Haus Vaterland in Berlin
around 1930 (Postcard Klaus
Lindow, Berlin).

seventeenth century that the companionship he illustrated found shelter under the roof of a coffee house. The patrons of these establishments gave a home to these manifold activities which previously had been carried out under the open sky. Furthermore, they greatly improved the heretofore rather patchy network of exchanging news, by giving it a more systematic and localized structure. By adopting the function of post boxes, the coffee houses became a collecting place for information via the messages sent to the respective recipients of letters. Opening their premises to lectures and readings also, the coffee houses placed teaching and education on a more democratic footing, which so far had been the sole privilege of the secular and ecclesiastical upper classes.

The coffee house thus improves social structures; mainly it serves as a provider of informal meeting places for the different representatives of the developing bourgeoisie, such as merchants, bankers, politicians, writers, artists and scientists. The character of this urban biotope was determined by the clientele, whose composition, on the other hand, was predetermined by the topographical position of the coffee house in the different parts of the city. Semi-permanent coffee shops at first were to be found at custom barriers on the arterial roads, at trade fairs or in harbour areas. Coffee house owners later chose permanent locations in fashionable streets and squares (the Piazza San Marco, Venice; the 'Piazza' at Covent Garden, London; the Palais Royal, Paris; the Parisian Boulevards; Berlin's Unter den Linden; Vienna's Ring Boulevard). An interesting phenomenon, almost a sort of synergy effect, can be observed here: coffee houses frequently were set up next

59 Setting the stage for modernity

56
'Sherbet', Arabian for drink, from which the Italian word 'sorbetto' derives. In the Orient it is a cool drink or lemonade, in Persia it is part of the daily meal

57
Clayton, op. cit., p. 64

58
Samuel Pepys, Memoirs of Samuel Pepys: Comprising his Diary from 1659 to 1669, London, 1825

59
Clayton, op. cit., p. 90

60
Ibid., p. 10

2.16
Gathering of a coffee house clientèle at a long table in "Manwaring's Coffee House". This pattern is superseded by the introduction of sitting niches for more intimate conversations (and better ways of listening in) (Woodcut, c. 1760).

to or facing each other or along a street. Another point of gravitation was the vicinity of scientific institutions or stock exchanges. As early as 1671, a coffee house opened next to the Marseilles stock exchange. New York's Merchant's Coffee House or later Crown or the de la Bourse in Brussels are examples of the same phenomenon. In London's streets around the Cornhill and in the vicinity of the Royal Exchange were to be found coffee houses that above all other purposes served trade activities, such as Garraway's, opened by Thomas Garraway in Exchange Alley in 1670. By candlelight, Hudson's Bay Company furs were traded here in the same way as sugar, indigo, textiles or spices. This allows us to speak of the liberalization of trade, equally important for the coffee houses as its attributed role as promoter of free speech. At Garraway's, the retail tea trade was introduced, too. Whole shiploads were auctioned here, thus coffee houses now compete with exchange trade, so far exclusively under royal control.

Edward Lloyd set up in business in 1686/87 in a lively thoroughfare on the way to Wapping. His clientele was mainly composed of sailors and ships' captains. He, too, auctions shiploads of goods in his coffee houses and develops an elaborate system of collecting news about ship cargoes, routes and harbours in Greece, Turkey and Egypt. These were distributed by word of mouth 'on the premises' and from 1796 three times a week in Lloyd's News, so that visiting their coffee house became a must for all sea traders. Soon the free-standing tables and chairs were complemented by niches where customers could cluster for more private discussions (Fig. 2.16). 'A staff of five distributed coffee, tea or sherbet,[56] as well as paper and ink for business minded clients.'[57] Soon cargoes are insured here and Lloyds gives his name to one of the most renowned insurance companies world-wide.

A totally different clientele crowded the coffee houses around Covent Garden Market. In 1631, Inigo Jones reshaped the area into a piazza following Italian examples in the Neo-Palladian style. The attraction of a coffee house here was still further intensified by the opening of the King's Drury Lane Theatre, designed by Christopher Wren in 1674. As early as 1664, Samuel Pepys,[58] the famous London chronicler, reports a visit to Will's, a coffee house, undertaken by William Urwin: 'Where I met Drayden [John Dryden] the poet I knew at Cambridge [Magdalen College] and all the wits of the town.'[59] Two phenomena can be observed here at the same time: first, the graduates of Oxford and Cambridge transfer their need to exchange opinions in a coffee house to the metropolis. Of Arthur Tillyard's Oxford coffee house, opened in 1655, one can read:

> The discussions on scientific and philosophical subjects that took place in this coffee house are believed to have inspired the formation of the Royal Society, many of whose members would later frequent the coffee houses of London in order to attend similar debates and to give public demonstrations.[60]

2.17.1
Famous habitués furthered reputations. Here we see the Paris café Procope surrounded by medallions of amongst others regulars George Louis Leclerc, Comte du Buffon, Denis Diderot, Jean Jacques Rousseau, François Marie Voltaire.

2.17.2 (overleaf)
Later, the list of celebrities grew considerably longer: Benjamin Franklin, Napoleon Bonaparte, Honoré de Balzac, Victor Hugo, Paul Verlaine, Anatole France.

A second phenomenon is to be seen in the act of 'holding court'. Of Dryden, it is said that visitors came 'to bow to the laureate' and to get his opinion, whether on Racine's latest tragedy or another work of literature. Other habitués at 'Will's' were Jonathan Swift or the young Alexander Pope. Characters such as Dryden, who in winter reserved a chair in front of the fireplace, held court in 'their' coffee house; they were literally 'courted' by landlord and waiters alike.

Here we have the first example of holding court in a coffee house, which will be continued by representatives of the Enlightenment in Paris, the 1900 literary world of Vienna or of the 1920s in Berlin, as well as by celebrities such as Jean Paul Sartre in the Paris of the 1950s, right up to the present day. The famous became advertisers of the coffee houses they frequented, about which they wrote and to whose fame they thus contributed. Famous clients, whom the coffee house owner tried to turn into habitués, are useful attractions (Fig. 2.17). While they are alive, the public comes to see them. When they are dead, commemorative plaques on their former chairs keep their memory alive. Even today one exploits the 'Here frequented ...', 'Here sat ...', or 'Here spent the night ...' (proof of this can be found in Agatha Christie's 'Pera Palace' in Istanbul or actor Otto Sander's 'Paris Bar' in Berlin). Thus, it became part of the commercial calculation of coffee house

2.17.3
Most egregious clients of the
Leipsic coffee house "Zum
arabischen Kaffeebaum" were
Saxonian king August The
Strong, August von Kotzebue,
Franz List, Richard Wagner.

61
Heise, op. cit., pp. 131–4; also
Franziska Lentzsch, Füssli: The
Wild Swiss, exhibition catalogue,
Kunsthaus Zürich, 2005

62
It was common to buy the right of
access and to a cup of coffee with a
penny, in more exclusive houses
with two pennies. Later tokens
became common.

63
Clayton, op. cit., p. 79

64
Hermann Westerfrölke, Englische
Kaffeehäuser als Sammelpunkte
der literarischen Welt im Zeitalter
von Dryden und Addison, Jena,
1924, p. 62

65
Ibid.

landlords, to increasingly cultivate the treatment of celebrities by reserving their accustomed seats for them, treating them to their favourite foods and beverages or surprising them with choice novelties. The personal greeting of a guest elevates the special visitor out of the crowd, a habit that had its beginnings in 'Will's' coffee house in London in the seventeenth century where it created a social norm.

Here the role of the 'meeting place' of the 'established wits' changed from 1712/1713 in the house founded by Daniel Button in Russell Street, Covent Garden, that bore his name. The political meeting places were situated in the Pall Mall part of the city, where Tories frequented Ozinda's and the Whigs the Cacao Tree coffee houses. The Spiritus Rector at Button's was Joseph Addison. His name and that of Richard Steele are associated with the beginnings of modern journalism. In 1709, Steele edited the coffee house gazette The Tatler, followed in 1710/11 by The Spectator which was edited at Button's, and The Guardian (Fig. 2.18) edited jointly by Addison and Steele.

Following Addison's and Steele's model, and in its title referring to this function of the coffee house, political economist Pietro Verri and public law specialist Cesare Beccaria, both held in high esteem by Empress Maria Theresia, in 1764/1765 published Il Caffè: Ossia brevi e vari discorsi in Brescia. Distributed from Venice and Milan, this weekly became the mouthpiece of the Italian Enlightenment. Painter and dedicated follower of the Enlightenment, Johann Heinrich Füssli probably read this publication in Rome's Café Greco, where he met Johann Joachim Winckelmann and Swiss painter Angelica Kauffmann. Enthusiastic about the provocative content, Füssli translates a selection of the articles, that appear in 1769 under the title Das Caffee oder vermischte Abhandlungen ... ('The coffee house or miscellaneous treatises ...') in Zurich.[61] This is an outstanding example of the multiplication effect of the influence of coffee houses (Fig. 2.19).

But there was more to the editing activities that took place in these institutions since the days of Button's. As well as writing articles, holding editorial meetings and organizing lectures and readings (an opening that gave coffee houses the nickname of 'penny universities'[62]), Addison introduced the 'letter to the editor'. In The Guardian he pointed out, in 1713, that a letter box in the shape of a lion's head – 'a proper emblem of knowledge and action, being all head and paws' received the correspondence. 'It opens its mouth at all hours for the reception of such intelligence as shall be thrown into', and he claimed, 'whatever the lion swallows, I shall digest it for the use of the public.'[63] 'In imitation of the antique Egyptian lion,'[64] the lion's head was made following the design of William Hogarth, the famous painter and graphic artist critical of society (Fig. 2.20). Fixed to the west wall of Button's in 1713, it showed an inscription adopted from the Roman writer Martial (40–104): 'Servantur magnis isti cervibus ungues: Non nisi delecta pascitur ille fera.'[65] Here we can see the association with the 'Bocca della la Verita', today touristically exploited, that in Rome was fixed to the wall of the early Christian church of 'Sta. Maria in Cosmedin', to serve

2.18
Central figures in London's
Will's and Button in the
early eighteenth century were:
John Dryden, Alexander Pope,
Richard Steele and Joseph
Addison.

2.19
In 1764/1765 in Italy
the cultural-political
enlightenment gazette Il
Caffè was edited, that Johann
Heinrich Füssli published
in 1769 in Zurich in the
German language.

IL CAFFÈ
OSSIA
BREVI E VARJ DISCORSI
DISTRIBUITI IN FOGLJ PERIODICI
Dal Giugno 1764.
a tutto Maggio 1765.
TOMO I.

IN BRESCIA. MDCCLXV.
DALLE STAMPE DI GIAMMARIA RIZZARDI
CON LICENZA DE SUPERIORI.

Si vende in Milano da GIUSEPPE GALEAZZI
Stampatore e Libraro.

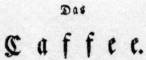

Das
Caffee.
Oder
Vermischte Abhandlungen.
Eine Wochenschrift.
Aus dem Italiänischen übersezt.
Erster Band.

Zürich,
bey Füeßlin und Compagnie, 1769.

2.20
In London's Button one could
find a collector of letters to
the editor in the shape of a
lion's head, that allowed
associations with the Roman
Bocca della Verità.

as a receptacle for petitions by the population. In fact, the sculpted piece of stone was a former ancient canal manhole-cover.

Over the course of the centuries, the coffee house increasingly changes its character from a place of literary production – except in the case of writers actually still writing there – to that of a distribution centre. In the course of the second half of the nineteenth century, subscribing to journals and newspapers becomes a must for the managers of coffee houses. The number of outlying national and international editions becomes part of the advertising strategy. The multitude and range of these publications were considerable, their degree of daily currency very high. Most newspapers appeared in the morning, at noon and in the evening. In 1913, the *Neue Züricher Zeitung* had no fewer than six editions a day. As Stefan Zweig writes as late as 1942:

> But our best place of education in everything new remains the coffee house. It is in fact a sort of democratic club, accessible for everybody for a cheap bowl of coffee, where each guest may remain for a small obolus for hours, may discuss, write, play cards, receive his mail and above all where he can consume any amount of newspapers and magazines.[66]

66
Stefan Zweig, Die Welt von
gestern. Erinnerungen eines
Europäers, Stockholm, 1942,
quoted in Thomas Martinek,
Kaffeehäuser in Wien. Ein Führer
durch die Wiener Kaffeehäuser,
Vienna, 1996, p. 19

Even today, coffee houses serve as distributors of daily print media and provoke more than one discussion. A recent Vienna coffee house guide,

67
Thomas Martinek, op. cit., p. 117

68
Hattox, op. cit., p. 32

69
Thomas Hobbes, Elementorum philosophiae sectio prima de corpore: sectio secunda de homine; sectio tertia de cive, Paris 1642. First English edition in 1651: "Philosophical Rudiments concerning Government and Society".

70
Clayton, op. cit., p. 16

71
Ibid.

72
Markman Ellis, The Coffee House: A Cultural History, London, 2004, p. 89

that comprises more than a hundred entries, mentions next to the address and hours of opening the number of newspapers provided.[67] As a device against theft, the newspapers in Vienna and other places are inserted into a backbone-like wooden device (Fig. 2.21).

From its beginnings, the coffee house is a place subject to close and mistrustful surveillance by those in power. Made more ardent by the stimulating effect of coffee, the news gathered and distributed here, tends to make political discussion more animated than in other places. As early as 1511, Mecca[68] and, in 1539 as well as 1544, Cairo were cities where bans were issued against the consummation of coffee. 'To draw a sharp line between religious and political concerns is perhaps a mistake,' Ralph S. Hattox writes. Both aspects played a role in the attempt to prohibit coffee consumption and coffee houses. In the end, the view prevails that those who drink coffee do not act contrary to the laws of the Sharia. However, in 1568, according to Wolfgang Jünger, once again an order was addressed to the 'kadis of Istanbul and Galata … to close all wine taverns and coffee houses, because vice and looseness prevail there'.

In most cases, attempts to close down coffee houses have a political background, in all cases, however, this is related to attempts to spy on conversations hold there. It was said about coffee houses: 'Certainly they have been linked with the spread of dissent and new political ideas such as the theories of Thomas Hobbes …[69] and constituted centres of opposition to the crown.'[70] So seriously did the authorities interpret the danger that on 29 December 1675, that Charles II issued a 'proclamation for the suppression of Coffee Houses'.[71] These places played a vital role as cradles of public opinion and therefore were places where the government infiltrated spies to gain a true insight into the political feelings of dissenters. This is exemplified by the case of Yarmouth – a town where a large concentration of Nonconformist Protestants lived. Soon after the Restoration, a certain Bower was employed as intelligence spy for the Secretary of State to describe the political situation. Around 1667, Bower established his wife in a coffee house. By listening over the tables, she gained confidential knowledge of town politics and ship movements to Holland. This was duly reported by letter to the Secretary of State Williamson.[72]

Coffee houses had encouraged a polyphony of conversations in public, which threatened authority by usurping the prerogative of the crown, i.e. political power. But the coffee house was not the only actor that played its role in a network. This was also the case in France before and during the French Revolution and again in 1830 and especially in 1848 all over Europe, or later in Italy during the time of Giuseppe Garibaldi. One of the most potent tools in this network of political emancipation is the literature of the Enlightenment. Here you find, among others, the works of the encyclopaedists Denis Diderot, Jean-Baptiste le Rond, called d'Alembert, and of Voltaire, who in 1716 spent eleven months in the Bastille because of a piece of satirical writing

2.21
Newspaper racks and holding
brackets were typical
ingredients of a Vienna
coffee house.

73
Jünger, op. cit., pp. 84–5

attributed to him, and of natural philosopher Jean-Jacques Rousseau – all of them regular customers at the Procope coffee house. These places were ideal sounding boards for the writings and teachings of this group of people. There they found fertile ground mainly among the so-called proletarian intellectuals who, due to the pressure of financial difficulties, had fled the provinces for Paris. They were lawyers, physicians, artists, teachers or students without work.[73] They waged fierce battles of words in the coffee houses and gardens of the Palais Royal. 'In the Palais Royal', one of these immigrant lawyers, Camille Desmoulins (like Voltaire, a fully trained jurist) wrote, 'those take turns every evening, who have Stentor's voice. They mount a table, people

66 Franziska Bollerey

2.22
Coffee houses also served
as stage settings for
politicizing and agitation. In
1789, Camille Desmoulins calls
for a storm on the Bastille in
Café de Foy. In 1848 critical
contemporaries gather in
Vienna (Etching by K. Gunther,
1848) and In den Zelten in
Berlin (Woodcut, 1849).

74
Quoted in Jünger, op. cit., p. 89

75
Joseph Roth, Zipper und sein
Vater, Munich, 1928, pp. 137–8

gather around ... they read to them the strongest stuff that was printed on the same day about things going on.'[74] On 12 July 1789, Camille Desmoulins himself stands on such a table in the Café de Foy and calls everybody to arms to storm the Bastille, after it was known that Jacques Necker the reform-friendly Minister of Finances had been sacked (Fig. 2.22).

One of the celebrities of the Café de Foy was also Théroigne de Méricourt (Anne Josèphe Terwagne) who, as the so-called 'Amazone of the Revolution', was of Flemish peasant origins and has been portrayed innumerable times. The cafés of the Palais Royal also became the scene for bloody activities. In the Café Caveau, rewards were distributed to those who delivered the severed heads of persons condemned to capital punishment by the people's tribunal (Fig. 2.23). From revolutionary times, Café de Foy and Café Corazza, also situated in the Palais Royal, pass into the Napoleonic era. The latter was used by Napoleon I himself as agent provocateur in his own interest. During the time of the Directory, Paul François, Count of Barras, ran an elaborate network of spies here. In his wake, Joseph Fouché organized the first modern secret police system. Representatives of his far-flung informant's network reaped rich harvests in the coffee houses. Thus, the place of unimpeded free speech and of bourgeois emancipation at the same time also becomes the source of organized spying by the state. This system of eavesdropping or listening in, practised in cafés till the end of World War II and later, and the control of telephone conversations today have been superseded by globally acting secret services that replace real people by electronic spying.

A hub for artists and writers

Even today, people come into Café Procope in Paris to sit at Voltaire's table:

By frequenting them, writing inside and about them, the representatives of literature, painting and later filmmaking contributeto the fame of coffee houses. Their owners, mentioned in connection with English coffee houses, tried to tie these customer attractions to their establishments, for some of the paying guests form the clientele of those eager to warm themselves in the sun rays of prominence. They form a backdrop for the appearance of those in the limelight, who played to their equals but also to the common folk. Appropriately, Joseph Roth, in his picture of the revenue clerk Arnold, in Zipper und sein Vater, portrays such a type.

He was interested in art. Being near to those who practised it, was part of his modest satisfactions. He certainly envied them. For only they, it seemed to him, had found a meaning in life and had a right to exist. It was only when Arnold entered the café that he had the feeling of finally escaping his daily life. His freedom began ... This world had nothing to do with the bitter and prosaic world of everyday.[75]

2.23
Café du Caveau, glamorous
place during the Ancient
Régime (Colour engraving,
eighteenth century), turns
into a bloody place in the
French Revolution: here
premiums for severed heads
were distributed (Copperplate
engraving, c. 1793).

The nearly sublime atmosphere of a place, apart from whirling metropolitan daily life, its specific 'esprit du lieu', is to be found in the following sketch of the Café Procope:

> An atmosphere of refined and elegant suppression pervades the place: ... Here all is peace and tranquillity, and that is why it is the haunt of many earnest and aspiring poets and authors: for hither they may bring their portfolios in peace and security, and there they may work upon their manuscripts, knowing that their neighbours are similarly engrossed ... And then, too, are they not sitting on the same chairs and writing at the same tables that have been occupied by some of the greatest men in all the brilliant history of France ...? Are not these ancient walls the same that echoed the wit, badinage, and laughter of the masters?[76]

76
W.C. Morrow, Bohemian Paris of To-Day, London, 1899, pp. 213–4

For more than a century, the fate of the Procope was intricately linked to that of the Comédie Française (Ancienne Comédie). Until their removal in 1770 they used a former 'jeu de paume' hall for their performances. It was the performers and playwrights who laid the foundations for the Procope's everlasting fame. As a café for artists and writers of the eighteenth century, it occupied an elevated position. 'From here, the entire public life of France was critically commented, epigrams were formulated und the judgment over the latest plays and operas cast. It had the reputation of a true newspaper of Paris.'[77] Voltaire was said to have gone to the Café Procope disguised as a clergyman to listen incognito to the opinions on his latest play *Semiramis*. After falling out of favour during the nineteenth century, it experienced a revival around 1900. Paul Verlaine was one of the fugitives from fashionable boulevard coffee houses as places of bourgeois hunger for consumption and attractions who looked for

77
Söhn, op. cit., p. 73

78
W.C. Morrow, op. cit., p. 219

79
Christophe, op. cit., p. 18

80
In the times of Procopio dei Coltelli the licensing costs for a licence for a cafetier or limonadier were considerably above those of the manager of a restaurant. More refinement was expected from the latter. This division was given up in 1791.

81
Léon-Paul Fargue, Le piéton de Paris, Paris, 1998 (1st edn, 1939), pp. 140–1

82
Molly Nesbit and Françoise Reynaud, Eugène Atget, intérieurs parisiens: Un album du Musée Carnavalet, Paris, 1992, p. 25

83
In 1920, Marcellin Cazes took over the brasserie Bord du Rhin, founded by Léonard Lippman in 1877 and rechristened it in commemoration of its first owner.

alternative retreats. 'He would sit in his favourite place in the little rear salon at Voltaire's table' (Fig. 2.24).[78] In the second half of the nineteenth century, it is mainly the artists' cafés in Montmartre that helped strengthen the fame of Paris as a cultural metropolis, as well as those mundane, elaborately furnished cafés along the boulevards, those flâneur runways, that held hundreds of customers. The Café Guérbois in the Grande Rue des Batignolles (today Avenue de Clichy) was the meeting place of the Impressionists. Here Eduard Manet would gather his friends around him. Next to the entrance, two tables were reserved for him. Later, the Café de la Nouvelle Athènes (Fig. 2.25) at Place Pigalle in the immediate vicinity of the ateliers of Edgar Degas and Auguste Renoir became the most important meeting place for artists. The Irish author, George Moore, calls it the 'veritable Académie française'.[79] Fugitives from Montmartre such as Claude Monet, Frédéric Bazille and others move to the Closerie des Lilas in Montparnasse. Paul Fort organizes literary lectures, Alfred Jarry, playwright and editor-in-chief of the literary periodical *La Plume* meets here young Pablo Picasso. From 1905 onwards, the Dôme is populated by the proponents of Fauvism and Cubism. Here Ilja Ehrenburg, Leon Trotsky and a young Lenin read the newspapers freshly delivered from St Petersburg. The Dôme's reputation in 1911 leads to the opening of La Rotonde (Fig. 2.26), an establishment of similar character. As the third star in this constellation, La Coupole appears in 1927, which will become the centre of the night life of 'les Années folles'. The gastronomic framework of all these places is formed by the combination of brasserie, restaurant and café[80] which since the 1920s had been influenced by the 'Bar Américain'. Josephine Baker, Jean Cocteau, Fernand Léger, Alfred Jarry and the many other extravagant celebrities draw clients like candlelight attracts moths:

> Each and every obscure poet or painter who wants to be successful in Bucharest or Seville, according to the actual situation on the old continent has to do a little military service in 'La Rotonde' or 'Coupole', those two pedestrian academies [here one is reminded of the London nickname 'penny universities'] that teach Bohème lifestyle, contempt for the bourgeois, sense of humour and heavy drinking.[81]

Although the ateliers crowded the back streets of Boulevard Montparnasse, mainly Rue Campagne Première – the renowned Eugène Atget[82] runs his photographic studio here – the congregation of artists and intellectuals moves on. It aims for St Germain des Près. Here, at the cradle of coffee house activity founded by Procopio dei Coltelli, since the 1930s the magic triangle of Café Flore, there since 1885, the Deux Magots, there since 1891, and Brasserie Lipp (under this name since 1920[83]) dominate intellectual life in Paris. Léon-Paul Fargue, who in 1939 reveals in his *Le piéton de Paris* the multifaceted life of Paris coffee houses, is a regular customer at Lipp's.

69 Setting the stage for modernity

2.24
Paul Verlaine occupies
Voltaire's former habitual
seat in 'Procope'.

2.25
Café de la nouvelle Athènes
in the 19th century became a
veritable 'Academie française'
because so many literates and
artists gathered here.

84
Léon-Paul Fargue, op. cit.

85
Ernest Hemingway, Paris: A
Moveable Feast, New York, 1964

'If I did not at least spend one night per week at "Lipp's", it would be impossible to write even thirty lines in a Paris newspaper, to create a painting or distinctly contribute one's opinion in the field of politics.'[84] Here, Léon-Paul Fargue once again clearly characterizes the give-and-take in the coffee houses. Creative productive energies are nourished here and those inspired here, in turn, elevate the place they frequent to fame by their presence and by their works. Parliamentary Deputies – who remain faithful after 1945 – or students of the Ecole des Beaux Arts rub shoulders in Lipp's with representatives of the theatre, films, literature and the fine arts. Among the customers are Pablo Picasso, Colette or André Gide.

In 1935, the literary award 'Cazes', named after Lipp's owner, Marcellin Cazes, was donated, an established feature of literary life. Also a contributor to the wealth of legends was Ernest Hemingway, a frequent customer of Paris coffee houses, through his posthumous book: *Paris: A Moveable Feast*.[85] Lipp's remains a literary fortress after World War II. It was visited by Michel Butor, Nathalie Sarraute and Alain Robbe-Grillet, the most important exponent of the French literary current of the 'Nouveau roman'.

The Deux Magots settles in the premises of a former fashion store. Part of the original furnishings were two wooden sculptures of

70 Franziska Bollerey

86
'Magot' – dog-ape or grotesque Chinese porcelain figure

87
Antoine de Saint Exupéry, Courier Sud: Paris, 1929

88
James Joyce, Dubliners, London, 1914

89
James Joyce, A Portrait of the Artist as a Young Man, London, 1917

90
James Joyce, Ulysses, Paris, 1922

91
Gianni Stupanitsch, 'Jeux d'ombre et de lumières au Caffe Garibaldi', in Gérard-Georges Lemaire, op. cit., p. 113

92
See the series 'Itinerari Triestini – Triestine Itineraries'

93
Christophe and Letourny, op. cit., p. 107

94
Hermann Kesten, Dichter im Café, Munich, 1959, pp. 12–3

2.26
The coffee house life of artists migrates in the beginning of the twentieth century to Montparnasse. Jean Cocteau in 1916 takes photographs of Amedeo Modigliani, Pablo Picasso and André Salmon in front of 'La Rotonde'. The following phase plays in St. Germain, where Picasso meets Dora Maar. Here a joint drawing of both on a serviette.

Chinese mandarins. They become the enigmatic reason for the establishment's name. In Deux Magots,[86] André Breton, who hated the charivari on Montparnasse, meets a carefully selected circle of Surrealists. Antoine de Saint-Exupéry is a customer here while he is working on his Courier Sud.[87] Pablo Picasso meets Dora Maar here. Foreign guests throw themselves without restraint into this intellectual and artistic turmoil. James Joyce gathers his apostles around him here. An excursion may be in order here to Trieste, where Joyce finishes his Dubliners,[88] commences work on A Portrait of the Artist as a Young Man[89] and continues writing Ulysses.[90] During his stays in Trieste in 1904–15 and again in 1919–20, the Caffè Stella Polare and the Pasticceria Pirona are both places he frequents. The city, the former Austrian Empire's door to the Mediterranean Sea, even today has a remarkable coffee house culture with numerous, partly not very aptly restored places:[91] Tommaseo, Tergesteo, Fabris, Garibaldi, Rosetti, Degli Specchi and, above all the rest, San Marco are linked with writers such as Italo Svevo, Umberto Sabba[92] and in more recent times, Giorgio Voghera, Claudio Magris and Fulvio Tomizza.

Joyce himself, who spent materially poor but creatively rich years in Trieste, we find back in Paris in Deux Magots, in the company of Bertolt Brecht, Alfred Döblin, Heinrich Mann, Joseph Roth and the permanently travelling, 'scorching reporter', Egon Erwin Kisch.[93] Mainly in the years after 1933 and until the occupation of Paris by German troops in 1940, coffee houses develop into the most important meeting places of the many exiles. What in the more peaceful times of the eighteenth century was a communicative amenity, namely to make the acquaintance on an international level of like-minded people (Benjamin Franklin met Isaac Newton in 1725 in Bathon's Coffee House in London; the El Greco in Rome as focus point of an early cultural tourism has already been mentioned), for the emigrants of the inter-war period becomes an existential necessity:

> In exile, the coffee house becomes house and home, church and parliament, desert and pilgrim's aim, a cradle of illusions and a cemetery. Exile makes you lonely and kills. In exile, the coffee house is the only continuous locality. I have been sitting in cafés in a dozen exile countries and it was as if I was always sitting in the same café, at the seaside, between mountains, in London, in Paris, next to Amsterdam's canals, between the monasteries of Bruges. I sat in the coffee house named exile and wrote.[94]

The third café of the mythical trio in St Germain in Paris is the Café de Flore. Here we find Raymond Queneau, author of Zazie dans le Métro, made into a film by Louis Malle in 1960, or Georges Bataille, Albert Camus, Alberto Giacometti and his brother Diego, Jean Louis Barrault, whose appearance in Les enfants du paradis made this a cult film. Among Flore's aficionados also counted actors such as Simone Signoret, Gérard Philippe and Brigitte Bardot, and film directors such as Roman Polanski,

95
The same kind of people, mixed
with Italian colleagues, were to be
found in the cafés of Rome's Via
Veneto in the 1950s.

Jean Rouch or Joseph Losey.[95] Jacques Lacan turned up there every day as well as Roland Barthes every morning. Every night Pablo Picasso sat opposite the door among his Spanish friends, in a sort of continuation of his sojourns in the Barcelona café, Els Quatre Gats, where he had exhibited his first paintings as a 16-year-old.

The intellectual, stimulating atmosphere of coffee houses certainly facilitated the production of sketches and notes for writers and artists, but this did not mean that every café automatically became an office. For the Café de Flore, however, this was nearly always the case. Jean-Paul Sartre, who lived next door to the Flore in the Rue du Seine in the Hotel Louisiane, used the café as his office. 'As a teacher with little money I lived in a hotel ... and like everybody that lives in a hotel, I spent most of the day in the café.' 'Simone de Beauvoir and I more or less settled down in the café' (Fig. 2.27).[96] On the marble table one found inkwells instead of drinks. Simone de Beauvoir wrote:

96
Noël Riley Fitch, Die literarischen
Cafés von Paris, Zurich, 1993,
p. 12

> We worked from nine in the morning till noon, when we
> went to eat. At two we came back and had conversations with
> acquaintances till four, whereupon we worked again till eight.
> After dinner we made appointments there with all sorts
> of people.[97]

97
Raoul Hoffmann, 'Die Cafés von
Paris – Bilder aus einer Tradition',
in Ausland 1981, pp. 439–40

98
Norbert Elias, Über den Prozeß
der Zivilisation. Soziogenetische
und psychogenetische
Untersuchungen, 2 vols, Frankfurt
am Main, 1978 (1st edn 1939)

99
Hermann Kesten, Dichter im Café,
op. cit., p. 14

100
Ibid., p. 14

101
Cf. Franziska Bollerey, Mythos
Metropolis. Die Stadt als Sujet für
Schriftsteller, Maler und Regisseure.
(The City as a Motif for Writers,
Painters and Film Directors),
Berlin, 2006, pp. 40–9

102
Lemaire, op. cit., p. 9

If Norbert Elias can talk of a 'housing in of human activities',[98] in a coffee house the exact opposite takes place. In it the privatized domain of dwelling is being enlarged by additional living space. 'My coffee house, is it not a handsome writing room for a poet?'[99] And: 'Already then I frequented the café mainly to do my writing,' Hermann Kesten notes.[100] The glimpse out of coffee house windows resembles the gaze out of the windows of an apartment upon the goings-on of a large city.[101]

'Within one hour I watch a dozen comedies and listen to the echoes of tragedies nobody will ever write down', Kesten notes during his exile.[102] To the curious and sensitive onlooker, the coffee house was both intimate theatre inside combined with wide-screen stage outside. In 1787, Carlo Goldoni reports on the Café de Foy, where the revolutionary Desmoulins had made history:

> A never-ending milling of the crowd, an amazing number of
> carts, small-scale retailers peddling manifold wares who throw
> themselves between the horses and wheels, seats on the
> pavement for those who want to watch and those who want to
> be watched, cafés with orchestras and Italian and French singers,
> pastry cooks, cooks, landlords, marionettes, acrobats and
> hawkers who advertise giants, dwarfs, wild beasts, sea monsters,
> wax figures, mechanical men and ventriloquists.[103]

103
Carlo Goldoni, Memorie del
Goldoni per servire all'istoria della
sua vita e quella del suo teatro:
traduzione dal francese, Florence,
1787–1789, quoted in Heise,
op. cit., p. 153

Goldoni is also one of the first to make the coffee house the centre of a prose comedy. In retrospective, the playwright declares that in the

2.27.1
The coffee house turns writing place for literates: A portrait of Fernando Pessoa around 1964 (Oil painting by José de Almada-Negreiros).

104
Walter Jens (Ed.), Kindlers Literaturlexikon, Munich, 1992, p. 578

centre of La Bottega del Caffe, which premiered in Mantua in May 1750, neither a story, nor a passion or a character is to be found, but the coffee house itself. 'The never changing stage in his comedy brings about that the acting personnel always meets in a public space and communicates there.'[104] This exactly mirrors the role that the coffee house itself occupied for a long time.

Examples of writers and artists making coffee houses their theme are many. One work, however, must not be omitted here: Johann Sebastian Bach's 'Kaffeekantate – Coffee Cantata'. Leipzig, being a major centre of trade fairs, possessed a wealth of famous coffee houses (Fig. 2.28). Each Friday night in Zimmermanns Caffee-Haus, the

2.27.2
The coffee house also becomes a locality for holding court, like for Jean Paul Sartre and Simone de Beauvoir in Café Flore.

105
Heise, op. cit., p. 152

106
Burkhardt Rukschcio and Roland Schachel, Adolf Loos, Vienna, 1982, pp. 66–9, 418–20

107
Heise, op. cit., p. 206

108
Evert van Straaten, Theo van Doesburg: Painter and Architect, New York, 1988, pp. 196–219

109
Arlette Kosch, Literarisches Zürich. Der Dichter und Denker Stadtplan, Jena, 2002

110
Ibid., pp. 35–6

111
Gudrun Arnd, Spaziergänge durch das literarische New York, Zurich, 1997, pp. 166–7

112
Ibid., pp. 35–6

'Collegium Musicum' would meet. This remained the case after Bach took over as leader of the Collegium between 1729 and 1740. It was here in all probability that in 1734 the première of Bach's 'Coffee Cantata' took place.[105]

There are, on the other hand, works of art too, that condemn the use of coffee, for example, Carl Gottlieb Hering's canon 'C-A-F-F-E-E'. In the realms of music, theatre and literature, many prominent members have dealt with the topic of the coffee house, but also among the ranks of the many architects and designers, who gave coffee houses their shape, we find well-known exponents of architectural history: Piranesi has been mentioned before, in England, we can name Robert Adam – the Adam brothers were close friends of Piranesi; it is to them he dedicates his Antichità Romane. In France, Claude Nicholas Ledoux and his Café des Officiers, in Germany, we find Karl Friedrich Schinkel and his Berlin coffee house, Fuchs, on Unter den Linden. In the twentieth century too, the design of coffee houses is an important commission for famous architects. Adolf Loos, who is also responsible for Vienna's American Bar, designs the highly austere Café Museum[106] in the same city. Its very character made critics rename this Karlsplatz café, 'Café Nihilism'. Never carried out was a project by Wladimir Tatlin and Alexander Rodtschenko for a 'Café Pittoresque' in pre-Revolutionary Moscow. This café was to 'treat basic aesthetic questions of the modern city and create the basis for a new style in painting as well as in the other branches of art'.[107] To agree in theory with the demands of a synthesis of art, literature and theatre was also the ambition of a coffee house in Strasbourg. In 1926/1927, Hans Arp won the commission for Café Aubette. Together with his wife, Sophie Täuber-Arp, and the Dutch De Stijl protagonist Theo van Doesburg, he worked for two years redecorating the place, which opened on 17 February 1928.[108] The café-brasserie, the café-restaurant, the tea room, the Aubette-Bar, the basement cabaret and the Bar Américain as well as the billiard room have been restored to their original state as befits this shining example of the architectural history of the 1920s (Fig. 2.29).

After this detour on the design of coffee houses, we return to them as refuges for artists and writers. An excellent source for this are literary guidebooks and literary portraits of cities with an anthological character. From the Literary Zurich guide,[109] we learn that in 1916 Tristan Tzara invented the term 'DADA' as an habitué of the Café Odéon.[110] Dadaism consequently was born in this city. If the birth place of existentialism was in the Café de Flore in Paris, where we find Sartre and de Beauvoir, the future authors of the 'Beat Generation', Jack Kerouac and Allen Ginsberg, met in New York's West End Café[111] on Broadway. Also in New York, in the Caffe Torino, Edward Albee was inspired to write his famous drama, Who's Afraid of Virginia Woolf? Behind the bar was a mirror covered in graffiti, and among those scribbles he found the question that he was to use as the title of his play.[112]

2.28
Up to 700 persons Leipsic's
Richtersches Coffe Haus
took at any one time.
Friedrich Schiller, in
this copperplate engraving
in all probability the
man with the hat in the
background, commends the
fruitful mental atmosphere.

113
Gérard-Georges Lemaire, Théories
des cafés, 2 vols, Paris, 1987

114
Pontus Hulten (ed.), Futurismo &
Futurismi, exhibition catalogue,
Palazzo Grassi, Venice, 1986

115
Filippo Tommaso Marinetti and
Albert Viviani, 'Gigantesque
bataille de poets, peintres et
sculpteurs', in Lemaire, op. cit.,
pp. 85–7

In *Walks through Literary New York*, one can read about the role that the bar and café-restaurant of the Hotel Algonquin on 44th Street played in the history of literature generally, and especially in the founding of the *New Yorker* magazine. The centre of the young 1990s New York literary scene, East 3rd Street's Nuyorican Poet's Café is also mentioned. Here, the famous 'Open Mike Nights' were invented, free reading or music events, where the public took over the stage. Thinking of the historical character of the coffee house as a stage, we should not speak of an invention here, but more of a reincarnation.

The two volumes of *Théories des cafés*, published in France, are also very informative.[113] Selected sources here illustrate the role of the coffee houses in the development of the Futuristic Movement in Italy.[114] Filippo Tommaso Marinetti gives an account of the 'gigantic battles' poets, painters and sculptors waged amidst gallons of coffee and choice Florentine ice cream treats in the Caffè delle Giubbe Rosse in Florence.[115] The true place of invention of the 'Futuristic Manifesto', however, was Caffè Centro in Milan. In the 1930s, the Bar Craja (see case study on p. 155) takes over as the meeting place of Milan's

2.29
Since the end of the
eighteenth century, the coffee
house becomes a challenge
for architects. Famous examples
from the Modern period are
Vienna's Café Museum by Adolf
Loos and Aubette in Strasbourg
by Hans and Sophie Arp and
Theo van Doesburg.

intellectuals and heart of the cultural life of the city. Carlo Dalmazzo Carrà wrote:

> It was in February of 1909, when Boccioni, Russolo and I met Marinetti who lived in Via Senato … a generation like mine interpreted the café as an extension of the atelier … in a salon lavishly decorated with Persian carpets we decided to address young Italian artists in a manifesto to invite them to free themselves from a lethargy that suppressed every ambition.[116]

In the next couple of days, the 'Futuristic Manifesto' was given its final shape.

I think it was the Irish writer George Moore, or was it Stendhal, who answered the question how art was to be furthered best with: "Open cafés!'"[117] How important coffee houses were to writers,

116
Carlo Carrà, 'Invention de la peinture futuriste au Caffè Centro', in Lemaire, op. cit., pp. 102–3

117
Réné Prévot, Bohème, Munich, 1922, p. 91

76 Franziska Bollerey

Karl Kraus makes clear. In a pamphlet of 1897, Literature Demolished, he writes:

> Vienna now will be demolished to a metropolis [here Kraus takes a similar position to that of Victor Hugo facing Baron Haussmann's destructive intervention in the Paris cityscape] … soon a disrespectful spade will level the venerable Griensteidl [coffee house]. Our literature is facing a period of homelessness, the thread of poetical production will be cruelly broken … more than one advantage has secured this venerable locality a place of honour in literary history. Who does not commemorate the truly overwhelming number of newspapers and magazines, that have made visiting our coffee house a real necessity for those writers, who did not ask for coffee? Is it necessary to refer to the complete volumes of Meyer's Universal Dictionary that – easy of access – enabled every literary person to obtain an education? Or to the lavish range of writing utensils that always were there for sudden inspirations? Namely the younger poets will miss that intimate, old-Vienna-like interior that compensated by the right mood what may have been lacking in comfort.[118]

118
Karl Kraus, Die demolirte Literatur, Vienna, 1897, quoted in Hans Weigel, op. cit., p. 62

Around 1900, in an atmosphere of 'dream and reality', Austrian literature reaches – also thanks to the coffee house culture in this country – a peak with writers such as Robert Musil, Arthur Schnitzler, Karl Kraus, Hermann Bahr, Alfred Polgar, Peter Altenberg or Felix Salten (Fig. 2.30). The history of the Vienna literary coffee house goes back to the eighteenth century. Here the literary scene exchanges the Kramersche Etablissement, which soon after its inauguration in 1771 is called 'the erudite coffee house' by Michael Hertl, for Kaffeehaus Neuner, that in 1820, because of the solid quality of its furnishings, was called 'the silver coffee house' by its owner, Ignaz Neuner. Nikolaus Lenau who has been called the Austrian-Hungarian equivalent to Lord Byron, whom he admired, lived at the same address and for more than 22 years was to be seen at Neuner's several times a day, busy with 'the fragrant Arabic beverage, a pipe in his mouth and always a fresh concept in his head'.[119] Among the many other illustrious guests were Franz Grillparzer and Ludwig van Beethoven, who in the same way as later the father and son Johann Strauß would, performed in coffee houses and their summer branches in the Prater gardens.[120] In 1847, Heinrich Griensteidl exchanged his professional role of apothecary for that of cafetier. Until its extinction as lamented by Karl Kraus, the Griensteidl that was situated in the Palais Dietrichstein, was the meeting place par excellence of artists (Fig. 2.31), where as well as the literary crowd, composers such as Hugo Wolf and Arnold Schönberg were to be seen. The new Parnassus from 1876 on will be the Café Central that, next to Café Herrenhof (from 1918 on) and Café Landtmann (from 1873), attained the rank of a primus inter pares. This happened mainly thanks to Peter Altenberg, who more or less made it

119
Jünger, op. cit., p. 145

120
A certain Martin Wiegand is said to have organized the first coffee house concert in Vienna in 1789.

77 Setting the stage for modernity

2.30 (bottom)
Adolf Loos and Peter
Altenberg (Photography
c. 1900) the architect with a
grudge against ornamentation
and the Bohème poet met in
Café Central and Griensteidl.

2.31 (top)
Café Griensteidl, founded
in 1847 (Water colour by
A. Vlkel, 1880) was demolished
in connection with urban
planning around Michaelerplatz
in Vienna. Karl Kraus
in an essay speaks of
'demolished literature'.

121
Hans Weigel, op. cit., p. 15

his residence, and around whom Adolf Loos, Egon Friedell and Alfred Polgar assembled. Karl Kraus, exiled from the Griensteidl, had a regular table here as well.

Later, Vienna relinquishes its role as the leading coffee house metropolis to Berlin. In the 1920s, Berlin coffee houses – after a phase dominated by large luxury establishments such as Café Bauer, for example – win the leading position in the German-speaking world as cultural meeting places. Two coffee houses can be named here as proxies for many: the Café des Westens (since 1893, the Kleines Café, but renamed in 1898) and the Romanisches Café (from 1916). Siegfried Kracauer gives an atmospheric description of coffee house life in his time. In Vienna, conditions comparable to the era of Griensteidl and Central arise only after World War II with the Café Hawelka (Fig. 2.32). Hans Weigel writes:

> There was one, outwardly unostentatious, in Dorotheengasse. This I used to frequent in the course of the afternoon. There I would write articles, work on books … this café was also one of the few keeping open after midnight, without music and the other bothersome attributes of the night café.[121]

It is Weigel who takes colleagues with him from the Café Raimund, a meeting place of journalists, publishers and writers, to Hawelka. Later, the usual process of the birth of a cult locality commences: local intellectuals, among whom we find the great Praeceptor Austriae,

122
Ferenc Bodor, Die Pressos der
Stad Budapest, Budapest, 1992

123
Michael Rössner, 'Aperçus
de la vie de café', in Lemaire,
op. cit., p. 57

124
Cf. Enrico Guagnini, Locali storici
d'Italia, Milan, 2000

125
Alfred Polgar, quoted in Hans
Weigel, op. cit., p. 69

Heimito von Doderer, are followed by international ones: Henry Miller, Günter Grass and others.

In Vienna and Paris, most historical coffee houses survived, but in Berlin they were destroyed in the bombings of World War II. In the London of the 1950s, an espresso culture flourishes, equally in Budapest.[122] With the rejuvenation of the Procope in Paris (1987) and in Vienna in the 1980s and 1990s with the reconstruction of Café Central and Griensteidl, the coffee house culture revival is treated as part of metropolitan branding. Whoever is looking for an atmosphere of authenticity should visit Prückel, Zartl, Sperl, Schwarzenberg (Fig. 2.33) or Landtmann. Schwarzenberg, situated near the parliament, the town hall, the university and the Burgtheater, even today is a focal point for politics, science and art. This is exactly the situation that Lipp's in St Germain in Paris finds itself in. In Vienna's Café Stein, Christian Ide Hintze recently established a 'school of poetry' following Jack Kerouac's New York West End Café example. Here once a week one can have discussions with Hintze either in person or via the internet.[123] In Berlin, after 1968, Café Einstein in Kurfürstenstraße revived the old coffee house culture, nowadays also in the central part of Berlin, Unter den Linden, where prominent politicians from the nearby Reichstag are part of the clientele. In the former West Berlin, the Café im Literaturhaus in Fasanenstraße represents a mixture of café, garden café, exhibition rooms and a bookshop. Selling books in cafés is a habit dating back to the eighteenth century, but in the Copenhagen of the 1960s quite a number of book-cafés came into being. One recent example of this is Café Litéraire in Berne, Switzerland (2005).

As well as all these famous metropolitan coffee houses as tourist attractions, there are the more anonymous historical coffee houses of Italy,[124] Vienna or Paris. Ambience and clientele here combine and form a convincing whole. In the period of an observable renaissance of the coffee house culture only those places will flourish culturally – no matter whether electronically connected to the whole world or not – that further a certain social togetherness. 'Coffee houses are visited by people who want to be on their own and need company to do so',[125] Alfred Polgar wrote. The secret of the coffee house was and is to be the stage for the 'L'être et Paraître'.

Conclusion

In its early stages as a place for public congregation, the main difference between coffee house, on the one hand, and taverns, pubs, inns and restaurants, on the other, lay in the fact that here predominantly coffee was consumed as a beverage that enlivens the spirit instead of dampening it as alcohol does. Today the borders are no longer so clearly drawn. In a coffee house all kinds of alcohol are served and it is no problem to get coffee in pubs or restaurants.

The global migration of coffee started in Ethiopia in the thirteenth and fourteenth centuries. Trade of this luxury good, as well as that of tea, cocoa or spices, is intimately interwoven with the aggressive

126
Hermann Kesten, op. cit., p. 8

2.32
In the 1960s and 70s 'Hawelka'
shelters intellectuals,
artists and students. It was
able to keep its patina and
its character. With Café
Central, renovated in the
1980s, the effect is more
that of a tourist-flooded
stage backdrop.

colonial policy of the European powers involved in it. Since the specific places for the consumption of coffee started to open, first, in the Ottoman Empire and later in Europe and North America, they have contributed to the social and political emancipation of their customers. The birth of the right to free speech as well as the liberalization of trade is, as has been shown, closely linked to the existence of the coffee house. For this reason, the respective political powers saw a grave threat here to their oligarchic claims and thus coffee houses become centres of intense spying activities, too.

In addition to being strongholds of political and civic emancipation, coffee houses at the same time served as Parnassus for many writers and artists. The specific and extraordinary atmosphere of coffee houses is equally characterized by a dialectic between restriction and independence as well as by the contradiction between leisure and activity.

In the biotope-like sphere of the coffee house, specific patterns of social interaction between owners, staff and client develop, from which all sides profit. To make this phenomenon flourish, a certain permanency is necessary, which opens the opportunity to put one's roots down, according to the deepest psychological disposition of the human being. The aura of familiarity and the framing preconditions for creative productivity are impossible to achieve when there is a permanent fluctuation of staff or a too limited span of time spent in a café – both circumstances common today.

In this context, it is interesting to observe, that in cities such as Paris or Vienna, where once more a certain metropolitan culture of the coffee house is alive and well, the type of quick-consumption-coffee place seems to have little chance of success. Here classic as well as creatively stimulating new coffee houses fulfil a civic demand for public gregariousness. Remake-type or over-renovated coffee houses such as the Procope in Paris and Central or Griensteidl in Vienna appear anaemic in comparison with places like Sperl or Spröckl.

To sum up, to be of real quality and justified reputation, a coffee house has to maintain a delicate balance between permanent staff, loyal clientele, a wide range of things to eat, drink and read, as well as a suitable location within the city, and above all a slowed-down movement of time. Only an atmosphere of leisure, a gentle slowing down, makes the coffee house a suitable observation post, from which to observe the hectic metropolitan stage. It embodies the opportunity for an outlook and at the same time for a retreat. 'Most people go to a café as if they go on holiday, leaving behind day-to-day life,'[126] Hermann Kesten writes as the voice of somebody representing the inter-war and early post-war point of view.

But what about the possible cultural and political relevance of coffee houses today? Does the revival movement of coffee houses since the 1980s reflect a true social need or does it merely represent the attempt to capitalize on a fashionable market niche? (Here it has to be said that what is true for the coffee house holds true for all such

2.33
Café Schwarzenberg in
Vienna (Photography of
the 1990s) is one of the
establishments that still
draw their inspiring
atmosphere from the
physical side-by-side of visitors,
sounds, smells, delights
and distinguished service.

commercial chains and brands: these standardized pre-fabricated offers completely lack any spirit.)

Without being nostalgic, it must be said that these coffee houses 'with a soul' are still to be found. But what role do those repositories of age-old bourgeois emancipation movements play today? It seems that even nowadays many of them, at least in the metropolises, are centres of informal meeting opportunities for the most diverse representatives of culture and the political sphere. But are rearguard actions fought here or have coffee houses become bastions of a counter-culture and thus won back their original historic functions? Can extended stays in a coffee house, in a consciously chosen atmosphere of leisure, be seen as evidence of a critical stance vis-à-vis the so-called 'efficient' use of time? Can coffee houses or, more precisely, the sojourn in them, help one to reflect on essential values? Could they help diminish the impoverishment of our basic psyche?

References

Christophe, Delphine and Letourny, Georgina (eds), Paris et ses cafés, Paris, 2004

Clayton, Anthony, London's Coffee Houses: A Stimulating Story, London, 2003

Hattox, Ralph S., Coffee and Coffee houses: The Origins of a Social Beverage in the Medieval Near East, Seattle and London, 1985

Heise, Ulla, Kaffee und Kaffeehaus. Eine Kulturgeschichte, Zürich, 1987

Jardin, Edélstan, Le cafetier et le café, Paris, 1895

Jünger, Wolfgang, Herr Ober, ein' Kaffee. Illustrierte Kulturgeschichte des Kaffeehauses, München, 1955

Lemaire, Gérard-Georges, Théories des cafés, 2 vols, Paris, 1987

Lepage, Auguste, Les cafés politiques et littéraires de Paris, Paris, 1885

Robinson, Edward, The Early History of Coffee Houses in England, London, 1893

Söhn, Gerhart, Von Mokka bis Espresso, Hamburg, 1957.

Ukers, William H., All about Coffee, New York, 1922.

Historical sources

Alpinus, Prosper, De plantis Aegypti liber, Venice, 1592

Clusius, Carolus, (Charles de l'Ecluse)

de la Rocque, Jean, Voyage de l'Arabie heureuse, Paris, 1716

della Valle, Pietro, Reiszebeschreibung in unterschiedliche Theile der Welt. Nemlich in Türckey, Geneva, 1671

de Thévenot, Jean, Relation d'un voyage fait au Levant, Rouen, 1665

Dufour, Sylvestre, Traitez nouveaux & curieux du café, du thé et du chocolate, La Haye, 1685 (1st edn. 1671)

Niebuhr, Carsten, Travels through Arabia and Other Countries in the East, Trans. Robert Heron, 2 vols, Edinburgh, 1792

Olearius, Adam, Beschreibung der neuen orientalischen Reise, Schleswig, 1647

Rauwolf, Leonard, Eigentliche Beschreibung der Raisz, so er vor dieser Zeit gegen Aufgang in die Morgenländer vollbracht, Lauingen, 1582

Tavernier, Jean Baptiste, Baron d'Aubonne, Six voyages de Jean Baptiste Tavernier qu'il a fait en Turquie, en Perse et aux Indes, pendant l'espace de 40 ans, Paris, 1676

**Scenes from the café –
gossip, politics and the
creation of personalities
A selection of texts from
and on cafés
Photographic impressions
and introductions by
Christoph Grafe**

As a place where political opinions and ideas about the world could be voiced and personal ambitions displayed, established and rejected, cafés have attracted writers and journalists who found ample study material to be made into essays, sketches or newspaper columns. The café may or may not be the birthplace of the modern public sphere, but it certainly was (and remains) a fertile ground for urban myth-making. Indeed, it could be said that there is a specific literary genre, of the light-hearted or serious moral sketch, which both originated in the café and circles around the experiences of public behaviour generated by it. Sometimes these descriptions are careful registrations of the physical appearance of the venue itself and of those for whom it provided a stage. Others are celebrations of the café, or particular cafés, as social condensers or cultural halls of fame. Finally, the evocation of café scenes can also be a vehicle for social analysis or a kind of social anthropology that takes the establishment as a microcosm reflecting broader tendencies or developments in the cultures that produce them.

This selection of fragments from various sources aims to present some of the aspects of café life witnessed and recorded by writers who were both participants and observers. Covering three centuries and establishments in London, Paris, Vienna, Berlin and Nice, these accounts reflect the influence of cafés on their respective urban cultures and the ways in which the position and physical structure of their premises interact with their use as places of urbane conversation, gossip, literary and other politics.

The first text by Joseph Addison is something of a travelogue set in early eighteenth-century London. The author describes his promenade from one coffee house to the next, recording the different and contradictory versions upheld in each of them of the news of the demise of the French king – a proper *canard*, as it turns out. Addison's account of the discussions and debates in the establishments he visits is an elegant ironical analysis of the cultural geography of the early capitalist metropolis that he inhabits, and of the emerging functional differentiation of administrative (St James), cultural (Covent Garden) and commercial (the City) districts.

Siegfried Kracauer's sketch of a café in Berlin's West End in the 1920s is limited to the locale itself. Spanning a day from the early afternoon to the late evening, the description of the goings-on in the café turns into a study not only of the unsettled, even neurotic, behaviour of Kracauer's fellow customers, who seem to move around constantly from table to table, but also of the instability of Berlin urban society in the Weimar years. The café is the home to mixed constituencies, émigrés and economic migrants, who take refuge inside its walls, and an exchange of vital information about job and other opportunities.

The fragment from William Chambers Morrow's *Bohemian Paris of To-day*, published in London in 1899, is an accurate description of the Café Procope, an institution and a symbol of French intellectual culture

3.1
Café Sperl, Vienna (2006)

and of 'Frenchness' in general. It is also a testimony of the inhibiting effect the café has on this American in Paris, who is intrigued and bewildered by the casual, yet explicit display of tradition present in the physical features of the establishment and the rituals of control and hospitality operating as common ground between the landlord, his wife and the guests.

The sketch of a bar in Nice by Siegfried Kracauer reflects the fascination of Northern Europeans with Southern Europe in general, and the lively scenes of bars and cafés in France, Spain or Italy. The small essay is also a highly perceptive and detailed description of the physical features of the bar and their cultural connotations, evoking a precise image of the establishment and its use as a place of continuous movement and social interaction.

The final document, fragments from Alfred Polgar's 'Theory of the Café Central', contains a description of this most myth-laden of the Viennese cafés of the last *fin de siècle*, but is above all an analysis of the collective psychology of the users. The Kaffeehaus is presented as something of a lived view of the world, a response to the fragmentation of Viennese urban culture and the disintegration of the Austro-Hungarian Empire. The Central offers shelter and a refuge from these realities and a home for the writers, businessmen and con-men, offering a place for creative work as well as the assumption of a personality.

Joseph Addison: Coffee house politicians

The writer, diplomat and politician Joseph Addison (1672–1719) was one of the prominent figures in eighteenth-century London culture. With his friend Richard Steele, he founded two of the most influential magazines of the period, The Tatler *and* The Spectator, *which appeared between 1711 and 1714. Addison also established a certain Daniel Button, a former servant of his wife, as the proprietor of Button's coffee house and installed a letterbox in the form of a lion's head where contributions to his magazine could be left for publication. Addison published this essay in* The Spectator *(No. 403) on 12 June 1712.*

When I consider this great city in its several quarters and divisions, I look upon it as an aggregate of various nations distinguished from each other by their respective customs, manners, and interests. The courts of two countries do not so much differ from one another, as the court and city in their peculiar ways of life and conversation. In short, the inhabitants of St. James's, notwithstanding they live under the same laws, and speak the same language, are a distinct people from those of the Temple on the one side, and those of Smithfield on the other, by several climates and degrees in their way of thinking and conversing together.

For this reason, when any public affair is upon the anvil, I love to hear the reflections that arise upon it in the several districts and parishes of London and Westminster, and to ramble up and down a

3.2
Caffè Florian, Venice (2006)

whole day together, in order to make myself acquainted with the opinions of my ingenious countrymen. By this means I know the faces of all the principal politicians within the bills of mortality; and as every coffee-house has some particular statesman belonging to it, who is the mouth of the street where he lives, I always take care to place myself near him, in order to know his judgment on the present posture of affairs. The last progress that I made with this intention was about three months ago, when we had a current report of the king of France's death. As I foresaw this would produce a new face of things in Europe, and many curious speculations in our British coffee-houses, I was very desirous to learn the thoughts of our most eminent politicians on that occasion.

That I might begin as near the fountain-head as possible, I first of all called in at St. James's, where I found the whole outward room in a buzz of politics. The speculations were but very indifferent towards the door, but grew finer as you advanced to the upper end of the room, and were so very much improved by a knot of theorists who sat in the inner room, within the steams of the coffee-pot, that I there heard the whole Spanish monarchy disposed of, and all the line of Bourbon provided for, in less than a quarter of an hour.

I afterwards called in at Giles's, where I saw a board of French gentlemen sitting upon the life and death of their Grand Monarque. Those among them who had espoused the Whig interest, very positively affined, that he departed this life about a week since, and therefore proceeded without any further delay to the release of their friends on the galleys, and to their own re-establishment; but finding they could not agree among themselves, I proceeded on my intended progress.

Upon my arrival at Jenny Man's, I saw an alert young fellow that cocked his hat upon a friend of his who entered just at the same time with myself, and accosted him after the following manner: 'Well, Jack, the old prig is dead at last. Sharp's the word. Now or never boy. Up to the wall of Paris directly.'

With several other deep reflections of the same nature, I met with very little variations in the politics between Charing Cross and Covent Garden. And upon my going into Will's, I found their discourse was gone off from the death of the French king to that of Monsieur Boileau, Racine, Corneille, and several other poets, whom they regretted on this occasion, as persons who would have obliged the world with very noble elegies on the death of so great a prince, and so eminent a patron of learning.

At a coffee-house near the Temple, I found a couple of young gentlemen engaged very smartly in a dispute on the succession to the Spanish monarchy. One of them seemed to have been retained as advocate for the Duke of Anjou, the other for this Imperial Majesty. They were both for regulating the title to that kingdom by the statute laws of England; but finding them going out of my depth, I passed forward to Paul's Churchyard, where I listened with great attention to a learned man, who gave the company an account of the deplorable state of France during the minority of the deceased king.

I then turned on my right hand into Fish Street, where the chief politician of that quarter, upon hearing the news (after having taken a pipe of tobacco, and ruminating for some time), 'If', says he, 'the king of France is certainly dead, we shall have plenty of mackerel this season; our fishery will not be disturbed by privateers, as it has been for these ten years past.' He afterwards considered how the death of this great man would affect our pilchards, and by several other remarks infused a general joy into his whole audience.

I afterwards entered a coffee-house that stood at the upper end of a narrow lane, where I met with a Nonjuror, engaged very warmly with a Laceman who was the great support of a neighbouring conventicler. The matter in debate was whether the late French king was most like Augustus Caesar of Nero. The controversy was carried on with great heat on both sides, and as each of them looked upon me very frequently during the course of their debate, I was under some apprehension that they would appeal to me, and therefore laid down my penny at the bar, and made the best of my way to Cheapside.

I here gazed upon the signs for some time before I found one to my purpose. The first object I met in the coffee-room was a person who expressed a great grief for the death of the French king; but upon his explaining himself, I found his sorrow did not arise from the loss of the monarch, but for his having sold out of the bank about three days before he heard the news of it; upon which a haberdasher, who was the oracle of the coffee-house, and has his circle of admirers about him, called several to witness that he had declared his opinion above a week before, that the French king was certainly dead; to which he added, that considering the late advices we had received from France, it was impossible that it could be otherwise. As he was laying these together, and dictating to his hearers with great authority, there came in a gentleman from Garraway's, who told us that there were several letters from France just come in, with advice that the king was in good health, and was gone out a hunting the very morning the post came away: upon which the haberdasher stole off his hat that hung upon a wooden peg by him, and retired to his shop with great confusion. This intelligence put a stop to my travels, which I had prosecuted with much satisfaction; not being a little pleased to hear so many different opinions upon so great an event, and to observe how naturally upon such a piece of news every one is apt to consider it with a regard to his own particular interest and advantage.

Siegfried Kracauer: Café in Berlin's West End

A trained architect, Siegfried Kracauer (1907–1966) worked as film and literature editor for the 'Feuilleton' of the Frankfurter Zeitung, first in Frankfurt and subsequently in Berlin. His analysis of the role of visual,

3.3
Café Westend, Vienna (2006)

85 Scenes from the café

3.4
Café Prückl, Vienna (2006)

performance and dramatic arts in modern mass culture appeared in 1927 as Ornament der Masse (Ornament of the masses). After he emigrated to the United States in 1941, he published major books on film and worked as a sociologist for various academic institutes. Kracauer wrote the text on a Berlin café for the Frankfurter Zeitung, where it appeared on 17 April 1932. Republished in: Siegfried Kracauer, *Schriften,* Inka Mülder-Bach *(ed.), vol. 5.3, Frankfurt: Suhrkamp, 1990.*

The one [café] I have in mind makes, on the face of it, a perfectly normal impression, is filled with people and newspapers, and forgoes all music. The only music to be heard there is produced by a nice little bell hanging above a handy slate, for noting the name of a guest wanted on the telephone at some stage. Whenever the page walks around with the slate and its bell, you hear a tinkling sound which, if the smoke were not so thick, might cause you to think you were lying in an alpine meadow among cow bells.

Yet, however ordinary the café may seem, it is bewitched inside. Otherwise how could you explain the fact that everyone who unsuspectingly comes in to drink a coffee in peace is rapidly drawn into a whirlpool of distracting events, which in the end totally confuse him? The chief cause of the tumult is undeniably the patrons, more specifically the regulars, for whom the ringing of the bell is usually intended. The obligation to describe the patrons to some extent again requires my discretion. Suffice to say, they are mostly of foreign extraction, without revealing the countries from which clearly originate. Because national prejudices are already far too strong to be further encouraged, I see far less harm in mentioning that the regular patrons in question operate in the fields of operetta and film. In fact, the café serves as an exchange for them. Evidently it only deals in low-priced commodities.

However, it is not the exchange trading itself that generates the whirlpool that swallows all outsiders. There is far more bubbling and fizzing in the post-working hours into which the actual exchange fades away. Then the regulars do not leave the meeting place like other people attending the exchange, to visit the café or go home, they simply turn the exchange into a café and make it their home. In that way they remain in the same space, day and night, using it for ever-changing purposes. Sometimes they make arrangements for hits and bookings, sometimes they are ordinary guests and sometimes they live here.

The residential function is their chief concern. I do not know if they still have a home of their own somewhere, but at all events they behave in the café as informally as if they were between their own four walls. It is as if they want to prove straight away to casual guests how comfortable they feel here. Since one does not have to eat and drink at home if not absolutely necessary, they usually manage without ordering anything; or else they order two glasses of water to do the waiter a small favour. Otherwise the waiter would be superfluous and possibly abolished. The pages are not in any danger in that respect, as they are exploited to the full. Not only do they have to swing the little bell incessantly, but they also drag to and fro all the newspapers appurtenant to the same nations as the regular patrons. The regulars are thus informed of events in the cafés of their far-off homeland.

The guests' tendency to move around constantly in the café suggests to me that their homeland is beautiful and encourages rambles. I have never experienced so much movement, and all the literary movements I know are greatly lacking in driving force compared with this. For example, when two people are sitting at a table, a third will greet them immediately, attracting other acquaintances as if pulled in by magnetic force. A whole crowd accumulates, dragging along spare and occupied chairs from nearby, ultimately forming an impenetrable throng, the components of which can no longer be distinguished. It is a pity for the table at the centre of it all. Suddenly and for no reason the company scatters again, and all that remain, abandoned messily, are cigarette ends and numerous empty chairs. The table is not badly damaged, but has lost its smart appearance. The members of the throng now roam singly through the café, but soon gang up again unexpectedly elsewhere. Many do not sit down at all, for fear of missing something, but stand chatting and, like flying troops, are always ready to decamp. Others take a seat in a way that enables them to command their entire surroundings. The chair is dragged abruptly from its own table and pushed up at another one close-by which is then commandeered accordingly. Regrouping of this type not only augments convenience, but also provides a better view of the companions throughout the café. Confidential exchanges occur quite often between two people at opposite sides of the café – the main thing is that one's voice carries far enough.

Towards the evening the residential operation flags and a gentle silence falls. Harmless guests leaf through magazines, pages giggle behind a balustrade and in the corners lovers whisper to each other. The habitués themselves have withdrawn, leaving a few at observation posts. I have reason to assume that they are recuperating meanwhile, to build up fresh strength for the evening. Since you barely have time to become aware of the intermission before the tumult starts up again, and more violent than before. The composers of musical hits, future operetta divas, stage extras, the gentlemen and the freshly imported young men and girls, who have nothing to call their own apart from their grandiose plans: they have all arrived and are endeavouring to double their achievements. They unconcernedly occupy the aisles, hum snatches of senseless melodies, fill gaps in conversations and shriek. Woe betide the guest who stumbles into their pack! He is in danger of being suffocated and can consider himself fortunate if he can follow the faint ringing of the little bell and reach the exit unscathed.

Translation: Wendy van Os-Thompson

3.5
Café Savoy, Vienna (2006)

William Chambers Morrow: The Café Procope

The American writer William Chambers Morrow (1853–1923) established a reputation in Parisian literary circles as a brilliant author of short stories and was called a new Edgar Allen Poe by Guillaume Apollinaire and Alfred Jarry. A descendant of a wealthy family in the South of the United States, Morrow moved to Europe and worked as a correspondent for the San Francisco Examiner. *This fragment is taken from: W. C. Morrow,* Bohemian Paris of To-Day *(from notes by Edouard Cucuel), London: Chatto & Windus, 1899.*

In the short, busy little street, the Rue de l'Ancienne-Comédie, which runs from the Boulevard St. Germain, in a line from the Théatre National de l'Odéon and connecting with the Rue Mazarin, its continuation, the heavy dome of the Institut looming at its end, is to be found probably the most famous café in Paris, for in its day it has been the rendezvous of the most noted French littérateurs, politicians, and savants. What is more, the Procope was the first café established in Paris, originating the appellation 'café' to a place where coffee is served, for it was here that coffee was introduced to France as an after-dinner comforter.

. . .

The front of the café is a neat little terrace off the street, screened by a fanciful network of vines and shrubbery that spring from green painted boxes and that conceal cosy little tables and corners places behind them. Instead of the usual showy plate-windows, one still finds the quaint old window-panes, very small carreaux, kept highly polished by the tireless garçon apprentice.

Tacked to the white pillars are numerous copies of *Le Procope*, a weekly journal published by Théo, the proprietor of the café. Its contributors are the authors, journalists, and poets who frequent the café, and it publishes a number of portraits besides, and some spirited drawings. It is devoted in part to the history of the café and of the celebrities who have made it famous, and publishes portraits of them, from Voltaire to Paul Verlaine. This same journal was published here over two hundred years ago, in 1689, and it was the means then by which the patrons of the establishment kept in closer touch with their contemporaries and the spirit of the time. Théo is proprietor and business manager, as well as editor.

. . .

The modern gas illumination of the café, in contrast to the fashion of brilliant lighting that prevails in the showy cafés of the boulevards, must nevertheless be a great advance on the ancient way that it had of being lighted with crude oil lamps and candelabra. But the dim illumination is in perfect keeping with the other appointments of the place, which are dark, sombre, and funereal. The interior of the Procope is as dark as a finely coloured old meerschaum pipe. The woodwork, the chairs, and the tables are deeply stained by time, the contrasting white marble tops of the tables suggesting gravestones; and with all these go the deeply discoloured walls and the many ancient paintings – even the caisse, behind which sits Madame Théo, dozing over her knitting. This caisse is a wonderful piece of furniture in itself, of some rich dark wood, beautifully carved and decorated.

. . .

The Café Procope was founded in 1689 by François Procope, where it now stands. Opposite was the Comédie Française, which also was opened that year. The café soon became the rendezvous of all who aspired to greatness in art, letters, philosophy, and politics. It was here that Voltaire, in his eighty-second year, while attending the rehearsals of his play, 'Iréne', descended from his chaise-à-porteur at the door of the Café Procope, and drank the coffee which the café had made fashionable. It was here also that he became reconciled to Piron, after an estrangement of more than twenty years.

. . .

Diderot was fond of sitting in a corner and manufacturing paradoxes and materialistic dissertations to provoke the lieutenant of police, who would note everything he said and report it to the chief of police. The lieutenant, ambitious though stupid, one night told his chief that Diderot had said one never saw souls; to which the chief returned, 'M. Diderot se trompe. L'âme est un esprit, et M. Diderot est plein d'esprit.'

3.6
Caffè Florian, Venice (2006)

Danton delighted in playing chess in a quiet corner with a strong adversary in the person of Marat. Many other famous revolutionists assembled here, among them Fabre d'Eglantine, Robespierre, d'Holbach, Mirabeau, Camille Desmoulins. It was here that Camille Desmoulins was to be strangled by the reactionists in the Revolution; it was here that the first bonnet rouge was donned. The massacre of December, 1792, was here planned, and the killing began at the very doors of the café. Madame Roland, Lucille Desmoulins, and the wife of Danton met here on the 10th of August, the day of the fall of the monarchy, when bells rang and cannon thundered. It was later that Bonaparte, then quite young and living in the Quai Conti, in the building which the American Art Association now occupies, left his hat at the Procope as security for payment for a drink, he having left his purse at home.

. . .

Since then have followed days of calm. In later times Paul Verlaine was a frequenter of the Procope, where he would sit in his favourite place in the little rear salon at Voltaire's table. This little salon, in the rear of the café, is held sacred, for its chair and table are the ones that Voltaire used to occupy. The table is on one side of the small room. On the walls are many interesting sketches in oil by well-known French artists, and there are fine ceiling decorations; but all these are seen with difficulty, so dim is the light in the room. Since Voltaire's time this table has become an object of curiosity and veneration. When celebrated habitués of the café died, this table was used as an altar, upon which for a time reposed the bust of the decedent before crepe-covered lanterns.

. . .

In the café are three doors that are decorated in a very interesting fashion. On the panels of one, well preserved in spite of the numerous transformations through which the establishment has gone, M. Théo conceived the happy idea of inscribing in gold letters the names of the illustrious who have visited the café since its founding. Many of the panels of the walls are taken with full-length portraits by Thomas, representing, among others, Voltaire, Rousseau, Robespierre, Diderot, Danton and Marat playing chess, Mirabeau, and Gambetta. There are smaller sketches by Corot, d'Aubigny, Vallon, Courbet, Willette, and Roedel. Some of them are not fine specimens of art.

M. Théo is a devoted collector of rare books and engravings. His library, which contains many very rare engravings of the eighteenth century and more than one book of priceless value, is open to his intimate friends only, with whom he loves to ramble through his treasures and find interesting data of his café.

Siegfried Kracauer: Bars in the South
Siegfried Kracauer's text on a bar in Nice first appeared in the Frankfurter Zeitung of 8 October 1926. Republished in: Siegfried Kracauer, Schriften, *Inka Mülder-Bach (ed.), vol. 5.1, Frankfurt: Suhrkamp, 1990.*

In *Nice* there is a bar that exemplifies the species [of a bar in the South]. At the entrance from which it evolves, there is a veritable clearance sale of architectural styles: a baroque cartouche sits above the pointed arch, renaissance mouldings encircle the imposts. Wooden scaffolding, which has been erected for repair work, projects from the façade into the opening. The scaffolding is probably always there, because there is no shortage of things to pull down, if not on this side, then on the other. The window contains a gigantic red temple in the form of a coffee machine, which reduces the beverage to its original ingredients. The swallowed 'dishwater' subsequently dissolves into the black molecules of the coffee beans. Hand-painted signs praising the quality of the wares wave like flags across the street; the hasty writing lays claim to permanence. Like any bar, this is a hall of mirrors. Mirrors seeking to multiply every little lamp enlarge the bar into a cave of treasures. It overflows with reflections in which everything is mixed up and quartered. Its complacent reality proves to be sham although the mirrors are impervious to anything that might be real. Additional decorations in the form of gilded tendrils trickle down over the frame around the panes of glass. On the counter bottles sparkle – soda water interposed between green anisette and the reddish-brown of vermouth. Spirits that evaporate quickly on the tongue long remain in the mind's eye as untouchable colour effects. Packets of cheap cigarettes have been stacked into triumphal pillars with an army of matchboxes at their feet. A momentary indulgence links the smoking requisites with the radiant aperitifs. Other things too are short-lived. Chairs and tables lack permanence as required in a living room. Visitors fail to recognise their purpose and keep on moving them around. Almost as soon as they enter the bar they shed social values and turn into vagrants. They stand next to one another, like the words in a crossword puzzle, equidistant and unrelated.

Translation: Wendy van Os-Thompson

Alfred Polgar: Theory of the Café Central

The Austrian writer Alfred Polgar (1873–1955) worked as a critic for the Wiener Allgemeine Zeitung and, from 1905, on the journal Die Schaubühne. *In the 1920s, he moved to Berlin and established a position as one of the leading critics of the Weimar Republic. After his emigration, he made a living as a writer of film scripts, but returned to Europe in 1949. 'The theory of the Café Central' was published in Alfred Polgar,* An den Rand geschrieben, *Berlin: Ernst Rowohlt, 1926, pp. 85–91.*

The Café Central is not a coffeehouse like any other coffeehouse, but a *Weltanschauung* (a view of the world); one the innermost essence of which is not to observe the world as it is. What is there to see anyway? I will return to this later. So much is certain from experience, that there is nobody in the Café Central who has not absorbed a piece of the Central: which is to say, on whose ego-spectrum the Central colour would not appear, a mixture of ash-grey and ultra-seasick-green. Whether the place adapted to the individual, or the individual to the place, is a moot point. I would imagine a reciprocal action. 'Thou art not in the place, the place is in thee,' says the Wandering Cherub.

If all the anecdotes that exist about this Kaffeehaus were smashed up, put in a distillation chamber and made into gas, a heavy, iridescent gas, faintly smelling of ammonia, would emerge: the so-called air of the Café Central. This defines the spiritual climate of this space, a rather particular climate in which unfitness for life, and nothing else, thrives in sustaining its unfitness. Here powerlessness develops powers unique to itself, the fruits of unfruitfulness ripen, and non-existing ownership produces interest. Only a real Central-ist will fully understand this, only he who has the feeling that he's been thrown out into raw life, subjected to the wild accidental arrangements, the anomalies, the cruelties of the foreign world outside, when his coffeehouse is shut.

. . .

The Café Central lies on the Viennese latitude at the meridian of loneliness. Its inhabitants are, mostly, people whose hatred of other human beings is as fierce as their longing for them, who want to be alone but need company for it. Their inner world requires a layer of the outer world to mark their own boundaries. Their unstable solo voices cannot survive without the support of the chorus. They are unclear natures, rather lost without the certainties provided by the sense of being a small part of a whole (the tone and colour of which they can influence). The Central-ist is a person to whom family, profession, and

3.7
Newton Bar, Berlin (2005)

91 Scenes from the café

political party do *not* give this feeling. The coffeehouse is helpful by appearing in as a substitute totality, inviting immersion and dissolution. . . . The Café Central thus represents something of an organization of the disorganized.

In this blessed space, each halfway indeterminate individual is credited with a personality – as long as he remains within the boundaries of the coffeehouse, he can cover all his moral expenses with this credit – and any one of them who shows disdain for others' money is granted the *Unbürgerkrone* (the crown of the Bohémien).

The Central-ist lives like a parasite off the anecdote that circulates about him. That is the main thing, the essential thing. Everything else, the facts of his existence, is small print, addenda, invented detail, all of which can also be omitted.

The guests of the Café Central know, love, and have disdain for each other. Even those who are bound by no association understand this non-association as a form of association – even mutual aversion possesses this power of association in the Café Central – accepting and practising a kind of Masonic solidarity. Everyone knows about everyone else. The café is a provincial nest in the womb of the metropolis, steaming of gossip, envy, and *médisance*. The fish in the aquarium must live like the habitués of this café, continuously circling at the closest distance around each other, always busy without purpose, using the slanting refraction of light of their environment for various small enjoyments, always full of expectation, but also full of anxiety that sometime an unknown object might fall into the tank, playing 'Sea' with a serious expression in their artificial miniature sea-bottom. They would be utterly lost if, Heaven forsake, the aquarium should turn into a banking house.

. . .

There are writers who are unable to do their daily chore of work anywhere else if not in the Café Central. Only there, only at the tables of idleness, is the worktable laid for them, only there, surrounded by airs of indolence, will their inertia turn into fecundity. There are creative types to whom only in the Central nothing comes to mind, and everywhere else far less. There are poets and other industrialists to whom profitable thoughts come only in the Café Central; constipated people to whom only there the door of relief opens; those who lost their appetite for the erotic long ago who only there experience hunger; the speechless who only in the Central find their own or somebody else's voice; and the greedy whose money gland secretes only there.

. . .

On the love life of the Café Central, on the elimination of social distinctions in it, on the literary and political currents by which its frayed shores are washed, on those buried alive in the Central-cavern eagerly awaiting their excavation yet hoping that it will never occur, on the masked play of wit and foolishness that in those rooms turns every night into a Carnival, on these and other things there is still much to

3.8
Café Central, Vienna (2006)

say. But those that have any interest in the Café Central know all this anyway, and in those who are not interested in the Café Central we have no interest.

It is a coffeehouse, everything taken together! Never will you come upon another a place like this. What Knut Hamsun says about the city of Christiania in the first sentence of his immortal *Hunger* applies to it as well: 'No one leaves her on whom she did not leave a mark.'

The question whether architecture is an art has produced some conflicting answers. Adolf Loos denied it emphatically; Josef Frank considered it pointless to wish to settle that question: 'The architect must have the ability and the desire to make something beautiful that is not a work of art.'

However, if architecture is art, it is certainly not restricted or debased in that people can use it or that it may not collapse. The idea that 'applied' art is in some way inferior to art 'proper', was already incorrect in classical art theory – architecture does not just have building materials, structure, light or space as its means, but, first and last, people's actual behaviour. 'Function' is not something given, determining the design, but it is only created by design.

A café sets conditions for the guests' behaviour; it is the means of expression of the person who addresses them – the host. By means of the food and the space he has the guest under control. The landlord does not have to cook himself, but delegates that to a chef, and similarly he can delegate the café idiom: to an architect, or whoever plays that part.

Sometimes a proprietor can cook, but hardly any entrepreneur is capable of sketching accurately his customary workspace – and even less of assessing the spatial relationships in a café for a conversion, let alone a new construction. And, like every layman, he mainly sees the architect's achievement as awaiting ideas, comparing the remuneration with the fee for an evening performance. Only when he witnesses the work does he know why he needed to delegate it.

The principle of delegating – familiar to every yuppie – for a building client is hard to accept, as this role is seldom performed. It means establishing *what* you want, but not *how*. (Yet even this distinction is always concrete and often contentious.) The client can fall back on supervision and control, but must also accept that the architect's solution is something unpredicted – incidentally, for the architect himself as well.

What is yet unpredicted has to consolidate into something obvious, so obvious that the guest may ask: *for this you really needed an architect?* Which indeed is the greatest compliment possible. After all, a café is not to be noticed, but remembered. It should be precisely to the point, and not annoy by pretentious ambitions.

This applies to architecture in general; however, there is hardly any other job that would confront the man (and woman) more directly than a café. It will be immediately apparent what is acceptable and what is not. Nevertheless, designing a café always remains a risky undertaking. Only an interior decorating company will know beforehand what the café will look like – uninteresting! The effect of profound obviousness that makes a deep impression only comes about when every problem has been worked on with blood, sweat and tears, and none is hushed up on behalf of preconceived 'ideas' – although one is never certain before seeing the result. So there is no scope left for considerations on how to make something 'cosy' or 'cool'.

After all, the prerequisites for people's behaviour are problematic and perplexing; and once you become involved, you will soon find 'design' decisions heartily stupid. Just consider the most elementary condition to be realized in a café (apart from the temperature): seating – the unstable position of the pelvis when one is seated, the necessity to support it in order to avoid rolling backwards or forwards, the contour-shaped classical upholstery of the nineteenth century, which was rediscovered in the 1960s as a result of ergonomic research – who would be interested in a 'designer' chair, with legs you stumble over as you walk behind it?

Not forgetting the ability to stand comfortably – how high is the bar, where is the footrest located? How wide is the bar? In spite of the customary deep chiller cabinets, is contact possible between the guest and the barkeeper? How close together can tables be placed? You have to know the rules of the design manuals if you want to break them, because what can actually be tried in practice is always a matter of experiment. The acoustics of a catering establishment – not the intelligibility of a speaker in a silent auditorium which is what the discipline of room acoustics addresses, but that of the person with whom you are conversing when everyone is talking. Why especially are small spaces often too noisy? Because punctual signals of noise – bursts of laughter, chinking glasses, moving chairs – stand out covering individual syllables of speech, which in turn leads to raised voices.

Mirrors in the room – the difference between a mirror hung on the wall like a painting and one creating the illusion of space. With the latter, it is not a matter of size, but of plausibility of the opening: its lasting appeal is due to the ambivalence between knowing it is a mirror and the repeatable illusion of the opening. Mirrors do indeed have a physical effect: the eye, for which any short visual distance requires effort, is able to adjust to the mirrored distance. And then fatigue and feelings of oppression occur less rapidly in small spaces.

This is a random series of subjects from the many behavioural elements that make up an everyday occurrence like a visit to a place. A cognitive psychological approach rightly questions if a computer ever could perform a visit to a restaurant – from entry, taking a seat, the menu and ordering, to payment and departure (which indeed is not an urgent demand). The freedom of choice in these behavioural elements has little to do with innovation, but much to do with continuity; and the many criteria for that can be summed up on one umbrella term: comfort.

Modern architecture, which has undoubtedly started out with the claim that it would make life easier, has only made limited progress in our everyday surroundings. For some, it may seem dim and unilluminated to take the 'mere' comfort of the user as a constituent of architecture. In fact, anyone who is not prepared for that must be accused of an inferior definition of architecture. For, if its intellectual content only existed beyond commonplace purposes, architecture after all would be an 'applied', contaminated art, since commonplace purposes can only rarely be by-passed.

However, it is just a mistake to deploy the purpose as a requirement enforced from outside. The 'function' does not precede the design, but is always *only mediated in the design*. Prior to that, it does not exist – on a par with space and structure. In the same way as music must be perceivable by the ears, architecture in its essence is usable.

Translation: Wendy van Os-Thompson

Case studies

Caffè Pedrocchi
Corner of Via VIII Febbraio and
Piazzetta Pedrocchi, Padua, Italy
1826–31
Architect: Giuseppe Jappelli

01 The Sala Tripartita, 2004

Around the year 1800, Antonio Pedrocchi took over his father's small coffee shop, which was located close to the University of Padua. Because of its convenient setting, this coffee shop was frequented both by students and professors, a circumstance that allowed Pedrocchi to build his fortune and at the same time develop his plans for the future. Padua counted a large number of cafés at the time and public life had gravitated around the Caffè del Duomo, which was patronized mainly by the old nobility. Pedrocchi realized, however, that the growing influence and self-assurance of the middle classes had created a demand for a new type of venue.

From 1815 onwards, Pedrocchi had been acquiring the land he needed to realize his plans. In 1826, he engaged Venetian-born architect and engineer Giuseppe Jappelli, who was a prominent figure in Padua, to build a new café. Jappelli had been most successful as a landscape architect until then, and none of the numerous designs he had made for the city of Padua had been executed. The new plans he made for this café, however, were a success. When Caffè Pedrocchi finally opened on 9 June 1831, it attracted huge interest among the bourgeoisie of Padua and its surroundings because of its beauty and comfort. Business was so good in these early years that a series of new rooms could be opened upstairs in 1842, roughly doubling the size of the premises.

The Pedrocchi became the arena for middle-class public life in Padua in this period, and an important meeting place for both scientists and artists. The café had many famous visitors; it seems, in fact, to have been a must-see for everybody travelling through Padua. The café also played a political role in the period of the Risorgimento (1815–70): local writers and poets met in the Sala Tripartita during this period and contributed to the unification of Italy from there.

Functional organization and layout

The footprint of the café occupied an entire building block and even a small part of the building opposite, the so-called *Pedrocchino*. The ground floor housed the most public rooms, the café and exchange, and the first floor a club, the *Casino Pedrocchi*, to which access was more restricted. The second floor contained the private apartments of the Pedrocchi family, along with a room where the coffee was roasted and another for making chocolate. Other storage spaces were located in the basement, which also featured an ice cellar. Two staircases connected the floors, a small spiral staircase on the side of the back street and a large ceremonial one starting from one of the entrance loggias. The triangular building had entrances on all sides, and walking through the café one could cut through the building block. This permeability and the fact that the café stayed open 24 hours a day illustrate the building's public character.

Interior decoration and fittings

The ground floor of the façades forms a simple plinth for the upper stories, but the three corners of the triangular site are

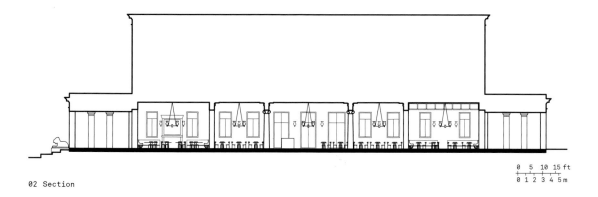

02 Section

0 5 10 15 ft
0 1 2 3 4 5m

99 Caffè Pedrocchi, Padua (1926–1831)

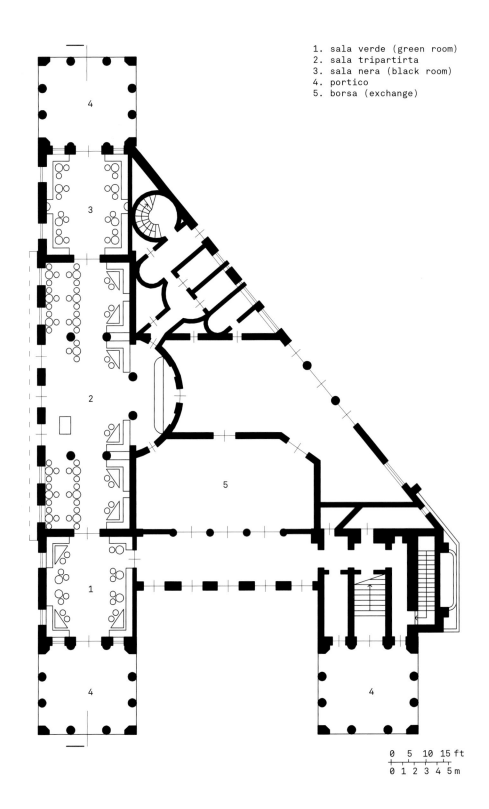

1. sala verde (green room)
2. sala tripartirta
3. sala nera (black room)
4. portico
5. borsa (exchange)

0 5 10 15 ft
0 1 2 3 4 5 m

03 Ground floor

100 Caffè Pedrocchi, Padua (1826–31)

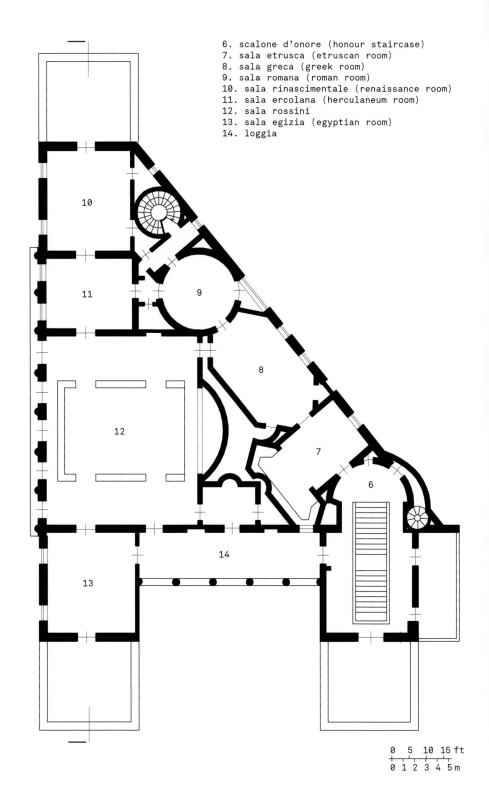

6. scalone d'onore (honour staircase)
7. sala etrusca (etruscan room)
8. sala greca (greek room)
9. sala romana (roman room)
10. sala rinascimentale (renaissance room)
11. sala ercolana (herculaneum room)
12. sala rossini
13. sala egizia (egyptian room)
14. loggia

0   5   10 15 ft
0 1 2 3 4 5 m

04 First floor

101 Caffè Pedrocchi, Padua (1926–1831)

05 Looking into the Sala
Tripartita from the Sala
Verde, 2004

06 The Pedrocchi seen from
the Piazzetta Pedrocchi, 2004

accentuated by identical Doric entrance loggias. The upper floors
are adorned with a Corinthian loggia on the northern façade and
Corinthian pilasters on the eastern façade. The exterior of the
Pedrocchino was designed in Gothic style to contrast with the
main building.

The public rooms on the ground floor were decorated in
neoclassical style. A dignified regularity in the plan was achieved by
aligning the public rooms along the two main façades and fitting all
the service spaces into the triangular leftovers of the site along
the back street. Along the Via VIII Febbraio, a suite of rooms formed
a perfectly symmetrical series increasing in importance towards
the centre. In keeping with the relative importance of the spaces the
decorations also increased in elaborateness. At the centre lay the main
café space, the *Sala Grande* or *Tripartita*. This room was subdivided into
three separate spaces by two screens of Ionic columns. The middle part
had three doors to the street on one side and an apsidal space screened

102 Caffè Pedrocchi, Padua (1826–31)

07 A detail of the marble bar, 2004

off by a third screen of columns on the other. This apsidal space was clad in marble and contained the bar, designed by Japelli in the shape of an elongated marble tub on lions' feet. At either end of the *Sala Grande* there was a smaller room, the *Sala Nera* and *Verde* respectively. These two rooms were themselves connected to the street through identical loggias. The colour in the names of these rooms referred to the colour of the upholstery of the original furniture. In keeping with the Neo-classical architecture, Jappelli designed the chairs in Roman style and the wall seats, small marble tables and mirror in Empire style. The floors of the rooms were tiled in marble, the ceilings and upper walls decorated with stucco ornaments.

The exchange where agricultural products were traded was housed in the *Sala Ottagona* or *Borsa,* in the interior of the building. This room was more businesslike, there were inkwells on the plain tables and lockers were available to the traders in two small adjoining rooms. The presence of such an overtly commercial space clearly signals that this establishment was intended to attract members of the middle class.

The rooms on the first floor were decorated to project an image of sophisticated eclecticism. The spaces formed a pattern book of styles, ranging from 'Greek', 'Roman', 'Baroque', 'Renaissance' and 'Herculanean', to 'Moorish' and 'Egyptian'. These styles were represented in every feature of the rooms: in the murals, the elaborate sculptures, the print of the wallpaper and the colour schemes.

The Pedrocchi did not just embrace the fashionable styles of the period, but also the physical improvements it brought. The café had been fitted with gas lighting, a plumbing system and even a big stove that could turn out enormous amounts of coffee very rapidly.

In 1891, the café was donated to the community of Padua and since then the café has continued in business. The interior has been changed on many occasions, and especially quite drastically in the 1950s. However, when the neglected café was renovated in the late 1990s, the original spatial lay-out was restored.

Charlotte van Wijk

Sources:

Architecture intérieure creé, 290, 1999: 114–5

Irace, F., *Domus* 658, February 1985: 20–3

Possamai, P., *Caffè Pedrocchi: Guida*, Milan: Skira, 2000

Riva, U., *Domus*, 815, May 1999: 64–71

Riva, U., *Lotus*, 102, September 1999: 63–9

Café Riche
Boulevard des Italiens/Rue Peletier,
Paris, France
1804/1894
Architect: Albert Ballu

Café de la Paix
Boulevard des Capucines/
Place de l'Opéra, Paris, France
1863
Architect: Alfred Armand

1. wine
2. beer
3. café
4. tea
5. absinth

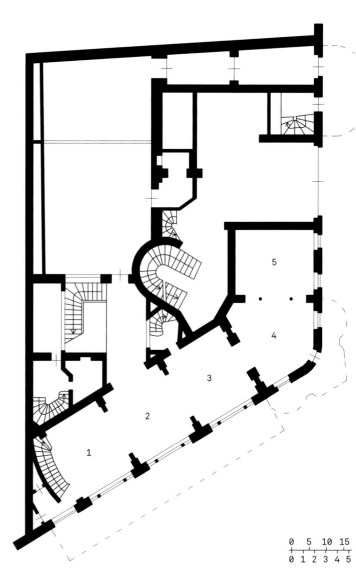

01 Ground floor

Café Riche

Both the Café Riche and the Café de la Paix have their origins
in the development and expansion of the Parisian boulevards, each
of them emerging during different stages of the construction of
these large metropolitan avenues. The Café Riche was launched as
a fashionable venue on one of the first proper boulevards and was
part of establishing the particular forms of use that these became
associated with. The Café de la Paix came into existence in the wake
of rearranging the area around the new Opéra under the aegis of
Baron Haussmann in the 1860s, when the boulevard system was
fully developed.

The boulevards replacing the mediaeval ramparts, including
today's Boulevard des Italiens and Boulevard des Capucines, had
already become a stage for the promenade during the *Ancien Régime*,

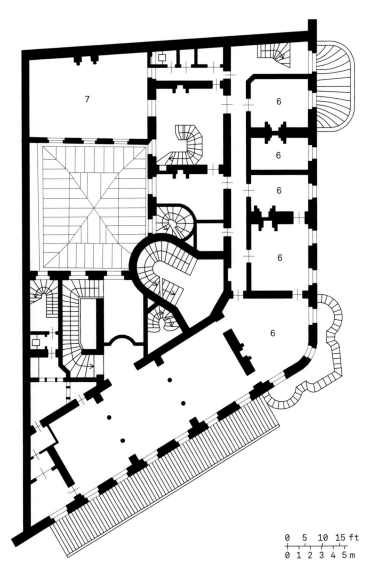

6. salon
7. grand salon

02 First floor

0 5 10 15 ft
0 1 2 3 4 5 m

but in the first decades of the nineteenth century they developed into the central location for the public display of the middle and upper classes. Newspaper offices, the stock exchange, theatres and luxurious boutiques were located on or near the boulevards. Cafés and restaurants competed for the attention of respectable citizens as well as artists who frequented the Café Tortoni, the Café Anglais or the Divan Peletier.

Among these establishments, the Café Riche was particularly known for the quality (and high prices) of its culinary offerings and for its late opening hours.[1] Founded in 1791 and relocated to the corner of rue Peletier and the Boulevard des Italiens in 1804, the Café Riche was also one of the most exclusively furnished cafés in this most fashionable part of Paris. Decorated by a Prix de Rome winner and 'artiste d'un talent exquis' who had also designed a Pompeian villa for the Prince Napoléon (1822–1891), the salons of the Riche were

1
Fosca, F., *Histoire des cafés de Paris*, Paris: Firmin-Didot, 1934 p. 134

105 Café Riche/Café de la Paix, Paris (1804/1894 and 1863)

03 Façade of the Café Riche, corner of Boulevard des Italiens and Rue Le Peletier, Paris, 1894

furnished to the best classical taste. The inventory made in 1846, when the establishment went bankrupt, presents a precise picture of the interior and the equipment that was necessary for running a Parisian Grand Café of the first half of the nineteenth century. Apart from the expensive glass, cutlery and crockery used for serving meals and beverages from the morning until well after midnight, the document lists a counter in mahogany with a marble top, a glass tourniquet, three glass showcases, a painted wooden buffet with a marble top, 27 oak tables, 11 decorative tables in marble on cast iron posts and 90 dark cherry wood chairs. Two pendulum clocks, one in bronze and adorned with a sculpture representing agriculture, and another in painted porcelain, had been visual attractions in the café.

Its commercial misfortune did not prevent the Café Riche from re-establishing itself as a venue for sophisticated dining and drinking. On the contrary, in the 1850s it developed into a focus for artists and writers, its habitués including Charles Baudelaire who 'appeared without a tie, showing his naked throat and with a shaved head, in a

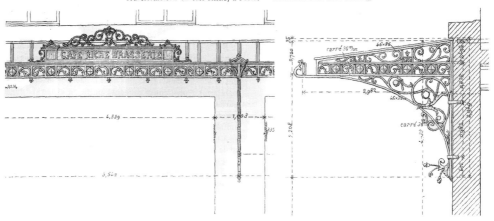

04 Front and side view of the canopy

2
Ibid., p. 64.

3
'Brasseries et cafés-concerts', *Construction moderne*, 15 December 1894: 121

4
'Le Café Riche, à Paris', *Construction moderne*, 27 October, 1894: 40

veritable *toilette de guillotine*', as the brothers Goncourt noted.[2] The luxurious interior did not fail to impress and intimidated even the bohemians among the clientele.

The refurbishment of the café in 1894 to the design of architect Albert Ballu was undertaken as part of transforming the establishment into a *café-brasserie*. The plans published in the journal *Construction moderne* show the result of extensive building works. What had been a series of separate rooms along the street was made into tripartite salons on all floors and at ground level the windows were replaced by large glass doors, rendering the café into a vast terrace open to the street in summer. Along the boulevard façade a glass and wrought-iron canopy offered the customers sitting on the terrace shelter while on the corner a similar structure was used for creating a loggia at mezzanine level and a balcony above. The *pièce de resistance* was a series of 17 mosaic panels depicting Parisian characters and designed by the well-known painter and caricaturist Jean-Louis Forain.

The author presenting the café to the readers of *Construction moderne* positioned the alterations made in the Café Riche in the larger developments in the design of commercial public interiors in Paris in the 1890s. For him the new project represents the phenomenon of the brasserie 'that kills the cafés, divans, estaminets of our childhood', along with the popular café-concert.[3] 'The democratization affects this branch of the industry and the *glacier-limonadier* of the old days is turned into the modern brasserie. The white and gold panelling gives way to leather and mosaics, transparent glass is replaced by stained glass panels.'[4]

Less than a decade later, in 1900, the entire building of which the Riche occupied the most prominent section, was pulled down. Its replacement, the 'Immeuble de la New York', was an exercise in the over-decorated, bombastic style of the turn of the century, covered in neo-baroque floral ornament with occasional hints of Art Nouveau. The Café Riche remerged as an exclusive restaurant that lost all the characteristics of a café.

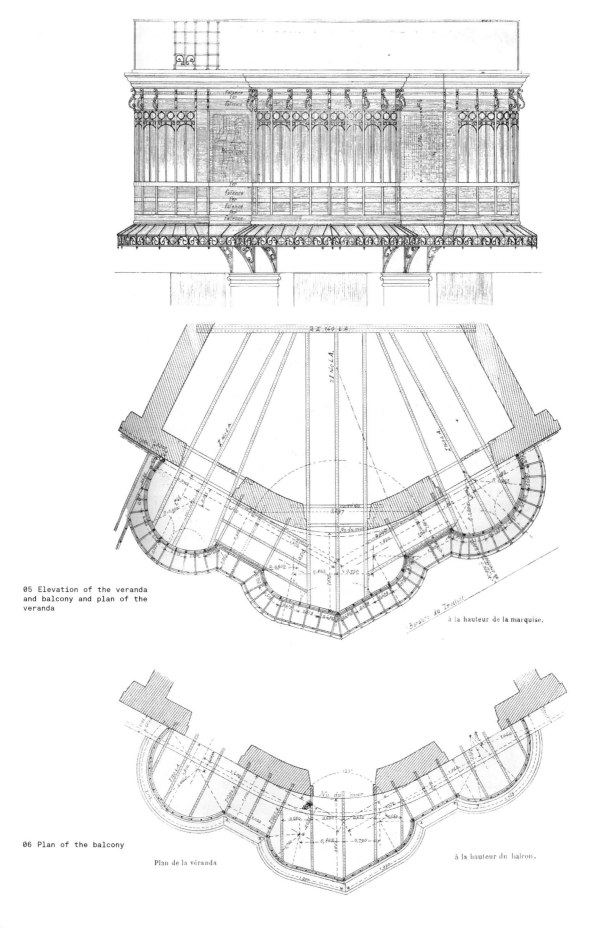

05 Elevation of the veranda
and balcony and plan of the
veranda

à la hauteur de la marquise.

06 Plan of the balcony

Plan de la véranda

à la hauteur du balcon.

07 The entrance, 1925

Café de la Paix

The Café de la Paix, a few blocks down the boulevard, represents the same development towards ever larger and more luxurious enterprises offering food as well as drinks. Opened as the Café-Restaurant du Grand Hôtel de la Paix, it was the result of the comprehensive reorganization of the entire quarter surrounding the Grand Opera by Charles Garnier. At its opening in 1863, the hotel had been devised for providing accommodation for demanding international visitors to the World Exhibition of 1867, offering the reliable service and comfort common in America and England. Situated on the most exposed corner of the new building designed by Alfred Armand and facing two boulevards and the Place de l'Opéra, the café provided the perfect vantage point for observing the newly created ceremonial centre of Paris during the Second Empire of Napoleon III.

The café was managed by the Société du Grand Hôtel (following a legal dispute, the name 'de la Paix' had to be dropped, while the café was allowed to retain its use) and could be serviced from the extensive kitchen facilities in the basement. This arrangement and the neutrality of the open ground floor made up by square modules defined by the grid of columns allowed for a large degree of flexibility. Less than 100 days after its first opening the café had become too small for the clientele attracted by its splendour and the management responded by enlarging it inside the building. The layout also allowed for functional and spatial differentiations between the restaurant area, the bar and the café proper, from which customers had access to the street terrace.

109 Café Riche/Café de la Paix, Paris (1804/1894 and 1863)

1. café
2. courtyard
3. covered passage
4. kitchen

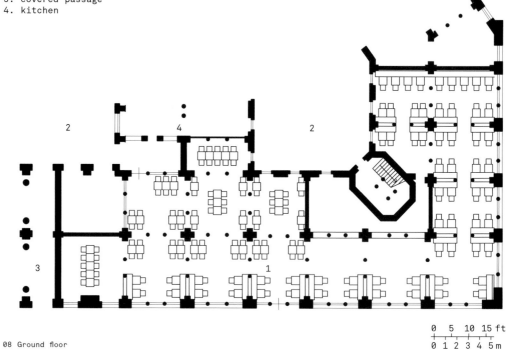

0 5 10 15 ft
0 1 2 3 4 5 m

08 Ground floor

The main structural and physical elements of the design were cast-iron Corinthian columns and the beams dividing the large space into square sections. Framed by the beams, ceiling panels showed paintings of Mediterranean skyscapes that could be illuminated by gas lighting. Panels decorated with mythological figures, Epicurean angels and floral ornaments covered in gold leaf completed the sumptuous decorative proposal.

09 The restaurant in the Café de la Paix, 1925

110 Café Riche/Café de la Paix, Paris (1804/1894 and 1863)

10 The Grand Hôtel, with on the corner the Café de la Paix and on the right the Opera, 2006

11 The terrace on Boulevard des Capucines, 1925

The Café de la Paix became a venue for the rich and powerful, but also attracted writers and artists including Emile Zola, Guy de Maupassant, Jules Massenet, André Gide, Oscar Wilde and Arthur Conan Doyle. In 1939, after 106 years of continuous service, the café was closed for the first time on the evening that France entered the Second World War, only to offer the venue for General de Gaulle's first dinner in 1944 in liberated Paris. Still a part of the Grand Hotel, the café is a listed monument and was renovated comprehensively in the 1990s as one of the few remaining interiors for this period during which Paris established itself as the centre of sophisticated high bourgeois culture.

Christoph Grafe

Sources:

'Brasseries et cafés-concerts', *Construction moderne*, 15 December 1894: 121

Christophe, D. and Letourny, G. (eds), *Paris et ses cafés*, Paris: Action artistique de la ville de Paris, 2004

Du palais au palace, des grands hôtels de voyageurs à Paris au XIX siècle, Paris: Carnavalet, 1998

Fosca, F., *Histoire des cafés de Paris*, Paris: Firmin-Didot, 1934

'Le Café Riche, à Paris', *Construction moderne*, 27 October, 1894: 40

Café Central
Herrengasse/Strauchgasse, Vienna,
Austria
1875
Architect: Heinrich von Ferstel

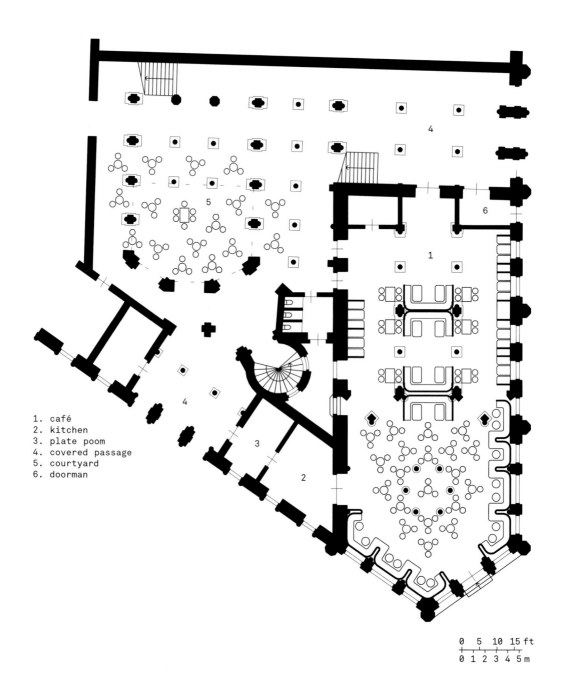

1. café
2. kitchen
3. plate poom
4. covered passage
5. courtyard
6. doorman

0 5 10 15 ft
0 1 2 3 4 5 m

01 Ground floor

112 Café Central, Vienna (1875)

Café Central is part of a multifunctional complex, known as Palais Ferstel, nestling between Herrengasse, Strauchgasse and the Freyung and one of the few buildings named, in homage, after its architect. It was built between 1856 and 1860, designed by the young architect Heinrich von Ferstel, to house the Stock Exchange and the Imperial and Royal National Bank. In 1855, during his travels in Italy, the 25-year-old architect received an invitation to take part in the competition for the exchange-cum-bank building. Ferstel, inspired by his experiences abroad, embarked on the first design, for the initially larger site. Eventually the existing Palais Hardegg, which had originally been earmarked for demolition, had to be integrated in the complex and the architect designed a second project for the irregularly-shaped site. He skilfully connected a narrow strip on the Freyung with Herrengasse and Strauchgasse by means of a shopping arcade (bazaar), placing at the centre a courtyard with a fountain from which the various wings could be reached. Ferstel forged ahead in the competition and, having made some minor alterations, was awarded the design commission.

Palais Ferstel is a splendid example of romantic historicism in Vienna and the last monumental structure prior to the construction of the Ringstraße. Apart from the Stock Exchange and the National Bank, the extensive spatial programme of the multi-purpose building contained retail premises, including Café Central. The *Kaffeehaus* was in keeping with a long tradition as well as the demands of the brokers, who had no desire to forego the familiar ambience: the café, therefore, was part of the initial brief. Yet the exchange required more space than originally thought and so a commodities exchange moved into the rooms intended for the coffee house. Even so, the exchange continued to be short of space and partially moved out of the complex in 1877 into a new building on Ringstrasse (Schottenring). The National Bank remained in the building until 1925. In 1876, the Pach brothers could at last open Café Central in the premises originally intended for that purpose. In 1943, the Café Central, in what was meanwhile a partially empty building, closed on account of the turmoil of the war and the concomitant loss of custom. After that, the premises were used for a long time for archives. The effects of war and time were damaging for the entire complex. Early in the 1970s, various experts were commissioned to revive the buildings. In the end, restoration work was started in 1978 and proceeded in stages until 1986.

Cultural context: the literary café

Café Central was not a centre for Viennese intellectuals from the start. It blossomed with the influx of intellectuals and artists who moved there after neighbouring Café Griensteidl closed. In the course of some 20 years, until 1918, it developed into Vienna's *fin-de-siècle* intellectual centre. Here, the Viennese literary avant-garde, including Karl Kraus, Hugo von Hofmannsthal, Arthur Schnitzler and Egon Friedell, and the European intelligentsia found their meeting place.

1
Anton Kuh, 'Central' and 'Herrenhof', in *Das Wiener Kaffeehaus*, Wien, 1978, p. 158.

2
Alfred Polgar, 'Theorie des Café Central', in Alfred Polgar: *An den Rand geschrieben*, Berlin: Rowohlt 1927. quoted from: *Das Wiener Kaffeehaus*, Zürich: Artemis 1978, p. 151.

Here, old-established literary celebrities collided with tempestuous young literati. Here, ideologies and world-views clashed. Here people read, eavesdropped, laughed, played chess, discussed, debated, worked, lived briefly. The table of the coffee house was a workplace for many literati. When asked for his address, Peter Altenberg, the coffee house poet, replied: 'Vienna I, Herrengasse, Café Central'.[1] Alfred Polgar wrote in his *Theorie des cafés centrals*: 'The Central is a place for people who have to kill time, so as not to be killed by it.'[2] Café Central was frequented by journalists like Theodor Herzl and Egon Erwin Kisch, painters like Oskar Kokoschka, architects like Adolf Loos and physicians like Theodor Billroth. The founder of Individual Psychology, Alfred Adler, the founder of Austrian Social Democracy, Viktor Adler, and the Russian revolutionary Leon Trotsky, as well as the deputy head of the Austrian secret service, Colonel Alfred Redl, drank their coffee here. Over 250 newspapers in 22 languages were provided, reflecting the cultural diversity of this intellectual centre in the multinational Austro-Hungarian state. 'On every other Thonet chair, a budding poet-genius, an Austro-Marxist, or nobleman, a twelve-tone musician or at least a psychoanalyst, behind every newspaper a mastermind, every debate a literary delight, every drop poured by a waiter a *Weltanschauung*.' This well-known description is an apt expression of the intellectual diversity of Café Central's microcosm.

The exterior and the functional arrangement

The café's young architect, Heinrich von Ferstel, envisaged in his design the large, impressive spaces in the wing at the corner of Strauchgasse and Herrengasse: the *Kaffeehaus* on the ground floor, immediately above it the large exchange area and, as the connecting element, a monumental staircase of spatially extraordinary interest, beneath a vast glass roof.

By placing the corner façade skewed to Herrengasse, Ferstel produced a polygonal shape, which he cleverly used inside to accommodate the café and exchange premises. The architectural solution is highly original. Large arched windows taking up three floors resemble loggias and reflect a very successful theme in Viennese architecture. The arrangement in threes, framed by the polygonal corner buttresses, is repeated in the street elevations and the rhythm is pursued in the ashlar walls, alternating with closed and open wall treatments. The forceful treatment of the fenestration, the corner buttresses developing from the octagon, as well as the straight roofline with its balustrade and the rows of star-shaped ornaments are direct references to Venetian and Florentine examples, such as the Loggia die Lanzi.

The actual access to the coffee house is located – logically – at the slanting corner of the building. You go through a storm door into a large space that is divided in two parts, the first of which is a 12-sided central area with a circulation route around six stone columns and fine vault in a cross- and triple-fan configuration and a triple-aisle, four-bay colonnaded hall with quadripartite vaults. The café's side rooms (storeroom, pantry) are situated at a slightly higher level connecting with the 12-sided central space and lit from Herrengasse. The exchange- or arcade-courtyard situated further inside the building and lit from above served as Café Central's covered 'free space'. For some, this was the real Café Central, the 'holy of holies', not only because 'Smoke and noise could become excessive' there,[3] but also because it was where the 'feuilleton' were to be found, whereas socialists, pan-slavists and adherents of other forms of *Weltanschauung* congregated elsewhere in the café. Today this area is still used as a 'Café im Freien', or outdoor café. Of course, its main importance was the fact that the arcaded courtyard could be reached in various ways via the warren of passages of Palais Ferstel, while the café proper was accessed from the street right at the intersection of Herrengasse and Strauchgasse.

The interior

Apart from the sculpture and the ornamental elements characterizing the exterior, the artisanal elements inside the spectacularly decorated building played a prominent role. Ferstel's edifice owes much of its artistic quality to the exceptional quality of the decorative workmanship. Ferstel, who propagated focusing on the materials in construction and reviving traditional arts and crafts,

3
Anton Kuh, op. cit., p. 158.

02 Façade on the corner of Strauchgasse and Herrengasse, 2006

designed all the fittings and hardware such as doors, lighting fixtures and wall coverings to create harmony between the sculptural and colour features of the individual elements and the overall building – forming a *Gesamtkunstwerk* or total work of art.[4] The attractive combination of iron and glass structures and majestic architectural forms in the bazaar (and in the Stock Exchange court) is particularly worthy of mention.

The café walls consist of grey or red-framed stucco-lustro expanses with red woollen velvet on the bands between the strips of fenestration matching the upholstery of the Thonet chairs. Wrought-iron chandeliers are suspended from the centres of the vaults with varying numbers of milk-glass bowls hanging from them. The floor is parquet light-coloured wood with dark-outlined strips applied in intarsia.

The rich spatial ambience of the café combined with a stock exchange, bank and shopping arcade may well have accounted for the

4
Renate Wagner-Rieger, *Wiens Architektur im 19. Jahrhundert*, Vienna, 1970, p. 130

03 The Arkadenhof, 2006

116 Café Central, Vienna (1875)

café's popularity with artists and literati alike. The large exchange court with its glass roof appealed greatly to the 'feuilleton' group: perhaps because the sky there seemed infinite. Yet the relative simplicity and elegance of the materials and their functionality may have inspired highly sensitive artistic souls such as Adolf Loos. Alfred Polgar, in his *Theorie des Café Central* would seem to have been correct in his assumption that no-one left the premises of the café without being affected by it.

Holger Pump-Uhlmann
Translation: Wendy van Os-Thompson

Sources:

Augustin, A. *Das Café Central Treasury*, Vienna, 1998

Brandstätter, C. and Schweiger, W., *Das Wiener Kaffeehaus*, Vienna 1978

Heering, K-J., *Das Wiener Kaffeehaus*, Frankfurt am Main/Leipzig, 1993

Jünger, W.,'Herr Ober, ein' Kaffee', in *Illustrierte Kulturgeschichte des Kaffeehauses*, Munich, 1955

Kuh, A., 'Central' and 'Herrenhof', in Heering, *Das Wiener Kaffeehaus*, Frankfurt am Main/Leipzig, 1993

Polgar, A., 'Theorie des cafés centrals', in A. Polgar, *An den Rand geschrieben*, Berlin: Rowohlt, 1927

Wagner-Rieger, R., *Wiens Architektur im 19. Jahrhundert*, Vienna, 1970, pp. 128–30

Café Bauer
Corner of Unter den Linden and
Friedrichstrasse, Berlin, Germany
1878
Architect: Ende and Böckmann

01 Downstairs in the Café
Bauer, looking towards the
rear (woodprint after a
drawing by G Theuerkauf,
1887)

1
Eduard Schmitt (ed.), *Handbuch der Architektur,*
IV/vol. 4/1 Gebäude für Erholungs-, Beherbergungs-
und Vereinszwecke, Stuttgart: Kröner, 1904, p. 86.

When Mathias Bauer, *cafetier* and restaurant owner from Vienna,
opened a café in the centre of Berlin on 13 October 1878, his new
établissement proved an immediate and complete success. The event
of the opening of the Viennese *Kaffeehaus* was noticed as a news
item of considerable importance: the correspondent of the *Vossische
Zeitung*, Germany's most important paper at the time, wrote a
detailed celebration of the luxurious interiors unprecedented in
the city. The café was successfully established as one of the prime
centres of respectable sociability in the German capital and Bauer
managed to secure its status for a long period. Almost 30 years
later, the author of the *Handbuch der Architektur* mentions that the
café is said to have been continuously operating since its first day
of opening.[1]

    After the 1873 World Exhibition in the Austrian capital,
the Viennese *Kaffeehaus* was eagerly copied and quickly replaced the

traditional Berlin *Konditorei* (cakeshop) which had existed since the eighteenth century. In adopting the *Kaffeehaus* for its superior elegance and style, however, the Berlin entrepreneurs profoundly altered the character and atmosphere to address the preferences of their clientele.

Mathias Bauer's enterprise could be regarded as one of the best examples of these changes that affected layout, decoration scheme, management and use of the fashionable Berlin cafés of the late nineteenth century. Its site on the corner of the city's ceremonial boulevard Unter den Linden and Friedrichstrasse, the main commercial street, afforded it a status of particular prominence. On the opposite corner another established café, Café Kranzler, had existed since 1825 (see case study on p. 172), which had been taken up by officers and members of the Prussian gentry. Café Bauer opened in a new building by the architects Ende and Böckmann who had associated in 1859 and were about to become one of the most successful German architecture firms in this period of rapid building. Ende was appointed president and later honorary president of the Berlin Akademie der Künste and designed the Japanese parliament and several ministerial departments. Ende and Böckmann were also appointed for the interior of the café and given carte blanche to design a café that was to become an attraction of the highest order.

Functional organization and layout

The building had five storeys, the lower two of which were occupied by the café. The second and third floor housed a small hotel, which was initially managed by Bauer but later rented to a hotelier. In its abundance of neo-baroque ornament, the design was typical for the commercial architecture of the late 1870s. Inside, the sumptuous decoration disguises a simple functional organization. The ground floor room of the café is a long, deep hall extending from the main front on the boulevard to a service courtyard at the back. Two rows of cast-iron columns supporting the beamed ceiling divide the hall into three bays, the middle of which is accentuated by a light well connecting the two floors and allowing daylight to enter from the roof light above. One of the notable technological innovations was the large glass window on the north side which could be slid downwards by means of a hydraulic mechanism, transforming the front room into an open-air vestibule on Unter den Linden – a concession to building regulations barring outdoor terraces along the boulevard.

The first-floor salon could be reached via the main staircase also accessing the hotel and another one at the back, next to the buffet, and was divided into a series of spaces around the light well. On the south side and separated by glass screens there was a billiard room with two large tables, while the section on the north side of the void was dominated by a large reading table. The extraordinarily extensive selection of reading material Café Bauer offered its customers – the specially published list mentions 348 daily newspapers from across the

globe and almost as many weekly and professional periodicals – was displayed along the side wall and on the reading table. Along the west side, facing Friedrichstrasse, there were three smaller reading rooms which could be reached from the main salon. One of the main attractions of the reading room on the first floor was the balcony running along the north and west façades and offering a privileged view of Unter den Linden, the balcony seats made available for rent on official holidays.

Interior decoration and fittings

The desire to establish Café Bauer as an institution in the social life of the Berlin middle classes is reflected in the elaborate decoration scheme and the wall paintings. The lower part of the columns were set on a plinth featuring elaborate intarsia work while the upper had been covered in darkened brass to match the copper and gold sparkles in the cast ornaments of the ceiling and the balustrades along the light well. In the middle of the area, lit from above, there was a fountain and further back the grand buffet appeared as a dark varnished wooden ornament set against the wall separating the café from the kitchen at

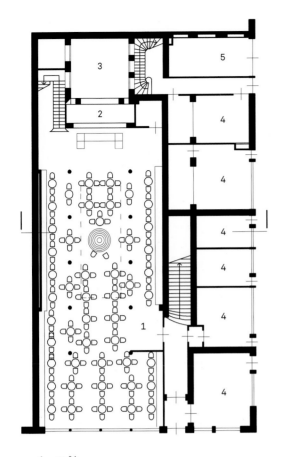

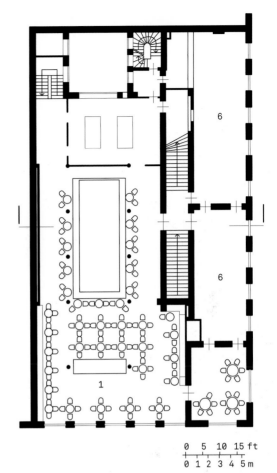

1. café
2. kitchen
3. courtyard
4. shop
5. delivery/storage
6. reading room

```
0    5   10  15 ft
├──┼──┼──┼──┤
0  1  2  3  4  5 m
```

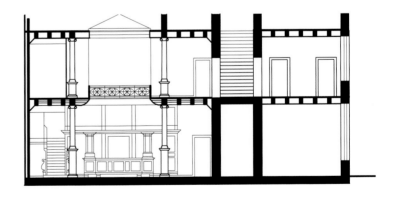

03 Ground floor

04 First floor

05 Section

```
0      5       10      15 ft
├──┼──┼──┼──┼──┼──┤
0   1   2   3   4   5 m
```

121 Café Bauer, Berlin (1878)

06 Downstairs in the Café
Bauer, near the façade,
c.1900

07 Unter den Linden in
front of Café Bauer by
night, c.1910

122 Café Bauer, Berlin (1878)

the back. Crystal chandeliers from Vienna and gas fittings were used to obtain an unprecedented level of lighting for the café at night. In 1884, Café Bauer was the first public space in Berlin to be illuminated by electric light, its energy generated by a steam engine constructed for this purpose on the adjacent site.

The wall paintings framed by dark varnished wainscoting were specially commissioned from two of the most established Berlin artists of the period. In the front part of the ground floor Anton von Werner, the official historic genre painter appointed to the Prussian court, contributed a cycle titled 'Roman Life', depicting scenes of banquets, song and dance events in ancient Rome. The walls in the area around the light well were covered by large Arcadian landscapes with ruins and temples by the artist Christian Wilberg.

Through the combination of these works of art by celebrated painters and the objects of state-of-the-art technology, Café Bauer established itself as a highly sophisticated urban institution and remained so until the early 1920s when its clientele moved to the newly fashionable west end of the city. In 1924 parts of the interior were sold off and the café reopened under a different name.
The destruction of the entire area in 1944 left no trace of this institution.

Christoph Grafe

Sources:

Berlin und seine Bauten, Berlin, 1896

Renate, P., *Das Café Bauer in Berlin*, Berlin: Verlag für Bauwesen, 1994

Schmitt, E. (ed.), *Handbuch der Architektur, vol. 4/1 Gebäude für Erholungs-, Beherbergungs- und Vereinszwecke* Stuttgart: Kröner, 1904

The Philharmonic Hotel
Hope Street and Hardman Street,
Liverpool, England
1898–1900
Architect (interior): Walter Thomas

01 Looking from the cocktail
lounge towards the bar

By 1900, Liverpool had a population of nearly 700,000 and had grown from its origins as a medieval harbour on the banks of the River Mersey into one of the world's largest ports and in Britain second only to London. Most of the goods traded between Britain and North America passed through the port, as did steadily growing passenger traffic. Liverpool had the population and complete apparatus of a successful Victorian city. It had been lavishly equipped by confident merchant and professional classes with public buildings and banks. Plans were under way for a grandiose new Anglican cathedral, its own university, local newspapers and a large, part-indigenous, part-immigrant working class employed mainly in the docks and served by 1,895 licensed pubs, a ratio of 1 pub per 361 inhabitants.[1]

1
Mark Girouard, *Victorian Pubs*, New Haven, CT:
Yale University Press, 1984, p. 246

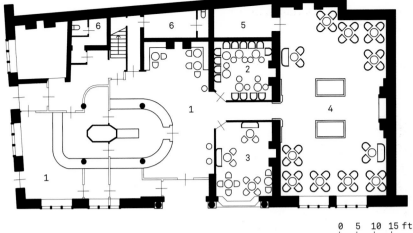

1. bar
2. Brahms room
3. Liszt room
4. grand lounge
5. ladies WC
6. men's WC

0   5 10 15 ft

0 1 2 3 4 5 m

The history of the planning, nomenclature and decoration of the nineteenth-century Liverpool pub was different from those both of provincial British cities and of London. At the peak of its development, the London pub exhibited its characteristic radial-concentric organization of a centrally-placed bar with its 'wagon', surrounded by individually articulated, served areas. The latter might be designed as completely independent rooms, or merely formed by subdivision with screens, and their names, for example the 'Smoking Room', came eventually to describe only loosely, if at all, their contemporary functions and intended sub-clienteles.

Brewer and architect: location, layout and design

The Philharmonic Hotel was commissioned by Robert Cain, who had recently established a Liverpool brewery and was developing pubs to serve his product in competition with the powerful existing brewers. His strategy, to attract the middle-class customer, was served by the Philharmonic's location, its layout, and its beauty, style and decorations.

Its site on Hope Street is in one of the city's better districts, well away and up the hill from the port and central commercial district, and opposite the Philharmonic Hall (erected in 1849, burnt in 1933 and replaced in 1939). For its design Cain commissioned the established and well-connected architect Walter Thomas who had earlier designed several of the city's pubs and was later to design another, The Vines in Lime Street, of 1907. Cain's brief to Thomas was for one of a series of buildings that would 'so beautify the public houses . . . that they would be an ornament to the town of his birth'.

Layout and interior

Thomas' layout is untypical. It is neither like that of contemporary pubs or its immediate predecessors in Liverpool, nor does it take

125 The Philharmonic Hotel, Liverpool (1898–1900)

03 The fireplace in the public bar

account of late-Victorian developments in London: it combines features of all of them. One half of the plan, on the southwest corner, has a radial-concentric arrangement, its various bars having entrances directly from the street, but the largest of these, the 'Lobby' also gives access via a short corridor to a very large billiard room which occupies a full one-third of the pub's ground floor. On either side of the corridor are two largish enclosed spaces, now called the 'Brahms' and 'Liszt' rooms, which have no direct access to the bar; these originally served as the specifically Liverpudlian 'News' and 'Smoke' rooms. The Lobby and these three latter rooms were equipped with profusely decorated fireplaces for the comfort of their intended middle-class clientele.

The combination of innovative layout and particular decorative treatment suggests that brewer and architect were attempting to propose a pub interior more like that of a gentleman's club than a nineteenth-century gin palace.

The surface treatment and apparatus of the interior are specially designed and use none of the standard decorative fittings with which pubs had usually been equipped. The walls are generally panelled up to the ceiling with heavily-detailed hardwood, and the plaster ceilings decorated with Jacobean designs. A refined glazed screen, modestly decorated with diffidently heraldic stained (rather than cut or etched)

04 A detail of the bar

126 The Philharmonic Hotel, Liverpool (1898–1900)

glass, divides the public areas into two, and separates the smaller public bars for 'perpendicular' drinking from the Lobby and Billiard Room with their probable table service.

A remarkable programme of sculptures was commissioned from prominent local artists and supervised by staff from the University's School of Architecture and Applied Arts, and their contributions were fully integrated into the interior design, placed over and around the fireplaces and doorcases. Made of repoussé copper or painted plaster, both cheap, eminently kitsch materials, their subjects portray various musical themes and allegories.

The exterior

The design of the building's exterior confirms the aspiring programme of the interior: in form and style it might be a successful merchant's large house, or a small institution such as a club or public library. Its style is now usually described as 'eclectic': developed by such architectural talents as Richard Norman Shaw and Philip Webb, lesser hands, as here, deployed reckless combinations of classical and English vernacular and domestic.

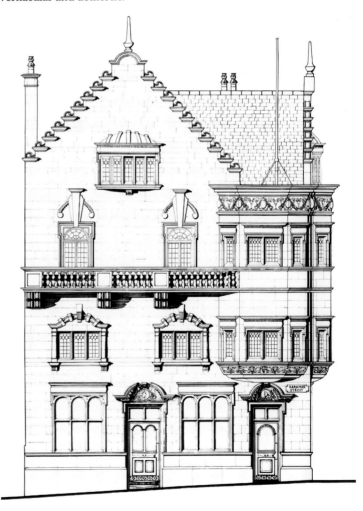

05 Hardman Street elevation, drawing by David A. Nicholson Cole, 1969

127 The Philharmonic Hotel, Liverpool (1898–1900)

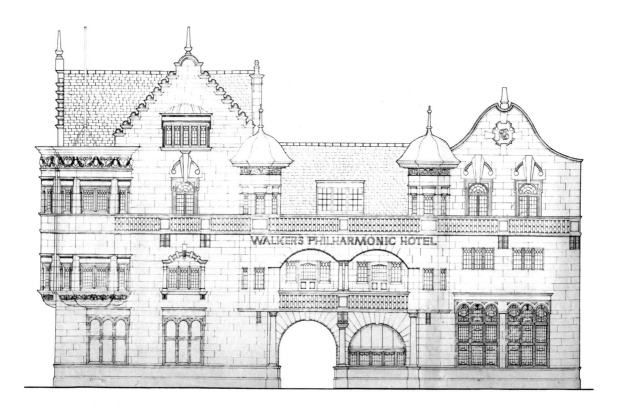

06 Hope Street elevation,
drawing by Anthea M.
Nicholson Cole, 1969

Stepped gables, perhaps derived from Flanders or Northern Europe rise to four storeys on either side of the street corner. Extending from these, the street elevations have artfully casually placed door and window openings unified by a continuous balustraded projecting balcony at second floor level. The front door is marked with turrets and is screened with the magnificent iron gates (by Henry Blomfield Bare), Art Nouveau in some of the details but with an overall design too stiff to qualify for comparison with continental examples of the style.

After a century in which its interior and its fittings have survived largely intact, the pub is now an essential part of what is marketed as Liverpool's heritage.

Christopher Woodward

Sources:

Cavanagh, T., *Public Sculpture of Liverpool*, Liverpool: Liverpool University Press, 1997

Girouard, M., *Victorian Pubs*, New Haven, CT: Yale University Press, 1984

Pevsner, N., *The Buildings of England: South Lancashire*, Harmondsworth: Penguin, 1969

Sharples, J., *Liverpool*, *Pevsner Architectural Guides: City Guides*, New Haven, CT: Yale University Press, 2004

Café Américain
Leidseplein, Amsterdam, The
Netherlands
1902
Architect: Willem Kromhout

1 Café Américain. Looking
towards the bar, across the
wide bay in the café room,
c. 1902

The Café Américain was realized as part of the 'American Hotel', an establishment that draws on Moorish and Maghreb architecture for its style, but the layout of which is inspired by examples from Berlin, Lucerne and London. When the hotel was opened in 1902, America and American cultural artefacts were becoming established as symbols for technological advancement and the emergence of a consumer-oriented leisure industry. Naming a hotel 'American' evoked associations with luxury and a high level of technical sophistication. More importantly, the predecessor of the hotel, which was located on a smaller lot in the same location, had also been called 'American'. It had been founded in 1881 by the entrepreneur C.A.A. Steinegeweg who, upon his return from the United States in 1875, wished to introduce the American establishment of the 'boarding house' to Amsterdam. He probably

02 The American Hotel seen
from Leidseplein, 1902

designed the building himself, and when his hotel opened its doors to the public in 1881 it struck its customers with its abundance of historical styles, marble bathrooms, a lift and the 'Belvedere' on the top. Steinegeweg's ambition was not matched by his business capacities and he had to sell the hotel to August Volmer in 1885, who decided to retain its name.

A few years later, the new owner decided to rebuild and increase the enterprise on the same site – now enlarged by filling in part of the Singelgracht, the canal that had formed part of the city's seventeenth-century fortifications. The new establishment was to become a first-class hotel, containing a café and restaurants, and rooms specially designed for entertaining larger groups. A regular visitor of the meetings of *Architectura et Amicitia*, an artists club that convened in the existing American hotel, Volmer looked for a building that would demonstrate its modernity, breaking away from the 'imitation' styles of the nineteenth century. The entrepreneur may have heard Kromhout's maiden speech for *Architectura et Amicitia* on the evening of 4 November 1891, when Kromhout fulminated against the mishmash of historical styles, demanding that they should be 'flushed away down the gutter'.

Kromhout was acquainted with the design of hotels and restaurants. In 1889, while working as an assistant for the architect Springer, Kromhout had been sent to London to direct the construction of 'Krasnapolsky's Restaurant and Wintergarden' in 1889, in the English capital. August Volmer, who was related to the Krasnapolsky family, was probably informed about Kromhout's work in London. In 1895, the architect had also contributed an imitation seventeenth-century Dutch town to the World Hotel Exhibition, and since he had also designed the urban decorations for the inauguration of Queen Wilhelmina, he had sufficiently demonstrated his ability to create entertaining public environments. Even so, Volmer decided to add his house architect H.G. Jansen to the design team. Jansen had been responsible for relatively minor changes to the existing building but was knowledgeable about the organizational and technical requirements of a hotel and restaurant. Jansen's name, however, is rarely mentioned and the new American Hotel was soon known as Kromhout's most important architectural project.

The hotel and its café-restaurant, the 'Américain' (the French name was adopted to market the quality of the cooking and service), were an instant success for their stylistic exuberance, a quality that is derived mainly from the outspoken Islamic inspiration of the design.

Rejecting the historicism of the later nineteenth century, Kromhout developed a style of his own, characterized by his ability to knead the volumes in clear cubic forms that prevented his designs from getting out of control, and his mastery in integrating decoration and construction. J.J.P. Oud, one of the pioneers of Dutch Modernism in the 1920s, liked the 'American Hotel' precisely for that, since Kromhout curbed its extravagance by the clear composition of volumes.

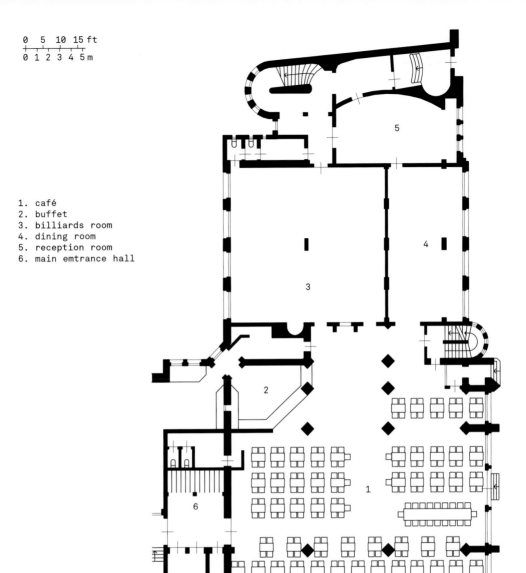

0 5 10 15 ft
0 1 2 3 4 5 m

1. café
2. buffet
3. billiards room
4. dining room
5. reception room
6. main emtrance hall

03 Ground floor

In this approach, Kromhout apparently oscillated between two opposite poles, and precisely here Orientalism came to the rescue. Islamic architects succeeded where most of his European contemporaries failed: they knew how to integrate construction and decoration and the Dutch architect used these references in his own attempt to reconcile structural and representational requirements in the design.

The site of the American Hotel borders on Leidseplein, a square that had become established as a centre of middle-class entertainment and was strategically located near the municipal theatre, the state museum (Rijksmuseum), the municipal museum (Stedelijk Museum) and the concert hall (Concertgebouw). These institutions had appeared

131 Café Américain, Amsterdam (1902)

04 Looking down the southern narrow bay in the café room, c. 1902

in the two decades before the construction of the 'American Hotel', and all the buildings had been designed in the historical styles so abhorred by Kromhout. Situated on the south-west corner of the square, the 'American Hotel' stands out as a sign of protest, a testimony to the ambition to overcome historicism and revitalize architecture. The square façade is most prominently present, but the two other façades are more equally notable and, according to some critics, less problematic since the façade facing the square shows the marks of an unresolved problem: the robust, large scale of the café and restaurant, and the slightly cramped floors of the hotel above.

The layout of the café resembles contemporary examples in London and continental Europe: it is a spacious hall with a high ceiling, beautifully decorated and typical of Kromhout's skill in merging architecture, interior architecture and decoration. The main space is divided into three by three bays by arches decorated by a band of coloured bricks. The three central bays have three times the width of those on the north and south sides, creating the effect of a nave dominated by a large stained-glass window at one end and two shallower aisles. The space between the outer arches and the façade with its tall arched windows establishes a transitional zone between the interior and the outside world. Kromhout designed special light fittings and furniture and a variety of artists provided contributions to the interior; the upper sections of the windows feature stained-glass panels. In 1929, the hotel was substantially refurbished and new Art Deco light fittings in opaque glass were installed while the inner walls acquired a series of wall paintings depicting scenes from William Shakespeare's *A Midsummer's Night's Dream*.

When the hotel and its café first opened their doors, the new institution was described as 'fresh, happy, sparkling, fantastic, beautiful, energetic, free, festive, attractive, joyous, vital'. The Café Américain immediately attracted writers, artists and a fashionable public and retained the status of a centre of Amsterdam's cultural life into the 1970s, its reading table operating as an informal exchange for literary ideas and gossip. Refurbishments in the following decade, informed by the views of modern hotel and café management, interfered with the original design of the café. During renovation in May 2004, however, the interior and the paintings were restored and additions removed, re-establishing the Américain as a rare example of a refined interior of the nineteenth-century *fin de siècle*, now mostly used by tourists.

Cor Wagenaar

Sources:

Jager, I., *Willem Kromhout*, Rotterdam: 010 publishers, 1992

Rebel, B. and Vermeer, G., *d'Ailly's historische gids van Amsterdam*, Amsterdam: Amsterdam Publishers, 2004

**The Willow Tea Rooms
Sauchiehall Street, Glasgow,
Scotland
1904
Architect: Charles Rennie
Mackintosh**

01 The Gallery Tea Room,
c.1904

1
D. Brett, *C.R. Mackintosh: The
Poetics of Workmanship*, London:
Reaktion Books, 1992, p. 13–7

In the late nineteenth century, Glasgow gave birth not only to the new tea room phenomenon, but also to a new decorative style, dubbed the Glasgow Style (also known as Northern Art Nouveau). The core of this Scottish stylistic group was made up of Charles Rennie Mackintosh, Herbert MacNair and the sisters Margaret and Frances Macdonald. The close collaboration between Mackintosh and Margaret Macdonald, who later married, contributed greatly to Charles's fame as a designer while putting Margaret somewhat in the shade.[1]

The Willow Tea Rooms, comprising several different salons, was not the first such establishment for which Mackintosh had designed the interior, but it was the first commission that gave him complete control over both interior and exterior. Apart from the Glasgow School of Art (1899), Mackintosh's fame as an architect and interior designer is associated with this building and in particular the extravagant interiors with their distinctive furnishings and the many decorative leaded glass windows and murals by his wife Margaret. In 1917, at the end of his short career as architect, Mackintosh designed the 'dug-out', an underground extension of the basement level of the Willow building.[2] Not long after this, the couple left Glasgow, whereupon Charles devoted himself entirely to drawing and painting.[3]

The emergence of the Glasgow tea room

The name of Catherine (Kate) Cranston, Mackintosh's patron, is inextricably linked to the enormous popularity of tea rooms in Glasgow and of artistic tea rooms in particular. Together with her brother Stuart, a tea dealer, she set up a tea room as an extension of the tasting room of his tea business in 1875. This was also a period when the Temperance Movement was very active in combatting alcoholism by offering alternatives to the pub and spirits in the form of outlets selling tea and chocolate.[4] Kate Cranston's business drive proved stronger than her brother's and, in defiance of contemporary conventions, she went on to establish a chain of artistic tea rooms in Glasgow which turned her into a household name. As well as business acumen, she also had a keen eye for artistic talent, which she detected in the young designer of ship interiors, Charles Mackintosh. When she married a wealthy industrialist late in life, she maintained her independent image as 'Miss Cranston'. Several unmarried Glasgow women followed in her enterprising footsteps and set up tea rooms, but none attained the artistic fame of their illustrious role model.[5]

Although their female proprietors may have caused a stir, tea rooms were not aimed solely at ladies, but also at Glasgow's numerous businessmen. At that time, the city of Glasgow was second only to London in the British Empire and it boasted a lot of heavy industry, in particular shipbuilding. The outfitting and internal design of the big ocean-going steamers and passenger ships for transatlantic and orient lines provided work for ship's carpenters and interior designers. Charles Mackintosh began his career as an apprentice designer of ship interiors.[6] In Glasgow's dynamic economic climate, the working day became ever longer, pushing the main meal of the day to the early evening. The gap between breakfast and dinner became so long that a few pints of beer in the pub began to be replaced by a more substantial midday meal.[7] In opening her first tea rooms-cum-luncheon rooms, therefore, Miss Cranston addressed herself in particular to businessmen: 'the situation is suitable for gentlemen attending the exchange, courts, banks and warehouses', adding 'Smoking room open next week.'[8]

Layout and interior design

The use of the plural 'tea rooms' reflected the desire to cater to different clienteles in separate rooms. It was not just for gentlemen and their business lunches that special rooms, sometimes

[2]
P. Kinchin, *Taking Tea with Mackintosh: The Story of Miss Cranston's Tea Rooms*, , Rohnert Park, CA: Pomegranate Communications, 1998, p. 70–1

[3]
Brett, op. cit., p. 146–9

[4]
P. Kinchin, *Tea and Taste: The Glasgow Tea Rooms 1875–1975*, Wendlebury: White Cockade Publishing, 1991, p. 21–7

[5]
Ibid., p. 36–9

[6]
Brett, op. cit., p. 13–20

[7]
Kinchin, *Tea and Taste*, op. cit., p. 27–30

[8]
Ibid., p. 38

1. dining room
2. gallery
3. room de luxe
4. servery
5. tea room
6. billiards room

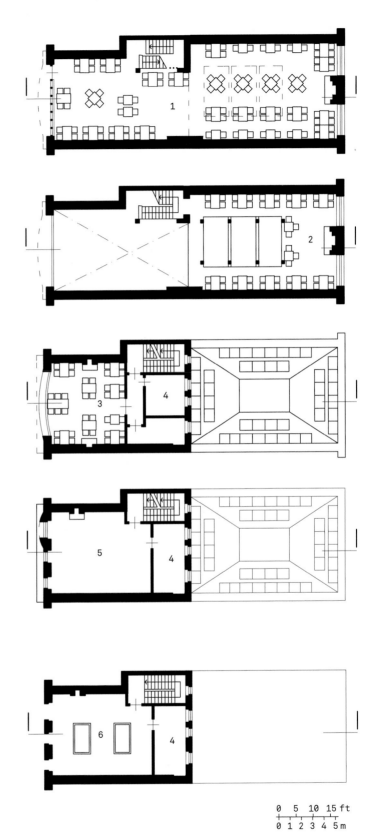

02 Ground floor

03 Gallery

04 First floor

05 Second floor

06 Third floor

0 5 10 15 ft

0 1 2 3 4 5 m

135 The Willow Tea Rooms, Glasgow (1904)

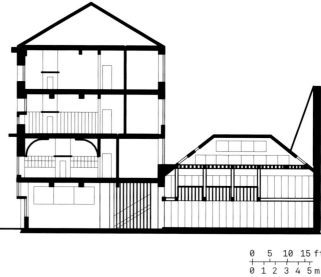

0 5 10 15 ft
0 1 2 3 4 5 m

with separate smoking and billiard rooms, were fitted out; women-only rooms were also provided where the ladies could enjoy their high tea without the need of a male chaperone. It was no accident that Miss Cranston opened the Willow Tea Rooms in a building on Sauchiehall Street, close to the new department stores where middle-class women had discovered the new pastime of shopping.[9] Pretty waitresses in elegant uniforms, also designed by Mackintosh, were an added attraction for the men, while at the same time giving the ladies a respectable, homely feeling.

The choice of colours and materials in the tea rooms reflected the contemporary gender-specific design of the different rooms of the Victorian house. The luncheon, smoking and billiard rooms were done in dark, masculine colours and heavy furniture, whereas light, feminine

9
Kinchin, *Tea and Taste*, op. cit., p. 30–3, 58, 68–77

08 The Room de Luxe, c. 1904

136 The Willow Tea Rooms, Glasgow (1904)

10
Kinchin, *Taking Tea*, op. cit.,
p. 16–7

11
Unlike Brett, Macleod views the
close collaboration as 'the
principal stumbling block in
Mackintosh's path to greatness'.
R. MacLeod, *Ch. R. Mackintosh*,
London: Collins, 1983, p. 145

12
'Ein Mackintosh-Teehaus in
Glasgow', *Dekorative Kunst*,
p. 269–73

colours and more delicate furniture were used for the ladies' tea rooms. However, under the influence of Miss Cranston and other female proprietors, the dominant interior style of the Glasgow tea rooms and thus of public tea rooms in general, was 'feminized from an early date'.[10] In particular, the extravagant, feminine interior design of the Willow Tea Rooms' famous 'Salon de Luxe' caused a sensation. It also represented the high point of the Glasgow Style, thanks in no small part to the close collaboration between Charles and Margaret.[11]

Descriptions and photographs in contemporary architecture journals give a picture of this ravishing interior.[12]

[Under an electric] chandelier of countless pink glass baubles . . . high-backed, silver chairs decorated with oval cutouts and squares of purple glass [were] carefully lined up at the central tables on the marked-out carpet. . . . At the sides of

137 The Willow Tea Rooms, Glasgow (1904)

10 The Oak Room, c. 1904

11 Sauchiehall Street façade,
c. 1905

the room [there were] chairs with lower curved backs, also silver and upholstered in purple velvet. . . . The lower walls were panelled with silvery purple silk, stitched with beads down the seams. . . . Round the walls ran a frieze of leaded coloured and mirror glass.

High on the wall opposite the fireplace was a decorative panel by Margaret Mackintosh, in gesso, 'representing three elongated ladies, dripping with strings of glass jewels'.[13] Margaret's title, 'O Ye, All Ye That Walk in Willowwood' referred to a Rossetti poem and was another manifestation of the pervasive willow theme, as were the oval leaf ornaments of the weeping willow in the leaded-glass windows and plastered wall decorations. As usual at that time, public credit for the handsome interior went to Miss Cranston, rather than Charles and Margaret Mackintosh.

The name 'Willow Tea Rooms' was an allusion to the Gaelic origins of the street name, Sauchiehall, which means 'alley of the willows'. The building had been a tenement house but the plain cement façade and open-plan interior devised by Mackintosh lent it a special and above all modern grandeur. Kinchin writes:

On entering, customers passed . . . behind a white enameled screen inset with elegant leaded-glass panels to a central cashier's station and [had] a choice: into a light ladies' tea room at the front or a darker general lunch saloon at the back, or up the stairs to the tea gallery built around a well over the back saloon. All these spaces were interconnected – separated only lightly by ironwork screens or an odd structure with the semi-circular order desk behind it. . . . The spaces were both coordinated and differentiated by their decor – white, pink, and silver for the ladies' tea room; dark grey canvas paneling with touches of pink in the stenciled decorations for the rear dining room; lighter gray, white, and pink for the general tea gallery. The areas were also articulated by the use of two main chair designs, both dark-stained: a ladder-back with curved rungs . . . and a contrasting boxy armchair. Up the stairs on the first floor, only customers willing to pay a bit extra would push open a pair of gorgeous doors to enter . . . the Salon de Luxe . . . the ultimate example of the tea room as a work of art.[14]

13
Kinchin, *Taking Tea*, op. cit., p. 53–9

14
Ibid., p. 52–3

15
Cooper, *Mackintosh Architecture*, London: Academy Editions, 1978, p. 70

Add to this the splendour of the specially designed floor covering and the tea service with willow motif and it is clear that a visit to the Willow Tea Rooms was in many respects a unique experience. The Salon de Luxe (popularly known as the 'Room de Luxe') is the only space that is still more or less intact, minus the furnishings, though no longer as a tea room but as a bridal salon for the adjoining department store which annexed the Willow building in the 1920s.[15]

Irene Cieraad.
Translation Robyn Dalziel-de Jong

Sources:

Brett, D., *C.R. Mackintosh: The Poetics of Workmanship*, London: Reaktion Books, 1992, pp. 13–7

Cooper, J. (ed.), *Mackintosh Architecture*, London: Academy Editions, 1978, p. 70

'Ein Mackintosh-Teehaus in Glasgow', *Dekorative Kunst,* 8, 1905: 257–73

Kinchin, P., *Tea and Taste: The Glasgow Tea Rooms 1875–1975*, Wendlebury: White Cockade Publishing, 1991, pp. 21–7

Kinchin, P., *Taking Tea with Mackintosh: The Story of Miss Cranston's Tea Rooms*, Rohnert Park, CA: Pomegranate Communications, 1998, pp. 70–1

MacLeod, R., *Ch. R. Mackintosh*, London: Collins, 1983, p. 145

American Bar (Kärntner Bar)
Kärntnerdurchgang, Vienna, Austria
1907–8
Architect: Adolf Loos

01 The bar, looking towards
the entrance, M. Gerlach,
c. 1930

1
Ludwig Münz dates the bar to
1907, Burkhardt Ruckschio to
1908. See L. Münz and G.
Künstler, *Der Architekt Adolf Loos*,
Vienna: Anton Schroll, 1964,
pp. 38-40, 185; B. Ruckschio and
R. Schachtel, *Adolf Loos, Leben und
Werk*, Salzburg: Residenz Verlag,
1982, p. 456-9

When Adolf Loos designed his American Bar in 1907,[1] he was still at the beginning of his career as an architect. Although he had been designing for ten years at this stage, he had yet to build anything from scratch. So far, his realized work had consisted of housing refurbishments and shop interiors, and the only free-standing house – Villa Karma in Montreux on Lake Geneva – was also a renovation job. He had, however, designed a Viennese café interior, Café Museum, near the opera house (1899). The American Bar fits into this series of smaller commissions and can be described as an internal conversion. Just two years later, in 1910, Loos successfully completed two new-build projects in Vienna, Haus Steiner and a shop plus dwellings for Goldman & Salatsch. Both buildings were rapidly constructed and the shop on Michaelerplatz earned Loos a lot of publicity owing to the scandal created by its taut, stripped, neo-classical façade.

Typology and context

An American bar in Vienna, in the twilight years of the empire, sits oddly with the image of the Central European drinking culture, with its cafés, beer halls and wine bars. Hard liquor was consumed on special premises where customers drank corn or fruit-based brandy (*Obstler*) standing at a zinc counter. A bar whose name alluded to the United States and which served 'American drinks' would certainly have been a novelty. In the twentieth edition of Louise Seleskowitz's Viennese cookbook in 1923, cocktails were still listed under 'Englisch-amerikanische Getränke' followed, in brackets, by 'American Drinks'.[2] Although the Viennese had had their first taste of mixed drinks in the American pavilion at the World's Fair in Prater in 1873 and the phenomenon of the American bar had already been mentioned in an 1894 architectural handbook,[3] cocktails only started to come into their own after World War I.

The commission for the American Bar coincided with Loos' cultural sympathies. He spent 1893 to 1896 in the United States, stopping briefly in England on his way home. His lifelong partiality for the Anglo-Saxon world found expression not only in his clothes and in his work for menswear stores like Knize or Goldman & Salatsch, which sold high-class English suits, but also via various themes in his essays. The subtitle of his short-lived magazine *Das Andere* (only two issues appeared, in 1903) was 'A magazine for introducing Western culture

2
L. Seleskowitz, *Wiener Kochbuch*, Vienna: Wilhelm Braumüller, 1923, p. 536

3
H. Wagner, 'Schankstätten und Speisewirtschaften; Kaffeehäuser und Restaurants', in J. Durm (ed), *Handbuch der Architektur*, Part 4 *Anlage und Einrichtung der Gebäude*, IV Vol. *Gebäude für Erholungs-, Beherbergugngs- und Vereinszwecke*, Darmstadt: Arnold Bergsträsser, 1894, n. 1, p. 13

02 The façade on Käzntner, 1908

141 American Bar (Kärntnerbar), Vienna (1907–8)

into Austria' and it is not hard to guess which culture he thought
should be introduced into the Austrian Empire.

Layout and interior design

The American Bar is one of Loos' smaller works, but it has been
well preserved. Although it is only 4.45 m wide, its external appearance
is particularly striking. Four columns of yellow Skyros marble flank
three glass doors in brass frames. The middle door is the main
entrance. Above the entrance is a canted fascia, emblazoned with a
stylized American flag in coloured glass and the name of the
establishment. Above this again is a wall of square slabs of translucent
onyx, also bearing the name of the bar, although the translucency of
the onyx slabs can only be appreciated from inside. Externally, the bar
stands out from its predominantly stuccoed neighbours and strikes a
rather frivolous note with its colourfulness. The relatively deep (1 m)
entrance lobby was used as a cloakroom, with a second inner door
providing access to the bar proper.

142 American Bar (Kärntnerbar), Vienna (1907–8)

04 Ground floor

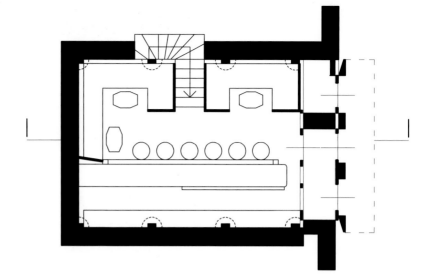

05 Section

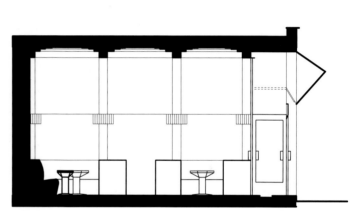

Once inside, one has the sense of having entered a genuine private
club room: subdued lighting, muted colours, wooden panelling and
leather settees. This inner sanctum measures only 4.45 x 5.15 m
but the modest proportions are not immediately apparent. To the left
is the bar, on the right, two low settees in green leather either side
of a low door leading down to the toilets. Customers can enjoy their
'American drink' at the bar, in which case they can lean on the 1.08 m-
high round mahogany rod and rest their foot on the brass rail along the
base of the bar. Alternatively they can choose to have their drinks
seated on one of the low (36 cm) but deep (50 cm) settees and place
their glass on the internally illuminated frosted glass of one of the two
fixed tables. Above the settee against the back wall hangs a single

143 American Bar (Kärntnerbar), Vienna (1907–8)

painting, a portrait of the poet Peter Altenberg, a friend of Loos, painted by Gustav Jagerspacher (nowadays a replica of the original).

The walls are panelled in mahogany to the height of the entrance door lintel. The back wall of the bar has bottle racks to the same height, and behind them mirrors that duplicate the number of bottles. Between the lintel line and the ceiling, the walls are lined with mirrors. The room is divided laterally into three bays by mahogany half-columns and this division continues across the ceiling in the form of beams. The ceiling is coffered in yellowish-brown marble, while the floor is paved with black and white marble tiles in a chequerboard pattern. With its subdued lighting, muted colours, sparkling bottles and glasses, the bar exudes a feeling of intimacy. But the most remarkable effect is achieved with the mirrors on three walls, which reflect the light-coloured ceiling in such a way as to make the space seem much bigger than it actually is.

The year of the bar's completion is memorable for another reason. It was in 1908 that Loos wrote what is possibly his best-known and most controversial essay, 'Ornament und Verbrechen' ('Ornament and Crime'). His dislike of ornamentation in architecture and applied art was later seen as a precursor of functionalism and was much quoted. In fact, Loos' criticism was directed primarily at the work of his Vienna Secession contemporaries, Joseph Olbrich and Josef Hoffmann, whose graceful Art Nouveau lines he abhorred. But by 1908 the difference between his work and that of his previously maligned contemporaries, especially Hoffman, was no longer so apparent. Like Hoffmann in his design for the Palais Stoclet in Brussels (1905–10), Loos used geometric shapes (ceiling coffers, panelling) and a combination of natural, preferably expensive, materials as a modern form of ornamentation.

Otakar Máčel.
Translation Robyn Dalziel-de Jong

Sources:

Münz, L. and Künstler, G., *Der Architekt Adolf Loos*, Vienna: Anton Schroll, 1964, pp. 38–40, 185

Ruckschio, B. and Schachtel, R., *Adolf Loos, Leben und Werk*, Salzburg: Residenz Verlag, 1982, pp. 456–9

Seleskowitz, L., *Wiener Kochbuch*, Vienna: Wilhelm Braumüller, 1923, p. 536

Wagner, H., 'Schankstätten und Speisewirtschaften; Kaffeehäuser und Restaurants', in J. Durm (ed.), *Handbuch der Architektur*, Part 4 *Anlage und Einrichtung der Gebäude*, IV Vol. *Gebäude für Erholungs-, Beherbergugngs- und Vereinszwecke*, Darmstadt: Arnold Bergsträsser, 1894, n. 1, p. 13

Café Worpswede
Lindenstraße 1/3, Worpswede
(near Bremen), Germany
1924–5
Architect: Bernhard Hoetger

01 The restaurant, view
towards the entrance, 1925

The Café Worpswede is possibly one of the more extreme examples of the artistic cafés or bars, a phenomenon that started to emerge in the late nineteenth century and became more widespread as an institution that could combine commercial and social functions with propagating, or marketing, particular tendencies of art and design. Designed by a sculptor with little previous building experience, but whose projects of the second half of the 1920s were among the most complex and extraordinary contributions to German architecture before World War II, the café reflects the uneasy internal tensions in a culture that was both undertaking radical artistic and social experiments and gripped by a deep anxiety about modernity. The programme of the building, a café with a gallery was part of what may now be described as a branding strategy; its architectural proposal blends images from film décor (notably Hans Poelzig's representation of the Prague Ghetto in the 1920 film, *The Golem*), traditional rural building and utopian projects of the early 1920s.

Context

In the 1890s, the inhabitants of the small village of Worpswede, mostly peat peasants and agricultural workers, witnessed the remarkable influx of a group of artists who took lodgings in humble farmsteads. Worpswede appeared remote enough to offer the young artists an environment onto which ideals of authenticity and rural primitivism could be projected. The proximity of Bremen, Germany's second largest port, with a sizable and wealthy middle class of merchants and shipping magnates, offered the 'colony' a regional base from which the artists could reach the emerging German arts market. By 1900, their presentation of the Worpswede landscape had been recast into a 'fully elaborated place myth',[1] responding to what Siegfried Kracauer described as 'the daydreams of society', celebrated in post-Impressionist and Jugendstil-inspired paintings of the village and its surroundings. Worpswede came to embody the promise of a reality somehow more authentic and complete than the present, and the village started to attract a growing number of visitors.

1
Nina Lübbren, *Rural Artists' Colonies in Europe 1870–1910*, New Brunswick, NJ: Rutgers, 2001, p. 121

Architect and client

The Café Worpswede was the first of a series of buildings that consolidated the role of Worpswede as a tourist destination. It is the work of the artist Bernhard Hoetger, but its history is essentially a major turning point in the relationship between the sculptor and his patron Ludwig Roselius, whose firm Kaffee Hag ranked among the world's largest coffee companies. Hoetger had come to Worpswede in 1916 and during the 1920s he became one of the more prominent artists in the colony.

In 1925, following the construction of a similar café in the Harz Mountains and a mainstream modern café on the boulevard of Zandvoort (Holland), Hoetger took the initiative for developing Café Worpswede as a part of an ensemble of workshops and galleries. In this, Hoetger had to rely on the financial support of Roselius, who supported the project and its later extensions with a 'Logierhaus' (hotel) and, finally, the 'Große Kunstschau', an art gallery that was completed in 1927. Several decades before cafés became a standard ingredient in public galleries, Roselius and Hoetger realized their own version of a museum café at Worpswede.

Lacking the formal training of an architect, Hoetger designed the café using plaster models and had to rely on the assistance of professionals. Much of the design was developed during the

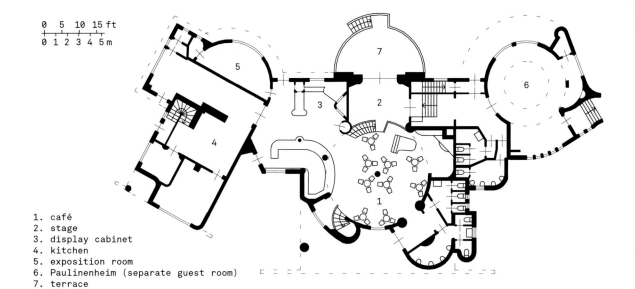

0 5 10 15 ft
0 1 2 3 4 5 m

1. café
2. stage
3. display cabinet
4. kitchen
5. exposition room
6. Paulinenheim (separate guest room)
7. terrace

02 Ground floor

2
W.E.W. Saal, *Bernhard Hoetger:
Ein Architekt des Norddeutschen
Expressionismus,* dissertation,
Bonn University, 1989,
p. 183–4

five-month construction period and involved improvisation on site.[2] As a building that grew from a process of intuitive design and traditional building techniques, the café epitomized Hoetger's ideas of a renewal of Northern German culture by evoking continuities with the pre-industrial, even pre-historic past. His anticlassicism was fuelled by highly idiosyncratic interpretations of theosophy and an increasing obsession with genealogy, all of these reworked into a delirious mélange of fairy-tale brick architecture and expressionist form making.

Architectural design and interior

The building appears to be a group of houses with high-pitched roofs, executed as a timber-frame and brick structure and based on the Lower Saxon farmhouses and their patterns of uniting man and animal under one roof. Inside, the café opens itself as a tall space, ignoring and almost contradicting the simple structural proposal of the hall house. Under the large roof supported by enormous oak posts and beams, the circular plan is developed in what could be described as a *plan libre* of convex and concave walls enclosing the interior. The smooth surface of the cave, covered in bright yellow plasterwork, renders the interior into a theatrically developed series of smaller niches around a tall cave. On the south side and originally accessed via the raised 'stage' there was the 'Paulinenheim', a second circular room illuminated by a lay light and probably intended for private parties. All rooms were furnished with chairs and tables designed by Hoetger, and the lower parts of the walls enclosing the main space were covered with raffia hangings from the local crafts workshop.

Situated in the centre of the hall, a wooden pole rises from the floor to the top of the cave, its wooden arms stretching out horizontally like abstract branches. This sculpture, a representation of the 'world

147 Café Worpswede, Worpswede (1924–5)

148 Café Worpswede, Worpswede (1924–5)

ash tree' Yggdrasil of Nordic mythology, divides the café into a series of smaller areas, one directed towards the large fireplace, another dominated by the bar and a third facing the entrance terrace, but it also introduces references to Hoetger's ideas about the pagan origins of Nordic culture. He and Roselius shared this ideology and it seems likely that the café at Worpswede played a role in the latter's decision to commission Hoetger for two buildings in the project for the Böttcherstrasse in Bremen. Anecdotal evidence suggests that the local and probably intoxicated artists occasionally mistook the sculpture as a giant toy and climbed on its branches.[3]

Representation and the branding of regional identity

The Café Worpswede and its gallery came to be identified as the rural equivalent to this project of the reinvention of North German culture by constructing a continuity with an imagined Nordic past. Like the Böttcherstrasse, the café in the artists colony was also part of a strategy employing references to regional identity in order to create consciously framed experiences for visitors from the region and abroad. The combination of the café with the gallery proved difficult commercially. In 1929 the entire enterprise was taken over by Roselius' firm, which continued exploiting it through the 1930s and after World War II.[4] The references to Nordic mythology and the ideological agenda had been met with suspicion by contemporary critics in the 1920s; they did not appeal to the National Socialists either, in whose catalogue of degenerate art Hoetger's work figured prominently as an example of the aberrations of what Adolf Hitler referred to as the 'Böttcherstrassenkultur'. Meanwhile, the café attracted a mixed clientele of respectable merchants who bought art works for their homes or ships, and artists for whom the café became a social focus in the village. The overt anachronisms in the design of the café and the eclectic use of images – Tafuri and Dal Co observed an 'authentic academism of fragmentation'[5] in Hoetger's work – were tremendously effective in creating the illusion that the building was indeed a remnant of some very distant past, a historical fiction in which most of its clientele were, and still are, only too keen to believe.

Christoph Grafe

3
Conversation of the author with Frau Ursula Köhler, whose father Martin Goldyga was managing director of both the café and the gallery, 28 December 2005.

4
Saal, op. cit., p. 197

5
Manfredo Tafuri and Francesco Dal Co, *Modern Architecture*, New York: Electa/Rizzoli, 1986, p. 143

Sources:

Lübbren, N., *Rural Artists' Colonies in Europe 1870–1910*, New Brunswick, NJ: Rutgers, 2001

Pehnt, W., *Expressionist Architecture*, London: Thames and Hudson, 1973

Pehnt, W., 'Das architektonische Werk von Bernhard Hoetger', in *Bernhard Hoetger 1874–1949*, Bremen: Hauschild, 1974, pp. 121–8.

Saal, W.E.W., 'Bernhard Hoetger: Ein Architekt des Norddeutschen Expressionismus', dissertation, Bonn University, 1989

Tallasch, H. (ed.), *Projekt Böttcherstraße*, Delmenhorst: Aschenbeck und Holstein, 2002

Tafuri, M. and Dal Co, F., *Modern Architecture*, New York: Electa/Rizzoli, 1986

Thiemann, E., *Hoetger*, Worpswede: Worpsweder Verlag, 1990

Hotel-Café Avion
29 Česká ulice, Brno, Czech Republic
1927–8
Architect: Bohuslav Fuchs

01 Looking down at the café
from the third floor, 1927–8

Between 1925 and 1929, the Moravian city of Brno acquired five functionalist cafés: the Savoy by Jindřich Kumpošt (1926), the Esplanade by Arnost Wiesner, the Café Era (1927–9) by Josef Kranz and the Zemanova Kavárna (Café Zeman 1925-7) and Hotel-Café Avion both designed by Bohuslav Fuchs. This concentration of 'modernist' commercial buildings was notable for a city of 230,000 inhabitants. Equally remarkable was the strong presence of modern architecture, from Wiesner and Kumpošt's Loosian classical modernism to Fuchs's radical avant-garde concept. Sadly, conditions after World War II were less favourable to modernism and none of the cafés exists in its original form. The Avion and Era buildings survived, albeit not as cafés, while Café Zeman was reconstructed in the mid-1990s.

But why were the 1920s so favourable to construction in general and to modern architecture in particular? To answer this we must go

02 The façade on Česká Street

back to the end of 1918 and the founding of the Czechoslovak Republic. After three hundred years, Bohemia and Moravia ceased to be part of the Austro-Hungarian Empire. The political and administrative changes brought with them a new energy that found expression on several fronts and a corresponding hunger for that which was newest and most modern.

One example of this hunger in architecture was the series of lectures held in Brno in late 1923 and early 1924, with J.J.P. Oud, Walter Gropius, Le Corbusier, Adolf Loos and Theo van Doesburg appearing as speakers. The regime change generated new posts and commissions. In 1920, for example, 29-year-old Jindřich Kumpošt was appointed city architect of Brno. He in turn invited Bohuslav Fuchs to come from Prague and work for the Brno City Council. Fuchs was 28 years old when he moved to Brno and he was by no means the last young architect to settle in a city where there was a lot of construction going on.

Around 1925, thanks to Le Corbusier and to a lesser extent Dutch architects and Adolf Loos, modern architectural ideas began to be translated into built form. In Brno this was not limited to cafés, but also extended to housing and schools, the 'Exhibition of Contemporary Culture' in 1928 marking the climax of this development. The modern pavilions built for that exhibition are still used for similar purposes today.

A modern hotel café

The commission for Hotel-Café Avion came in what was for Fuchs a busy and successful year. He built six other projects in 1927–8, including his own house, a block of three one-family homes for a model housing scheme and the City of Brno pavilion (the last two for the aforementioned exhibition). But the hotel-café project is the most interesting owing to the difficulty of the task and its spatial resolution.

The plot was long and narrow: 8.5 m wide at the street end, 7.5 m at the rear, but 34 m deep. These dimensional constraints called for a creative spatial solution. On the street side the building has nine storeys, including the basement. The total height from basement to roof is 40 m. The ground floor housed a refreshment bar, hotel reception and stairs to the café, and a staircase and lift to the hotel rooms. The hotel and café circulation routes were independent but connected. The café areas were located on the first and second floors and above them were six standard-height storeys containing 40 hotel rooms and one apartment. The top two floors were set back to leave room for a roof terrace with a fine view of the cathedral and fortress. Offices, the kitchen and ancillary spaces were located at the rear. The spatial heart of the building is a vertical well with a glass ceiling, the voids allowing daylight to penetrate the two café floors.

151 Hotel-Café Avion, Brno (1927–8)

1. buffet
2. café
3. hotel

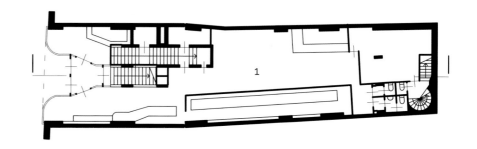

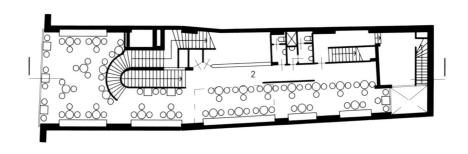

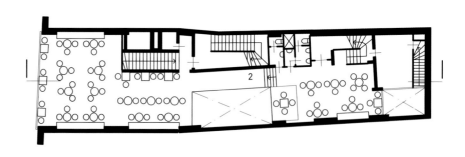

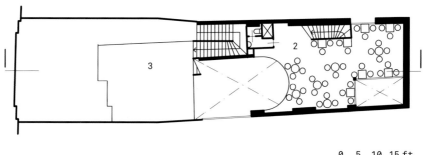

03 Ground floor

04 First floor

05 Second floor

06 Third floor

0   5   10 15 ft
0 1 2 3 4 5 m

152 Hotel-Café Avion, Brno (1927–8)

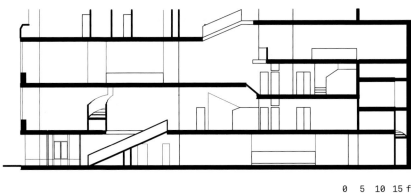

0 5 10 15 ft

0 1 2 3 4 5 m

These two café floors, identifiable on the outside by large window areas – in contrast to the narrower window bands of the hotel rooms – are the most spectacular part of the building. The well divides these floors into front and back areas connected by galleries, allowing interesting views, the most beautiful of which is obtained from the third floor at the rear (where the floor height is reduced to create an additional level) which looks right down to the ground-floor entrance.

08 On the first floor, looking towards the front

153 Hotel-Café Avion, Brno (1927–8)

Materialization

The interior was uncluttered and simple: beechwood Thonet-style chairs and tables with round marble tops; banquettes against the walls, interspersed with the central heating radiators; wall lamps of opalescent glass and polished brass from the Inwald company to a design by Miroslav Prokop; a modest cream-coloured accent in the form of the 'Salubra' wallpaper; a clever use of mirrors in order to give an illusion of greater width.

Because of its central location, the Avion fulfilled the classic function of a Central European café: a place to grab a cup of coffee and read the paper, to have a bite to eat perhaps, but above all to meet one's friends. The clientele spanned all age groups but the young predominated. Before the war Café Avion was also a meeting place for Brno's younger avant-garde.

Almost two decades after the velvet revolution the hotel is still operational but in effect only for enthusiasts of modern architecture, since the level of comfort is rather low by the standards of the early twenty-first century. The ground floor contains a restaurant, the café floors are occupied by an amusement arcade and a Chinese restaurant, while a new owner has considered restoring the (listed) building. Given the high cost involved in such a project, however, the future of the Café Avion remains uncertain.

Otakar Máčel.
Translation Robyn Dalziel-de Jong

10 On the second floor,
looking from the front room
towards the back

Sources:

Crhonek, I., *Architect Bohuslav Fuchs: The Lifework*, Brno: Petrov, 1995, pp. 26, 31, 60–3

Šlapeta, V., *Die Brünner Funktionalisten*, Innsbruck: University of Innsbruck, Institut für Raumgestaltung, 1985, pp. 22–3, 32–3, 46–7

Kudělka, Z., *Bohuslav Fuchs*, Prague: Nakladatelství Československých výtvarných umělců, 1966, pp. 72–3

154 Hotel-Café Avion, Brno (1927–8)

Bar Craja
Piazza Cardinal Paolo Ferrari
(Via San Dalmazio), Milan, Italy
1930
Architects: Luciano Baldessari with
Luigi Figini and Gino Pollini

01 The entrance zone with the
till and counter, c. 1930

If there was a single architectural construction in Italy connected strongly to a particular movement and literally inhabited by some of the most important exponents of that movement, it may well be Bar Craja in Milan. The clientele in question were the protagonists of the Milanese 'novecento': not only the rationalist architects of *Gruppo 7*, founded in 1926, and later the M.A.R. (*Movimento Architettura Razionale*, 1928) and M.I.A.R. (adding '*Italiano*' to it in 1930), but also philosophers, typographers, sociologists, critics, sculptors, writers, poets, musicians, thinkers and painters had found in Craja a place to meet. It constituted an oasis in the Italy of the 1930s that was not in the cultural shadow of Benedetto Croce, or the architectural one of Piacentini, but was tuned in to the rest of Europe across the Alps. Craja was part of the same avant-garde scene as the Millione Gallery across from the Brera Academy. In the evenings, the in-crowd sat down according to a fixed seating arrangement,

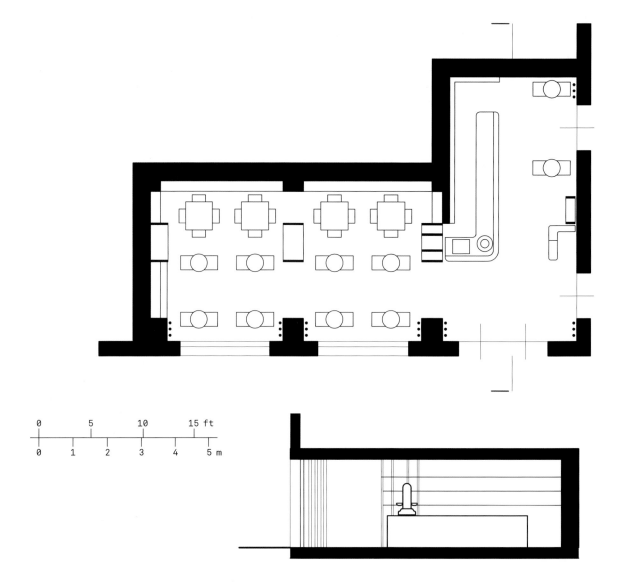

1
Carlo Belli, in *È riapparso l'impero sui colli fatali di Roma, Café Craja*, Milan: libri Scheiwiller, 1962

02 Ground floor

03 Section

reflecting the subtle hierarchies and dynamics of the group. According to Carlo Belli, the painters came in first at nine, followed by Persico (editor of *Casabella*). The architects joined them (much) later: Pollini and Figini, and on Saturdays sometimes Terragni, the painter Rho and also Lingeri and the young Cattaneo came in from Como. When in Milan, Savinio, painter and brother of De Chirico was present as well. Besides being the first 'rationalist' space in Milan, Craja was also the last bar to close.[1]

Architect and client

For the design, architect Luciano Baldessari collaborated with Figini and Pollini. Baldessari had contacted Gino Pollini in 1930 about the commission, which he considered important enough from the start to gather a small group of like-minded artists around him. In addition

04 The façade in 1930

to the young architect duo, the artists Fausto Melotti (a common friend of both Baldessari and Pollini) and Marcello Nizzoli were asked to join the effort together with the engineer Ernesto Saliva (to resolve some static issues related to the refurbishing of an old building).

The client, Antonio Craja, was already a famed restaurant owner in the Via San Dalmazio, where the rich industrial elite met with the artistic world just a few steps from the Scala. Craja himself achieved the status of enlightened patron in the eyes of the Italian modernists; his café became a radical manifesto for rationalism in a city where the academicism preached at the Brera was very much alive. On completion of the bar in 1930, according to Belli, it faced a few difficult months, as the sterile interior was at first only appreciated by the avant-garde itself. The interior had been kept intentionally cool and not cosy and was perceived as the bar version of the minimalist existentialism across the Alps. Craja persisted, however, and started to attract elite customers with its distinctly modern theme.

Layout and organization

The bar had an asymmetrical L-shaped plan, with the short side on an alley (now called passaggio Giovanni Malagodi, leading to Via Santa Margherita) and the long side on the Piazza Cardinal Paolo Ferrari, where the Via San Dalmazio leads onto the Via Filodrammatici. It faced both streets with large shopfronts set in a band of panelling, applied to the lower part of the façade without intermediate cornice to the plaster above. The storefronts displayed the inside both night and day, showing off a shiny modern interior in which the electric lighting conjured up futuristic associations. The theatrical effect of mirrors and metallic surfaces was visible from the outside – Baldessari had joined the futurists together with Depero in 1913, only one year before his 'Luminator' design for a lamp stand had been on display in the Italian Pavilion of the International Exhibition in Barcelona.

The L-plan divided the interior in two parts. Out of three bays with the same width, perpendicular to the long façade on the piazza, the first one was deeper: it featured the standing bar, with two entrances from the alley and a wider one from the piazza. The space here was characteristic of the conventional Italian bar still omnipresent today, with a separate cash point near one of the entrances. The other section, consisting of the remaining two, almost square bays, was accessed here. The second space resembled a train car with compartments, the seating arranged around two larger tables in each bay against the back wall and four smaller tables in each bay on both sides of a 'gangway'.

The length of the seating area was accentuated by chrome finishes and mirrors. The division in bays was articulated by means of pilasters and the neoplastic decorative system on the floor, the walls and the ceiling. The identification of the constituent surfaces was often referred to as reminiscent of 'De Stijl',[2] but the neoplastic treatment of the space is combined with a general attention to detail and structure

2
A. C. Quintavalle, *Marcello Nizzoli*, Milan: Electa, 1989

05 View from the entrance.
In the background the metal
sculpture by F. Melotti.

3
F. Irace, in V. Gregotti and G.
Marzari (eds), *Luigi Figini – Gino
Pollini, Opera Completa* Milan:
Electa, 1996, p. 258–61

4
Ezio Bonfanti, R. Bonicalzi,
A. Rossi, M. Scolari and D. Vitale,
*Architettura Razionale. XV
Triennale di Milano*, Milan: Franco
Angeli, 1973, p. 16–20

06 Interior with the metal
sculpture by F. Melotti

more in line with Josef Hoffman (articulating the edges of the surfaces) and a conspicuous materiality not unlike Mies. This 'machine à jouir'[3] may have been rational, but it had nothing to do with economy of materials. It was a dense interior where art and new materials were on display as if in an exhibition stand.

The fantastic aesthetic of Craja (Baldessari's input according to De Seta) is closer to the 'shiny' diners in America than the transalpine rationality and geometric ingenuity so admired by Figini and Pollini. Hidden lighting behind the opaxit ceiling panels was reflected by the shiny floors, filling the space with an almost hostile atmosphere (Belli), intentionally not cosy – to stir a polemic. The floor consisted of small ceramic mosaic tiles: white, light green and dark green, laid out in a gridded, tatami-like pattern with shiny black fittings between the rectangles. The ceiling followed the same pattern, but inverting light and dark. The treatment of the walls picked up on the grid by means of pilasters in grey opaxit interspersed with plates of green marble (*cipollino apuano*). The space was thus prepared for the insertion of red leather divans designed by Melchiore Bega, black wooden frames dividing the two bays, a bar caged in a galvanized frame and yellow floor-to-ceiling tubes for heating near the windows.

Sculpture

A fountain was situated at the end of the en-suite bays, designed by sculptor (and musician and painter and poet) Fausto Melotti: three athletic, galvanized-steel female figures just larger than life in and out of a water basin, placed in front of a large mirror: *Icaro che sfugge alle stelle*. In the centre window stall sits a double-faced mannequin by Marcello Nizzoli (designer, draughtsman and architect influenced by Futurism and later responsible for fashion items, posters for Campari and Martini and the famous Olivetti typewriter).

When Bar Craja was demolished in the 1960s, nobody seems to have noticed or been sufficiently bothered. It really was only with the preparations of the exhibition for the 1973 Milan Triennale 'Architettura Razionale', curated by among others Aldo Rossi,[4] that something of an interest in revisiting and consequently preserving the architecture from between the two wars emerged. But for Bar Craja, this came too late.

Filip Geerts

Sources:

Belli, C., in *È riapparso l'impero sui colli fatali di Roma, Café Craja*, Milan: libri Scheiwiller, 1962

Bonfanti, E., Bonicalzi, R., Rossi, A., Scolari, M. and Vitale, D., *Architettura Razionale. XV Triennale di Milano*, Milan: Franco Angeli, 1973, pp. 16–20

Gregotti, V. and Marzari, G. (eds), *Luigi Figini – Gino Pollini, Opera Completa*, Milan: Electa, 1996

Irace, F., in V. Gregotti and G. Marzari (eds), *Luigi Figini – Gino Pollini, Opera Completa* Milan: Electa, 1996, pp. 258–61

Quintavalle, A.C., *Marcello Nizzoli*, Milan: Electa, 1989

La Maison du Café
Corner of Place de l'Opéra and Rue
du Quatre-Septembre, Paris, France
1933
Architect: Charles Siclis

01 Interior view along the bar, 1934   **159 La Maison du Café, Paris (1933)**

Although Charles Siclis counted many members of high society among his clients in the 1920s and 1930s, his name is not widely known today. Born in 1889, Siclis studied architecture at the École des Beaux Arts and graduated in 1920. During his career, Siclis refused to adhere to either the rules of classicism taught at his school or to those of modernism. However, he met with widespread appreciation from his contemporaries, even among important representatives of other styles. Robert Mallet-Stevens, for instance, praised Siclis for his imagination and his ability to reach exactly the result that he had envisaged.[1]

The designs for the pavilion and garden at the Place de Clichy for the 1925 *Exposition International des Arts Décoratifs et Industriels Modernes* were an early achievement of Siclis's. This exhibition was intended to establish French interior design as leading in Europe and the French designers impressed the commentators with their opulent interiors. The style they presented became known throughout Europe as Art Deco, after the title of the exhibition. The work of Siclis, with its luxurious aura, rich materials, the lighting tricks and the appreciative integration of technological innovations, shows it was strongly influenced by this style.[2]

As well as the Maison du Café, Siclis designed many more successful cafés in Paris,[3] but his cafés and bars were considered minor works and are not even mentioned in the list of works in a 1931 monograph. Other projects such as villas for the rich and famous and a large project on the Basque coast, consisting of a casino, a hotel, around forty villas and several public monuments, feature prominently on this list.[4] Siclis's real fame, however, came from his many designs for theatres and cinemas. In this field he benefited greatly from the support of Philippe de Rothschild, who commissioned a number of theatre designs from him.

Functional organization and layout

In 1930, Nino Frank described how new types of bars started to appear in Paris. He divided them into two categories: proper bars where one drinks standing up and bars *de luxe* which have appropriated that name falsely, although, he adds, an attempt was made to camouflage this by the introduction of 'high stools, on which, sitting down, one can at least appear to be standing up'.[5] La Maison du Café belongs to the first category; it does not contain any other furniture than the bar itself with its eight enormous coffee machines and some tiny high tables. The bar was divided into a part where coffee was sold and a smaller part for pastry. The visitor entered through one of four doors in the transparent façade, ordered a coffee at the nearest of the percolators, enjoyed his drink while standing at the bar, and was off again.

Interior decoration and fittings

The commission for La Maison du Café had challenged Siclis to make an exceptional effort and a contemporary critic described the result as 'the most sumptuous bar in Paris'.[6] The tiny venue was well

1
Architectures de Biarritz et de la côte basque, de la Belle Époque aux Années 30, Liège/Brussels: éd. Mardaga/IFA, 1990

2
Rybczynski, W., *Home: A Short History of an Idea*, New York: Penguin Books, 1986

3
A.B., 'Café "Le Triomphe" aux Champs-Élysées', *L'Architecture d'Aujourd'hui*, December 1934–January 1935: 5

4
Janneau, G., *Ch. Siclis*, Geneva: éd. 'Les Maîtres de l'Architecture' S.A., 1931, p. XIV

5
Frank, N., *Art & Décoration*, 57, 1930: 179

6
Sabatou, J.P., *L'Architecture d'Aujourd'hui*, 1934(2): 679

1. espresso bar
2. patisserie

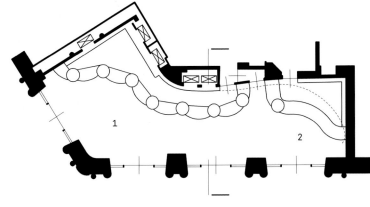

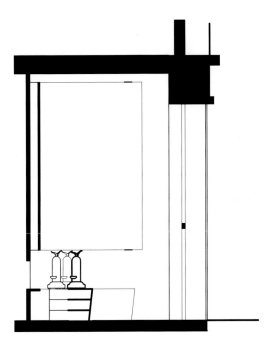

located in Parisian street life, but its surroundings also meant that it had a lot of competitors. In order to make it stand out, Siclis made the façade resemble a grand portico, worthy of a much larger interior. In fact, the entire shallow space of the bar was revealed by this transparent façade, which allowed the lush materials and the shiny percolators in the interior to attract passers-by.

Inside, Siclis strived to make the space seem larger by a number of spatial and decorative means. The bar is placed along the back wall in a series of curves in order to create the impression of greater depth. An undulating fresco over the bar seems to disengage itself from the wall because of the hidden lighting above. The mirrors beneath the fresco allow the space to appear wider than it actually is. Siclis used the

161 La Maison du Café, Paris (1933)

04 The façade seen from
across Rue du Quatre
Septembre, 1934

available height to maximum effect, emphasizing it by illuminating the pilasters with vertical light lines.

The fresco shows human figures producing and consuming coffee, executed in warm colours on a blue-green field. Both in the façade and in the interior, the pilasters were covered with onyx. This colourful material full of sparkling quartz crystals was combined with gold-coloured metals, from the huge percolators to the smallest details in the interior. The bar and counter were executed in elm with copper and bronze elements. Outside, the corner of the façade was decorated with a bronze bas-relief by Drivier, continuing the remarkable decorative scheme of the interior.[7]

Drivier, a former collaborator of Rodin, belonged to a prominent group of young sculptors known as the *bande à Schnegg*.[8] The fresco over the bar was painted by Angel Zarraga, a Mexican painter of international stature who had received the Légion d'Honneur in 1927.[9] By integrating the work of two such well-known artists in this bar, Siclis showed once more how seriously he took decorative features for his design, stimulating casual visitors to remember the bar, and visit it again.

Charlotte van Wijk

7
Christophe, D. and Letourmy, G. (eds), *Paris et ses Cafés*, Paris: Action Artistique de la Ville de Paris, 2004

8
http://gastonschnegg.chez-alice.fr/bandasch.htm (accessed 5 June 2006)

9
http://www.mexartmasters.com/cvzarraga.html (accessed 5 June 2006); http://www.mexicodes conocido.com.mx/english/cultura _y_sociedad/personajes/detalle. cfm?idsec=20&idsub=0&idpag= 2511 (accessed 5 June 2006)

Sources:

A.B., 'Café "Le Triomphe" aux Champs-Élysées', *L'Architecture d'Aujourd'hui*, December 1934–January 1935: 5

Architectures de Biarritz et de la côte basque, de la Belle Époque aux Années 30, Liège/Brussels: éd. Mardaga/IFA, 1990

Christophe, D. and Letourmy, G. (eds), *Paris et ses Cafés*, Paris: Action artistique de la Ville de Paris, 2004

Frank, N., *Art & Décoration*, 57, 1930: 179

Janneau, G., *Ch. Siclis*, Geneva: éd. 'Les Maîtres de l'Architecture' S.A., 1931

Rybczynski, W., *Home: A Short History of an Idea*, New York: Penguin Books, 1986

Sabatou, J.P., *L'Architecture d'aujourd'hui*, 2, 1934: 67–9

http://gastonschnegg.chez-alice.fr/bandasch.htm (accessed 5 June 2006)

www.mexartmasters.com/cvzarraga.html (accessed 5 June 2006)

www.mexicodesconocido.com.mx/english/cultura_y_sociedad/personajes/detalle.cfm?ids ec=20&idsub=0&idpag=2511 (accessed 5 June 2006)

05 The façade lit up at
night, 1934

**Seagram Executive Bar
Chrysler Building, East 42nd
Street/Lexington Avenue,
New York, USA
1936
Architect: Morris Lapidus**

01 Looking towards the rear
with the bottle display.
Photograph Gottscho-
Schleisner, August 1939

1
M. Düttmann and F. Schneider,
*Morris Lapidus: Architect of the
American Dream*, Basel:
Birkhäuser, 1992

The ban on the sale and consumption of alcohol in the United States during the Roaring Twenties and subsequent Depression, is the most likely explanation for the dearth of stylish bars from that period, even though the then popular Art Deco – gleaming and reflective materials, evocative lighting, painted walls and ceilings, decorative details – would have been ideally suited to the task.

The emergence of Art Deco should be seen from the perspective of technological advances that demanded a new cultural identity. Late nineteenth-century inventions such as electricity, the steel frame and the lift provided the preconditions for a new metropolitan life in skyscrapers, as eloquently described in Rem Koolhaas's Retroactive Manifesto for Manhattan, *Delirious New York*.[1] The design of the exterior of the skyscrapers of this period was a *Gesamtkunstwerk* in which teams of architects, engineers, artists and artisans collaborated

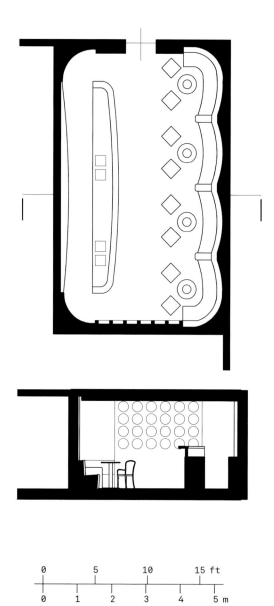

2
'Restaurant and Bar Design, Time-saver Standards, Case Studies',
Architectural Record 87, January 1940

to express the dynamism of the new age (energy, speed, automobiles, planes, trains, mass production) in combination with the old symbols of strength (such as labourers, predators, the rising sun). Interior design commissions for the skyscrapers of the 1920s and 1930s were chiefly for lobbies and lifts. Art Deco was also associated with the design of theatres, such as Radio City Music Hall.[2]

The brief: entertaining and impressing business partners
    When Prohibition was lifted in 1933, the warehouses of the Canadian Distillers-Corporation Seagram were full of fine old whisky just waiting to be exported to their southern neighbour. Such was their eventual success that in 1958 they built their own status symbol, the

164 Seagram Executive Bar, New York (1936)

04 Looking towards the
entrance. Photograph Gottscho-
Schleisner, August 1939

Seagram Building on Park Avenue in New York, designed by
Ludwig Mies van der Rohe. But in 1933 they still had to capture the
American market and to this end Seagram rented an office floor in
the Chrysler Building in New York, a quintessential Art Deco skyscraper
designed William van Alen for the eponymous car manufacturer.

To design the bar, which was intended to put clients in an
appropriately congenial mood and to provide a relaxing atmosphere
for its own personnel, Seagram engaged Morris Lapidus, who was
then 34 years of age and working for Ross Frankel, an architectural
firm specializing in retail design. The son of Russian Jewish
immigrants, Morris Lapidus had initially wanted to be an actor, but
had ended up, via the design of theatre sets, studying architecture
at Columbia University in New York. As a retail designer he applied
himself to developing concepts, techniques and forms for sales-
boosting layouts.

The notion of turning the shop interior itself into a display
window, using light and curving walls to sweep people into the store,
was one of the innovative ideas that made him famous. In 1943,
Lapidus finally set up on his own, designing many hotels with exotic,
dream interiors that contemporary architecture critics dismissed as
'eclectic'. In the 1940s, Lapidus's designs, which catered to consumers'
desires, were regarded as an offence against good architectural taste.
In the 1960s and 1970s, however, when a younger generation of
architects learned to value complexity and irony, Lapidus' œuvre
was duly rediscovered and has since received the attention of design
historians in academic publications and exhibitions. For the
design of the Seagram Executive Bar, Lapidus automatically resorted
to the vocabulary of his shop designs. The bar is a showroom of and for
its own product: bottles of alcohol. The bar represents the Seagram
image, not unlike the glass *bonbonnière* on the roof of the famous

05 Detail of the bar.
Photograph Gottscho-
Schleisner, August 1939

165 Seagram Executive Bar, New York (1936)

1931 Van Nelle factory (for coffee, tea and tobacco) in Rotterdam, albeit that the Executive Bar is hidden away in the heart of the skyscraper.

Layout and interior design

The Seagram Executive Bar measures 4.6 x 8.75 m and has a ceiling height of 2.5 m. It consists of two zones: a series of four leather settees along a curving wall and opposite these a long, free-standing bar. The bar is designed for 'leaning on' so there are no stools, just a steel foot-rail. On the wall behind the bar, a mirror reaching from counter to ceiling makes the room seem twice as big as it is and allows customers to see what is behind the bar. The walls are covered in panels of bleached rift-sawn oak and East Indian rosewood and North American plywood, combined with brown rubber tiles for the floor and leather for the settees along the wall. Bottles and glasses are casually arranged on glass shelves. The murals above the banquettes by Stuyvesant van Veen depict the production and tasting of spirits and can be seen as a nod in the direction of the Art Deco of the Chrysler Building. All illumination is in the form of fluorescent lighting and indirect: arched glass boxes directed towards the mirror are installed in the bottle display, in a cove along the curving wall and in the ceiling. The rounded corners, curving walls, indirect lighting and large round holes used as display cases can be found in all of Lapidus' store interiors.

Willemijn Wilms Floet
Translation Robyn Dalziel-de Jong

Sources:

Düttmann, M. and Schneider, F., *Morris Lapidus: Architect of the American Dream*, Basel: Birkhäuser, 1992

Koolhaas, R., *Delirious New York*, Rotterdam: 010 Publishers, 1994

'Restaurant and Bar Design, Time-saver Standards, Case Studies', *Architectural Record*, 87, January 1940

Varian, E.H., *American Art Deco Architecture*, New York: Finch College Museum of Art, 1974

Coco Tree Bar
Laemmle Office Building, Hollywood
and Vine, Los Angeles, USA
1933
Architect: Richard Neutra

01 View down from the
mezzanine, 1937

1
www.socialhistory.org/Articles/
Hoffman2a.htm, accessed
21 March 2006.

At the beginning of the twentieth century, Los Angeles truly was a
boomtown: it had grown from 100,000 inhabitants in 1900 to over
1,000,000 in 1930.[1] This attracted innovative industries such as film
production, but also the aircraft industry and numerous famous
immigrants, among them Igor Strawinsky, Thomas Mann and Bertolt
Brecht. German émigré Carl Laemmle, founder and president of
Universal Studios was also one of them.

In the 1920s, the radio and movie industries had concentrated
around the crossing of Vine street and Hollywood boulevard.

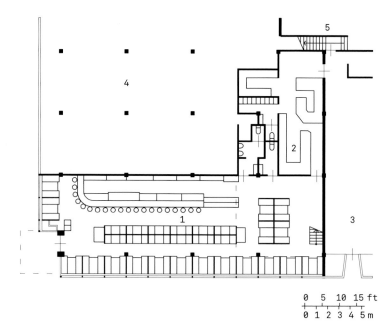

1. restaurant
2. kitchen
3. shop
4. storage
5. delivery yard

0 5 10 15 ft

0 1 2 3 4 5 m

Carl Laemmle had bought a piece of land at the northwest corner of this crossing and asked architect Richard Neutra to design a building on it. Neutra had just achieved international fame with the Lovell Beach House (1928) in Los Angeles. He was originally from Vienna, where he graduated in 1917 from the Technische Hochschule, having studied under Adolf Loos. Loos' influence proved to be profound and left a sense of richness and elegance in Neutra's work. Loos had previously worked in America and told his students enthusiastic stories about American architecture and culture. In 1923, Neutra decided to emigrate to 'this fantastic living culture of some yet unknown people'.[2] He worked briefly for Frank Lloyd Wright and with his old university friend Rudolf Schindler. In 1926, Neutra opened his own practice in Los Angeles.

2
E. McCoy, 'Richard Neutra, New York, 1960, and London, 1961', in R. Spade, *Richard Neutra*, London: Thames and Hudson, 1971 p. 11; W. Boesiger, *Richard Neutra, Buildings and Projects*, Zurich: Editions Girsberger, 1951

A bar on a street corner

Carl Laemmle wanted the design to epitomize his company: modern and up-to-date. Neutra designed a simple and elegant building with several sleek shops on the ground floor and office spaces above. Right at the intersection, he located the Coco Tree Bar, with a striking cantilevered entrance. High atop the building on either side, billboards were integrated, announcing Universal's newest release. Laemmle liked the result.

The Coco Tree Bar was a typical American lunch bar, serving simple breakfasts and lunches for employers and business people. It was likely in this case that service extended into the evening. The Viennese *Kaffeehaus* was its European predecessor and counterpart, both providing a place where one could sit down during the day, have a snack and meet informally for pleasure or business.

168 Coco Tree Bar, Los Angeles (1933)

03 The entrance on the corner
of Hollywood and Vine, with a
billboard in the top left
hand corner

The most distinguishing feature of the bar was a result of its strategic location in the building. The façades on either side of the corner with a combined length of some 25 m were made entirely out of glass. With an estimated ceiling height of 5 m, the light inside must have been striking. As a result, the bar became an integral part of the street and therefore of public life. This blurring of inside and outside was to become one of Neutra's lifelong themes and lead to truly innovative designs for private residences in the 1950s and 1960s.

The entrance of the café was on Hollywood Boulevard. A modern steel cantilever together with a big clock high above marked the entry. Once inside, the cantilever disappeared from sight and the glazed corner dematerialized. The café itself had a clear and functional layout. It was an elongated space of about 20 m deep, with a mezzanine at the back and around the corner a kitchen, adjacent to the delivery yard. The long bar in front of the party wall ran the whole depth of the café and seated 20 people.

169 Coco Tree Bar, Los Angeles (1933)

170 Coco Tree Bar, Los Angeles (1933)

Materials and interiors

The materialization of the bar was twofold. At eye level soft and lush material provided comfort and privacy, while above glass and stucco gave the café a distinctly modern and spacious atmosphere. The two rows of booths parallel to the bar contained sophisticated leather benches that were reminiscent of Loos' Kärtner Bar, a place Neutra had visited frequently as a student. But whereas Loos' bar was very much an interiorized space, with mirrors expanding the room endlessly, Neutra's café was radically turned inside out and mirrors were replaced by the transparent façade. Neutra always wanted the users of his buildings to feel comfortable. Therefore curtains were hung at eye level behind the glass to shield visitors from curious passers-by and to ensure adequate acoustics.

The food could be ordered at the bar where it was displayed in small glass showcases. Behind the bar were ice-cream machines and toasting machines; the meals were prepared in the kitchen at the back. For cigarettes, there was a special point of sale beside the counter, next to the entrance. Above the entrance was a second clock, suggestive of quick and efficient service.

At night, the bar was equally bright. The cantilever above the entrance was filled with lines of fluorescent lighting that together with the dramatic lighting of the clock and the billboards positioned the Coco Tree Bar in the nightlife of Los Angeles. Inside, concealed lighting in the ceiling ran along the perimeter of the space, ensuring a bright and brisk atmosphere and lighting the white concrete columns and beams. The cabinet behind the bar also contained concealed lighting from above. The bright interior and the lighting on the façade turned the café into a beacon in the cityscape.

[3] Spade, op. cit., p. 10

Loos' doctrine of 'lastingness'[3] in architecture, as a direct rejection of fashion and his rejection of ornament, profoundly influenced Neutra's thinking and his work. In his 40-year practice, Neutra's style remained remarkably consistent. The architect was best known for his numerous residences for wealthy clients. Tragically, one of the few bars he made had a short lifespan. Soon after Carl Laemmle's death in 1940, the building changed hands. It was entirely redecorated, the glass façades were closed and the corner was rounded. The Coco Tree Bar was turned into a fashionable cocktail bar.[4]

[4] www.lottaliving.com/bb/viewtopic. php?t=3456& (accessed 21 March 2006)

Eireen Schreurs

Sources:

Boesiger, W., *Richard Neutra, Buildings and Projects*, Zurich: Editions Girsberger, 1951

McCoy, E., 'Richard Neutra, New York, 1960, and London, 1961', in R. Spade, *Richard Neutra*, London: Thames and Hudson, 1971, p. 11

www.lottaliving.com/bb/viewtopic.php?t=3456& (accessed 21 March 2006)

www.socialhistory.org/Articles/Hoffman2a.htm (accessed 21 March 2006)

Café Kranzler
Kurfürstendamm/Johannistaler
Strasse, Berlin, Germany
1958
Architect: Dustmann, Schwebes &
Schoszberger

01 Café Kranzler on the
corner of Kurfürstendamm and
Joachimstaler Straße, 1958

In 1825, Johann George Kranzler, the Austrian confectioner
who had been promoted pastry cook to the Prussian court, opened
a coffee house in Berlin. The café-cum-patisserie was at the corner of
Unter den Linden and Friedrichstrasse (formerly known as Kranzler
Eck) and soon became a rendezvous whose popularity reached far
beyond Berlin's city limits. In 1932, following the renovation of an
existing five-storey building (dating from the post-1871 great German
economic boom) a second Kranzler business was opened. It took over
the premises that since 1900 had housed the Café des Westens,
popularly known as Café Größenwahn (Megalomania), again at a
significant street corner, called Neues Kranzler Eck on the corner of
West Berlin's main boulevard Kurfürstendamm and Joachimstaler
Strasse. And again it had its own patisserie on the ground floor and a
restaurant furnished in Biedermeier style on the first floor. After the

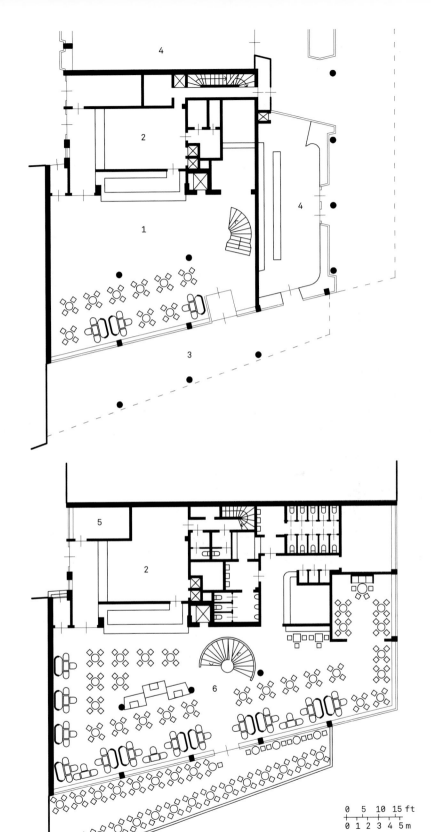

1. cake shop
2. kitchen
3. terrace
4. shop
5. office
6. café

7. espresso bar

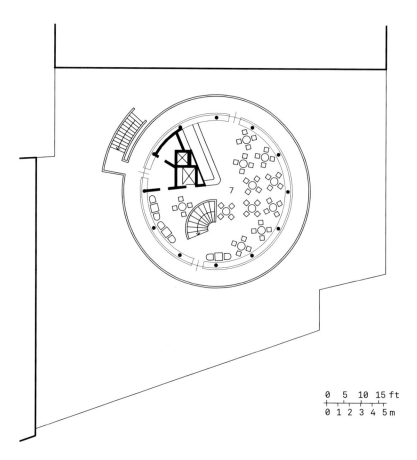

0 5 10 15 ft

0 1 2 3 4 5 m

war, a temporary café was opened in 1951 on the ruins of the old premises which soon had to make way for an entirely new café as a consequence of the post-war urban reconstruction programme.

Kranzler Eck: urban planning symbol for West Berlin
West Berlin, once the 'front-line' city, created its own, new centre in the Cold War period. Two established urban landmark structures, in close proximity to each other, marked the new centre of the western section of the divided city: the Kaiser Wilhelm Memorial Church and Café Kranzler. Both became symbols of the city of West Berlin. Even after 1961, when the building of the Berlin Wall finally cut off the historical centre, this new city considered itself the showcase of the West, the laboratory of freedom, which, significantly, also entailed freeing itself from the pre-war cityscape with its homogenous scale resulting in the development at the Zoo, Europacenter, Ku'dammeck, the Allianz high-rise offices and the Victoria Areal with Café Kranzler.

In urban planning terms, Café Kranzler is of special note. It came about in 1957–8 (opened on 17 December 1958) and was designed

174 Café Kranzler, Berlin (1958)

by Hanns Dustmann as part of the new-build of what is known as the Victoria Areal between Kantstrasse, Joachimstaler Strasse and Kurfürstendamm. A two-storey perimeter bordered the block as a whole and encompassed two courtyards. An eight-storey management and administration building carrying on from the existing neighbouring buildings and a three-storey, blank-walled cube formed the architectural border of the 'Areal'. The complex as a whole was intended to be perceived as a coherent ensemble comprising shops, offices, apartments, an indoor car park and the café, none of which stood out visibly from the rest. The original idea for a 17-storey high-rise dominating the complex was dropped.

The café was integrated in the corner of the block at Kurfürstendamm and Joachimstaler Strasse. At the intersection there was sufficient land to create a café from which one could see and be seen. A two-storey row of shops with plenty of glass, the ground floor of which is set back to form a colonnade, connects the corner structure with a department store at the corner of Joachimstaler Strasse and Kantstrasse. The street elevation at Kurfürstendamm is stacked. This seminal point of the new city in the West by no means radiates false monumentality. The only features adding a special, cheerful look to the café are the projecting gallery and balcony above, and a rotunda on top, as well as large, red-and-white striped awnings. In this way, the café part of the building stands out somewhat from the rest.

Internal arrangement: unimpeded view to the outside and open-air seating

It is clear from studying the floor plan that there were two leading themes in the spatial conception. One was to create an extremely bright, informal atmosphere in a spacious, well-lit interior, from which guests could gaze out unhampered. The other was to provide the luxury of open-air seating on every floor, as intended by the architect.

The architect Hanns Dustmann, who had made a name for himself with homes for the Hitler Youth in the Nazi era, designed a building which was not reminiscent of the war and post-war years. The character of this design was one of brightness and lightness.

For his design he applied the well-established pattern of preceding cafés: a patisserie on the ground floor, a café area opening onto a heated terrace via drop windows and a retail outlet for Sarotti chocolates. The primary spatial features of the architecture were its round columns clad in cheerful mosaic and a spiral staircase winding elegantly to the upper storeys. The first floor comprised the principal part of the café: the large space with its large balcony overlooking Kurfürstendamm and what was known as the 'china cabinet'. Large windows overlooking Kurfürstendamm characterized the spacious café area. A long wall integrating the bar and the glazed kitchen cabinets concealed all the ancillary rooms (including the washrooms) which faced the interior of the block. The spiral staircase led further to the

05 The first floor on opening day, 1958

175 Café Kranzler, Berlin (1958)

rotunda of the rooftop tea room, which afforded a splendid panoramic view of the neighbourhood. A rooftop gallery covered with a red-and-white awning served as an outdoor extension to the café, similar to the spaces on the floors below.

Ambivalence in interior design: lightness versus conventionalism

The architectural practice of Dustman, Schwebes, Schoszberger was commissioned by the operators Hotelbetriebs-Aktiengesellschaft (later Kempinski AG) to style the interior. The contemporary press praised the 'pleasant synthesis of conservative and modern taste'.[1] However, for the architects that was dubious praise, since the original design concept and the actual interior design differed considerably. The spacious, light rooms contrasted markedly with the appointments. The style did not reinforce the spatiality of the rooms, but generated a traditional respectability. In accordance with the operator's intention, the furnishings were abundant and conventional: the walls on the ground floor were panelled in cedar and on the upper floor they were covered with silk. Top-quality velvet carpet was used on the floors and chandeliers with porcelain ornaments and Murano glass provided the opulent finishing touch. The wall and picture ornamentation tied in with the tradition of the establishment and recalled highlights of Prussian architectural history: on the ground floor a marquetry picture of wall height of the old 'Unter den Linden' café at the old Kranzler Eck, a plaster engraving of Sanssouci Palace in the café on the upper floor, an artistically polished mirror in the china cabinet depicting Charlottenburg Palace.

In the china cabinet on the first floor there were changing exhibitions of china products of the *Staatliche Porzellan Manufaktur*. The ceiling in that room had china decorations with figurines, the chandelier was embellished with china ornaments. The original seating in the tea room also illustrated the ambivalence between a modern approach to architecture and traditional interior design. The space, flooded with light, which housed only an espresso bar, was originally intended to be furnished with light, randomly arranged

1
Der Tagesspiegel,18 December 1958.

06 Design for the round Tea Pavillion, by Dustmann, Schwebes & Schoszberger, 1958

176 Café Kranzler, Berlin (1958)

07 Design for the first floor, looking towards the East, by Dustmann, Schwebes & Schoszberger, 1958

tables and chairs. However, it in fact contained large tables and curved chairs in white-lacquered tubular steel. Their upholstery and design, reminiscent of the Biedermeier style, contrasted uncompromisingly with the intended lightness and delicacy, as did the heavy saddlecloth curtains and high Venetian blinds at the large window elements.

Destruction of a cultural monument

Today, following a highly controversial urban remodelling of Neues Kranzler Eck (1994–2000 Murphy/Jahn Architects, Chicago), not only has the complex been deprived of its prime architectural features, but so has Café Kranzler. The only restoration to be carried out was to the rotunda of the tea room. The ground and upper floor have been taken over by textile outlets. The exterior of the café, once an emblem of West Berlin, has suffered greatly. The delicate forms and fanciful details, such as the red-and-white striped awning and gilt mouldings which unmistakably characterized the building and made of Kranzler a synonym for the architecture of the 1950s and early 1960s, have only partially been retained. Today only the rotunda is a reminder of what was once the showcase of the West.

Holger Pump-Uhlmann

Sources:

Berlin und seine Bauten, Part VIII, *Bauten für Handel und Gewerbe*, Vol. B *Gastgewerbe* Berlin: Ernst und Sohn, 1980, pp. 94–5, 120

Rave, P.O. (ed.), *Die Bauwerke und Kunstdenkmäler von Berlin. Charlottenburg*, Vol. II: *Stadt und Bezirk Charlottenburg*, Berlin, 1961, pp. 562–4

Pitz und Hoh (Werkstatt für Architektur und Denkmalpflege), *Das Victoria-Areal. Denkmalpflegerischer Maßnahmenkatalog*, Vol. I, *Original – Veränderungen – Bestand – Empfehlungen zum Umgang mit einem Baudenkmal*, Berlin: December 1995, pp. 14–6

Splügen Bräu Beer House-Restaurant
Corso Europa, Milan, Italy
1960
Architect: Achille Castiglione

01 The café room with seating
on three different levels,
1961

The Milanese designers, the brothers Pier Giacomo and Achille
Castiglione, born in 1913 and 1918 respectively, created many
important interiors, exhibitions and objects. They practised together
from the 1930s until Pier Giacomo's death in 1968; Achille continued
the practice until his own death in 2002. Many of their celebrated,
characteristically innovative and simple designs, particularly for
furniture and lamps (such as the ubiquitous Arco), continue to be
produced today.

Birra Poretti, a Varese-based brewery, commissioned the Castiglioni brothers to design the Milanese beer house-restaurant 'Splügen Bräu': Splügen Bräu beer was prominent among its several brands. The Castiglioni brothers had designed an open-air pavilion for Poretti at a Milan trade fair the previous summer, which was a great success.[1] The restaurant was designed in 1960, and situated on the ground floor of the first of a pair of office buildings (1953–5) designed by Luigi Caccia Dominioni, an architect with whom the brothers had collaborated on several occasions.[2] It was situated in *la Racchetta*, now known as Corso Europa, a new route carved out of the historic urban fabric in the 1950s. Dominioni's buildings, with their façades of finely detailed curtain walling, faced both the new boulevard and the ancient

1
Sergio Polano, *Achille Castiglioni: Complete Works 1938–2000*, Milan: Electa, 2001, p. 145.

2
Paola Antonelli, *Achille Castiglioni,* www.moma.org/exhibitions/1997/castiglioni/essay.html

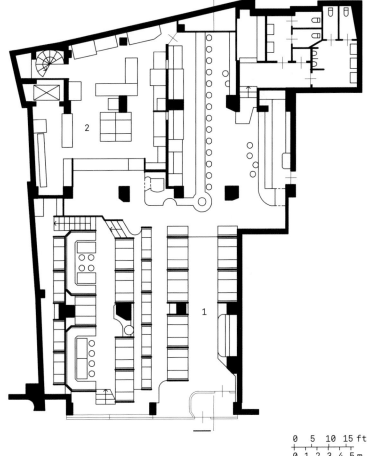

1. beerhouse/resturant
2. kitchen

02 Section

03 Ground floor

0 5 10 15 ft
0 1 2 3 4 5 m

179 Splügen Bräu, Milan (1960)

3
Astrid Staufer, *On the Work of
Luigi Caccia Dominioni, 9H no. 9
(On Continuity)*, Cambridge, MA:
Harvard University Press, 1995,
p. 130, 134

4
Antonelli, op. cit.

5
Gío Ponti, *Milano oggi*, Novara:
edizioni Milano moderna,1957,
p. x

urban fabric. They signalled the first presence of an 'American-style' architecture in the city, and were significant for their part in the representation of Italy's 'economic miracle',[3] the hard-won achievement of the concerted efforts of industry, business and culture to rejuvenate post-war Italy.

With the stated objective of 're-casting' the country arose a wealth of opportunities for the designers of products and environments.[4] Private design commissions, however, were not at the scale of public commissioning of large-scale reconstruction: they were frequently modest, limited to the design of interiors and everyday artefacts. Milan was the centre of Italian industry, business, intellectual activity and design: it hosted speculations and debates surrounding Italy's future. Milan, however, was also an ancient city with a highly developed, stratified and deeply ingrained social life.[5] Splügen Bräu's design was made in an optimistic climate with latent conflicts. Its very site was emblematic of an emerging, difficult reality.

05 Detail of the lower two
levels of the café room, 1961

A *birreria* in post-war Milan

The situation of a large *caffé* or *ristorante* in the midst of an important civic setting is utterly typical of Italian cities in which more attention is accorded to the quality of public life than financial return. Splügen Bräu's appearance in a brand-new construction and setting was significant in that it represented the enduring, flexible character of the Italian urban model. In the new cutting-edge state made by Corso Europa, new constructions abutted old, reiterating a condition typical of Italian cities in the nineteenth century, in which the demolition of city fortifications exposed edges of ancient urban centres to confrontations with large-scale urban extensions. Rather than being antagonistic, such meetings were typically softened by the inclusion of many traditional elements and aspects. The placing of Splügen Bräu in Caccia Dominioni's obviously modern building, set in the face of Milan's historical centre, is representative of this phenomenon.

Splügen Bräu was an example of the common Italian urban brewery-sponsored beer house-restaurant. Typically, such venues were simply yet solidly furnished and appointed and brightly lit, but by no means as rowdy as taverns. They served to promote breweries and their identities to urban markets. As such, they were dependable if somewhat predictable places to eat and drink, serving lunch and early dinner to a predominantly male clientele. Splügen Bräu's design, like its site, was singular in all respects. Its demands, Perotti's previous experience with the distinctive Castiglioni brothers and the association with Caccia Dominioni, contributed to their commission.

Layout and interior design

Splügen Bräu afforded a forum for the Milanese to eat, look at each other and talk. According to Achille Castiglioni, the Milanese 'are big-mouths; they like to be seen and heard'.[6] One might have expected the Castiglioni brothers to have provided an environment that reflected the manners of a modernized Milan. Yet, they recognized that Milanese manners ran deep, and their design instead recalled other aspects of the city's character. It made associations with Milan's past, its social and architectural history. Conceived very much *as* an interior, it occupied a long, high and deep space with a curtained window that obscured visibility of the street and, from outside, the interior's occupants.[7] Seating areas were distributed on three levels in tiers, as in a small auditorium or theatre. A variety of pendant lamps hung down at different heights; electrical conduits and air-conditioning ducts were painted glossy dark brown, left exposed and simply fixed to the ceiling, which was painted a tobacco colour.[8] Below this, tables were primarily arranged in narrow booths seating four people, with high backs and curvaceous side profiles in walnut, recalling the *fin-de-siècle* Liberty Style. These backs were numbered with enamelled plaques, lending the interior, according to Sergio Polano, the quality of a railway dining car. The 'accidentally' decorative accumulation of ordinary

6
Polano, op. cit., p. 158

7
Ibid., p. 160

8
Ibid., p. 158

181 Splügen Bräu, Milan (1960)

06 The corner of the bar, with a nostalgic clock and stools, 1961

elements in the heights of the room evoked the interiors of railway stations and nineteenth-century industrial architecture.

Imagery that reflected the historical process itself arose from the eclectic array of elements and their treatments. The extensive use of walnut for floors, booths and wainscotting; of polished brass and trachyte stone, baize-green upholstery and tobacco and brown paint; of traditional contours to booths and the bar; of convex mirrors, as well as the studied nostalgia of the restaurant's graphic identity (devised by Max Huber)[9] were clearly intended to speak of another time. Yet modern effects also appeared – polished aluminium pendant lights (still produced by Flos) hanging directly over each booth among ordinary modern pendants, Saarinen-esque table pedestals, and other pieces of furniture that one could only describe as contemporary reconsiderations of standard equipment such as bar stools, umbrella stands and standing ashtrays (all still in production by Zanotta) – happily settled alongside 'old-fashioned' effects. The mixture of 'Pop' and nostalgia, and the attention paid to the specific qualities of each apparently ubiquitous component – from the beer glass and bottle opener (still in production by Alessi) to the bar footrail – accorded a sense of quotidian normality to the setting. The Milanese customers, of course, also played their part.

The interior design of Splügen Bräu summarized the frequently surprising character of the Castiglioni brothers' design ethic. They valued existing, 'ready-made' objects and arrangements – particularly those 'without design' – for their usefulness, the forms that these solutions assumed and retained through time, their embodied ideas and their beauty.[10] They applied their intelligence to the repositioning, redeployment and improvement of objects for daily use, drawing lessons from other disciplines to make them fresh and alive to those who used them.

Despite protests, the interior of Splügen Bräu was demolished in the early 1980s.

Mark Pimlott

9
Ibid., p. 160

10
Alberto Bassi, *Italian Lighting Design 1945–2000*, Milan: Electa, 2004, p. 107

Sources:

Antonelli, P., *Achille Castiglioni*, www.moma.org/exhibitions/1997/castiglioni/essay.html

Bassi, A., *Italian Lighting Design 1945–2000*, Milan: Electa, 2004

Polano, S., *Achille Castiglioni: Complete Works 1938–2000*, Milan: Electa, 2001

Ponti, G., *Milano oggi*, Novara: edizioni Milano moderna, 1957

Staufer, A., *On the Work of Luigi Caccia Dominioni, 9H no. 9 (On Continuity)*, Cambridge, MA: Harvard University Press, 1995

07 Foot-rail along the bar, 1961

Niban Kan
Kabuchi-ko, Shinjuku, Tokyo, Japan
1970
Architect: Minoru Takeyama

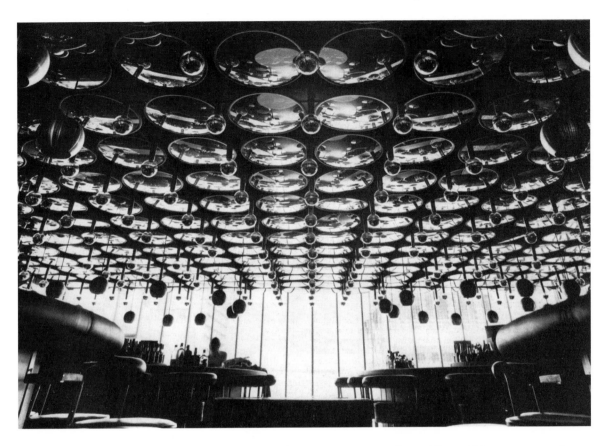

01 The ceiling finished with
light bulbs and convex traffic
mirrors, 1970

In 1964, the young Japanese architect Minoru Takeyama returned to
Tokyo, after completing a Fulbright scholarship at Harvard and
working for a variety of well-known Western architects, such as Joseph
Lluis Sert, Jorn Utzon, Arne Jacobsen and Henning Larsen. In 1970,
one of the first projects by his new office was completed: the Niban Kan
(Japanese for 'Building no. 2') in the Shinjuku district in Tokyo. This
building, which houses several bars, restaurants and a sauna, became
world famous, not in the least because it appeared on the cover of
Charles Jencks' book, *The Language of Post Modernism*.

The same two years were also crucial for Japanese post-war
culture. In 1964, the Olympics were held in Tokyo. This international
event marked the beginning of a well-organized campaign to end
Japan's isolation from the West. In order to secure the continuous
growth of the economy, the Japanese government needed to turn
around the mentality of the traditionally rather ethnocentric Japanese
people. Six years later the Osaka World Expo can certainly be regarded
as the peak of this campaign: a huge exhibition that showed an

unprecedented eagerness to assimilate the modern culture of the Western world, combined with a strong national self-confidence. More than 60 million Japanese visited this stunning circus of futuristic architectural sublime in the year 1970.

Takeyama was well aware of the debate on architecture and semiotics that started to develop at the beginning of the 1970s.

At Harvard, he came to know Charles Jencks, who picked the Niban Kan as an icon for that newly acclaimed eclectic style called Postmodernism. However, Jencks merely focused on the outer appearance of the Niban Kan and especially on the colourful graphics that cover it. The specific character of the building, regarding both its content and its context, is not taken into consideration, although both are actually quite interesting.

The Niban Kan is situated in Kabuchi-ko, a red light district that developed after World War II. It is to be found in Shinjuku, a part of Tokyo that traditionally had been a nest of vice and sin. After the war it developed into a lively quarter with a mix of housing, entertainment and commerce, attracting young people in particular. The booming economics in the late 1950s and 1960s and the immediate social and cultural effects this had could be experienced here. Both the number and the variety of more or less half-decent places of entertainment grew considerably: already in the 1970s, there were thousands of them to be found in Shinjuku. A lot of these bars, pubs and nightclubs were quite tiny: the Ichiban Kan, also done by Takeyama for the same client who commissioned the Niban Kan, offers no less than 49 rentable spaces, distributed through eight floors.

Excessive as it may seem, one has to realize that Japan has a large and rather complex nightlife-culture. Since alcohol and sex are widely accepted as a form of masculine entertainment, there is a certain openness about bars, clubs and sex joints. Most of the time, men will go out in groups, often as colleagues, but also in other socially related company. They visit a number of these places in the course of an evening and their host, often the company they work for, will spend large sums of money to entertain them. The sites for their enjoyment all share two characteristics: they are highly expensive and strive to attain an aesthetic perfection in their appearance, both in the interior and in the service and looks of the female personnel. Although less delicate and exclusive than the more traditional bars and clubs in other parts of Tokyo, the new Shinjuku joints in the early 1970s made an attempt to create a striking sensual appearance that would relate to a young audience.

In 1970, unlike today, the Niban Kan certainly stood out among the surrounding buildings, which consisted of a Japanese mix of traditional wooden houses, Western style Art Deco cinemas and other structures. Not only was it significantly taller, but it also had a feature that linked it to that burst of brand new 'communication-architecture' that was being celebrated in nearby Osaka that year. From a distance one simply could not ignore the colourful 'dazzle painting'

02 Niban Kan seen from the street, 1970

184 Niban Kan, Tokyo (1970)

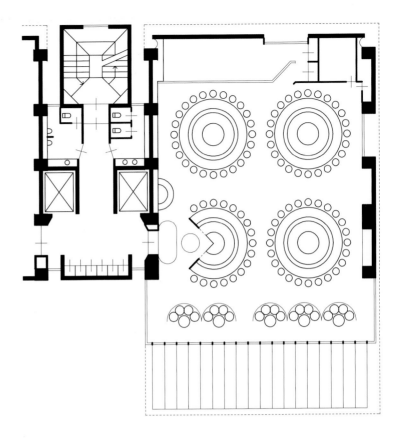

0   5   10 15 ft
+---+---+---+
0 1 2 3 4 5 m

that covered it. Not the architect himself, but a graphic designer, Kiyoshi Awazu, was commissioned to give this collection of bars and restaurants a striking appearance that could cope with the immediate urban landscape in this seedy area.

But a closer look reveals that, besides the highly effective paint-job, the volumetric composition of the building itself is also quite impressive. Basically, it is a silo-like structure, with an exaggerated vertical tower containing stairs and elevators and an enormous full glass bay window, facing the main street. The first two floors feature rental spaces on what appears to be two small open decks with direct access to the street by an open staircase. Here, Takeyama merely provided the outdoor space with features like heavy concrete railings and tiles that resemble the pavement of the surrounding streets. An elevated part of the railing indicates the entrance to the upper floors, where a number of bars, restaurants and a sauna are to be found, all managed by the client himself.

Takeyama not only designed this entrance and the various spaces for circulation behind it, he was also responsible for some of the interiors, like one particular bar on the third floor. If a visitor came in from the street and took the stairs to the third floor, he would immediately be surrounded by a multitude of small concave mirrors stuck on the adjacent walls and ceiling. After entering a bright red, heavy pivoting door with rounded corners and all, he would enter

185 Niban Kan, Tokyo (1970)

04 Interior view showing
round bar and the reflection
of the entrance in a mirror,
1970

a room with a shiny black floor and four large circular bar elements. Each element is a bar in itself, situated around a circular plateau with all kind of bottles on it, as a celebration of alcohol. The circular furniture, all done in the same bright red leather, is excessively reflected in what certainly is the main feature of this 180 m^2 bar: a continuous repetition of ordinary convex traffic mirrors, 450 mm in diameter, suspended from the dark ceiling and stuck to three of the walls. Light bulbs on stainless steel tubes, positioned in between every four mirrors, enhance the psychedelic effect that would knock even the most hardened drinker off balance after the first sip. One façade is completely glazed and provides a view to the street. Near this façade one finds five small tables with some chairs. Placed against the railing in front of the glass façade is a tilted mirror, which reflects the light effects created by the hundreds of mirrors in the interior to the upper floors, as is suggested by a section drawing published by the architect. This bar, officially called a 'restaurant' so that its opening hours extend into the night, clearly displays the psychedelic 1970s style that somehow quite precisely expressed the image that Japan wanted to encourage in those years. Unlike the better-known Metabolists, who linked a Pop style with utopian ideas of some kind of overall planning, Takeyama undoubtedly took a more realistic position that explored issues of communication and a popular language within both the limits and challenges of commercial architecture.

Jurjen Zeinstra

Sources:

Bognar, B. (ed.), *Minoru Takeyama,* London: Academy Editions, 1995

Seidensticker, E., *Tokyo Rising: The City Since the Great Earthquake*, New York: Alfred A. Knopf, 1990

Takeyama, M., 'Omni-Rental-Stores: Ni-Ban-Kahn', *JA-The Japan Architect*, 45(8-166), August 1970: 63–70

van Wesemael, P., *Architecture of Instruction and Delight: A Socio-historical Analysis of World Exhibitions as a Didactic Phenomenon*, Rotterdam: 010 publishers, 2001

05 A wall covered with convex
traffic mirrors, 1970

Café Costes
4-6 Rue Berger, at the corner of
Place des Innocents, Paris, France
1984
Architect: Philippe Starck

01 View of the staircase and
mezzanine, 1984

The appearance of Café Costes marked a turning point in the
development of café interiors. In a Paris that boasted countless
numbers of traditional neighbourhood cafés, this café that aimed at a
young clientele was exceptional. It came about through the cooperation
between Costes and Starck, who both have since established
themselves in their respective fields. Like many of the café owners in
the French capital, the proprietor, Jean-Louis Costes, came to Paris
from the Auvergne to open a bistro, together with his brother. They
have since opened a series of places-to-be in Paris (cafés, restaurants,
a hotel, all aimed at a young, fashionable and privileged clientele),
but the Café Costes was the first, and it put their name on the map.

1. café
2. kitchen
3. bar

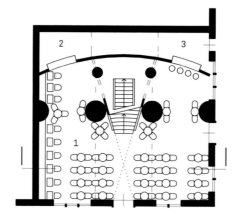

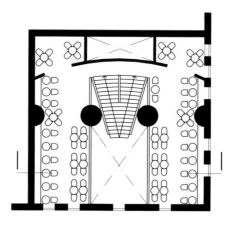

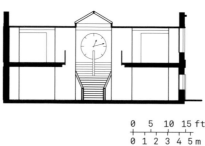

Paradoxically, according to the Costes brothers, it was also their least successful project. The café existed for ten years but it was eventually closed as the area of Les Halles had started to attract a different kind of visitor who was not interested in the café. The collaboration with Starck started with a chance encounter when Jean-Louis Costes had just bought the first shop of three that were to become the Café Costes. Altogether it took three years to buy all the property that was needed to make the 600 m^2 café. During this time the design kept evolving, until eventually the first floor was bought as well and the design was executed.

Starck started his career in the 1970s as a designer for Italian furniture producers, his real breakthrough, however, coincided with the

188 Café Costes, Paris (1984)

05 The corner of Place des
Innocents and Rue Berger,
1984

design of the café. Besides working on the Costes, Starck had designed
the Élysée offices and apartments of President Mitterrand (1982).
His success, reflected and enlarged by the attention of the media,
earned him nicknames such as 'the messiah of French design'.
His success continued, for instance, through his designs for Alessi in
the 1980s and 1990s.

Functional organization and layout

Outside on the ground floor, the façades of the three different
shops were unified by a smooth finish and by windows of the same
height and crisp detailing. The two identical public entrances were
emphasized by lighting and a pediment. Along both façades, three rows
of terrace tables and seats were placed closely together.

Entering the café from the Place des Innocents one was met by a
view of the central staircase flanked by two gigantic columns, a view
made iconic because it appeared in so many publications. An abstract
version of this fragment of the floor plan literally became the icon of
the café, appearing on the menu and the awnings. The two columns
flanking the stairs were in fact the middle ones in a row of four that
roughly divided the premises in half. Their function was to provide
stability for the construction, a structural necessity resulting from
joining together three rickety old buildings.

Functionally, the available space was divided at roughly three-
quarters of the depth, where on the ground floor a curved screen hid
the kitchen area from view. The spaces communicated through a
buffet-type opening partially hidden behind the stairs. Bar stools

06 Downstairs; on the right,
behind the column the curved
screen with the opening to
the kitchen is just visible,
1984

provided alternative seating here. The same screen was continued
upstairs, where it created two more intimate niches. The back walls of
these niches were entirely covered with mirrors, which created the
impression of a continuous space. The screen was made to appear as
a loose element rather than a wall, the sides and top not touching
the walls and ceiling.

The seating arrangements on the ground and first floor
mezzanines were similar; a long leather bench ran along the wall
and small café tables with three or four chairs filled the space.
Rows of small mirrors were hung along the walls over the benches.
The chairs used were the specially designed 'Costes' chairs, three-
legged, with a leather seat and curved plywood back. These chairs
became a design success of their own accord, appearing in a lot of
other cafés and restaurants.

Interior decoration and fittings

Underneath the grand staircase to the first floor a more modest
flight of stairs led to the toilets in the basement. The toilets were
not the cramped and unpleasant spaces they tended to be in cafés.
At the foot of the stairs one first reached an antechamber with two
symmetrically placed black columns and design objects displayed in
cases embedded in a mirror wall. On either side of the right-hand
column was a door, one to the ladies and one to the men's room.
Beyond that point men and women were in very different worlds, the
ladies room was entirely clad with glass and mirrors, very bright and
crisp. The men's room was darker and featured a highly reflective
stainless steel urinal in the shape of a water wall. According to Starck,
the thought behind the toilets was that if the spaces looked good and
clean, people would keep them tidier. Interestingly, the toilets were so
successful that many people visited the café just to see them, resulting

07 A row of wash basins in
the ladies toilets, 1984

in a trend of designing remarkable toilets (not just in Paris, but also elsewhere, especially in Barcelona). The newly established Japanese Association for the Improvement of Public Toilets even made Starck their honorary chairman.

The staircase itself was made out of pistachio-coloured terrazzo, and appeared to be of a piece with the floor of the same material. Its shape, narrow at the bottom and wider at the top, combined with the narrow cleft left between the stairs and the columns, made it look as though the staircase had been squeezed in. The columns themselves were of a huge scale and unrefined finish that appeared to belong to a utilitarian building rather than an intimate space intended for socializing. Together these elements created the impression that the café had been inserted into a leftover space underneath a towering superstructure.

The drab colours of the interior, the artificial skylight and the homogeneous way the ground floor ceilings are lit make the atmosphere appear rather flat. Intentionally, because Starck wanted the space to be melancholy; the project's working title was: 'Sad and beautiful as the buffet of Prague's railway station'. The text that ran along the top of the wall on the first floor read 'QUE DOMINE UN PETIT FORTIN', which does not actually mean anything, just something to occupy the visitor for a while. The overall intention was to create an interior that would involve and challenge the visitor. With that in mind, its elements, although all functional, are shaped and finished in a way that is out-of-the-ordinary and thought-provoking. This strategy may have worked even better than expected; the out-of-scale clock at the top of the stairs is a good example. At the time, a lot was made of the fact that it always showed the wrong time, but according to Starck, this was just due to a faulty mechanism.[1] Starck's point was that when everybody could see what he or she wanted in it, the café would make everybody feel at home, an essential requirement for a successful social space.

Charlotte van Wijk

1
Domus, 880, supplement, April 2005: 78

Sources:

Bertoni, F., *The Architecture of Philippe Starck*, London: Academy Editions, 1994

Bouvard, H., *NRC Handelsblad*, 17 August 2003

Breitman, M., 'Philippe Starck, designer-architecte', *Arch, mouvement, continuité*, 7, March 1985: 26–31

Colin, C., *Starck*, Tübingen: Wasmuth, 1989

'Die Erinnerung an das Bistro', *Werk, Bauen und Wohnen*, 72/39(3), March 1985: 32–5

Fitoussi, B., 'Chance and Necessity', *Domus*, 880, supplement, April 2005: 74–8

Schomberg, B. (ed.), *Philippe Starck*, Cologne: Taschen, 1991

Zsa Zsa Bar
Carrer del Rosselló 156, Barcelona,
Spain
1988
Architects: Dani Freixes and Vicente
Miranda

01 View towards the back,
in the background the wooden
shelves in front of the
toilet block, 1988

1
Dani Freixes, interview 10 March
2006

The cocktail bar Zsa Zsa in Barcelona was commissioned in the late 1980s, a period characterized by the economic boom and newly gained freedom after the repression of the Franco regime had come to an end. These circumstances brought about a blossoming of cafés, bars and nightclubs – their number increased fifty-fold in a little more than a decade[1] – attracting (new) young urban professionals with a diverse range of highly designed interiors that were influential beyond Spain. Though part of this general trend, Zsa Zsa distinguishes itself from most of the new bars by exploring subtle innovations in typology and decoration that are achieved with a minimum of means.

192 Zsa Zsa, Barcelona (1988)

Zsa Zsa was designed by Dani Freixes, a Catalan architect who started his practice in Barcelona in 1971. Freixes established himself as an exhibition designer, but soon started to work – currently together with his office *Varis Arquitectes* – on diverse projects, ranging from interior commissions to architecture and landscape design. Exhibition design continues to be a substantial part of his office's portfolio.

A central feature of designing exhibitions is the staging of objects and information through the careful control of artificial light. Freixes exercised this skill in his early commissions and continued it in the design of commercial interiors. In these, the manipulation of artificial light and, in addition to this, of surface textures is used to construct atmospheres rather than to stage objects and information. Zsa Zsa, which was realized in 1988, might be seen as exemplary of this approach.

Context

The Zsa Zsa Bar is located in Carrer del Rossello, which is part of the *Eixample*, Cerda's grid that was adopted for the extension of Barcelona in 1866. The neighbourhood lies to the west of the major axis *Passeig de Gracia* in the historically less affluent part of the grid. It typically consists of residential tenement buildings with a commercial ground floor. The on-average six-storey buildings were erected around 1900 in a moderate industrialized eclecticism.

The narrow and deep ground floor of Zsa Zsa (7.3 x 28.5 m) is characteristic of commercial space in this type of city fabric. Less typical, however, is the arrangement of the street frontage, divided into three sections by a centrally-placed core providing access to the apartments on the upper floors, leaving no more than a corridor of 2.5 x 11 m on either side.

The client was a private entrepreneur without any previous experience of running a licensed bar. He did not particularly want an ambitious project; in the brief, however, he expressed the desire for a flexible space to be able to suit different types of customers.

Typology

Freixes observed that the character of the Barcelona bar had changed in the early 1980s:

In 1982, in the time span of a single year, three important modifications took place: Chairs were taken out of the bars; coffee was no longer available; and the music became much louder. Socially, too, the bar turned into a different place. People would no longer visit a bar only in a group of people that they knew, but now they would also go on their own looking for opportunities to flirt as well as to find out about job possibilities. The bars in Barcelona started to become showrooms of the city dwellers, where you would go to see and be seen.[2]

2
Ibid.

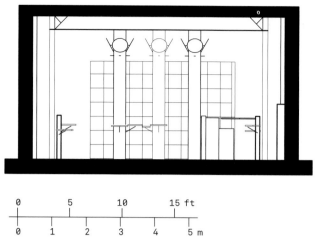

1. bar
2. crate storage
3. bottle
   showcase

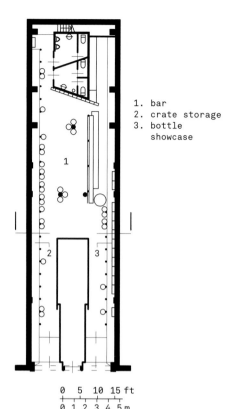

0   5   10 15 ft

0 1 2 3 4 5 m

02 Floor plan

03 Section

0   5   10   15 ft

0   1   2   3   4   5 m

3
H. Wagner, 'Schankstätten und
Speisewirtschaften; Kaffeehäuser
und Restaurants', in: J. Durm
(ed.), *Handbuch der Architektur*,
Part 4 Anlage und Einrichtung der
Gebäude, IV Vol. Gebäude für
Erholungs-, Beherbergugngs- und
Vereinszwecke (Stuttgart: Kroner,
1904), p. 16

4
Ibid.

5
www.barcelona.to/bars.htm
(accessed 28 May 2006)

The *Handbuch der Architektur* would probably have classified this bar as a modification of the typology of the American Bar, a type that was considered appropriate for an active business crowd preferring short bar visits.[3] The *Handbuch* describes how drinks were consumed standing or leaning against stools as the most characteristic feature of the American Bar. The spatial solution of this type of bar is simple. A single rectangular room is dominated by a long bar counter, where the customers order and consume their drinks. Subordinate spaces are organized in such a way as not to disturb the main space. The *Handbuch* also depicts a distinctive decorative feature of the American Bar: 'The open shelves behind the bar counter [are] equipped with long rows of twinkling bottles of finely cut glass, filled with multi-coloured content and mostly very flashy inscriptions.'[4]

The Zsa Zsa Bar shows these typological and decorative principles employed in an innovative way. The plan is simple: a box against the back wall contains the lavatories, leaving space for an anteroom on one side and the kitchen on the other; both are open to the main space. This configuration, which mirrors the situation at the street front, allows the experience of the lot to its full depth.

A typological novelty is constituted by the way in which the storage rooms have been integrated into the scheme. They are contained in an unconventionally proportioned space of 70 cm wide and 28.5 m long. The impetus for this *poché* space that is created by glass walls placed in front of both sheer walls is in first instance rational rather than artistic: because of this setup the main space of the bar is kept as deep as possible.

Decoration and interior effects
Entering the Zsa Zsa, a patchwork made of reused, cut-up and then reassembled rugs is what first catches the visitor's eye; it dresses

04 Calle Rossellon; the entrances to the bar are hidden behind steel shutters during the day, 2006

the apartment core. But the predominant decorations determining the gist of the atmosphere are those that are related to the two long glass walls delineating the *poché*.

Directly behind the glass wall opposite the bar counter, 4 mm-thick resin panels are suspended from the ceiling with cast-in birch-wood veneer. In a Miesian fashion, the grain of the material itself becomes the decorative pattern of the wall. Backlit, it fills the bar with an amber-coloured haze, establishing a warm and almost domestic atmosphere, while in actuality, it is only hiding the profane crates of non-alcoholic beverages. In contrast, the luxurious and expensive spirits are stored unhidden in the *poché* on the other side of the room. Here the 'long rows of twinkling bottles of finely cut glass' extend from behind the counter into the storage space, thus forming the decoration of an entire wall.

The light conditions on either side of the glass screen, which are made of Cool Lite glass, determine whether their appearance becomes either hyper transparent or reflective. When illuminated from the back, they become the backdrop decoration described above; lit from the front the bottles disappear and the glass walls appear as dark mirrors, visually widening the space of the bar and reflecting the decorations on the opposite wall. Technically, this is achieved with conventional light fittings (simple light bulbs, halogen down lights and wall washers), whose luminosity is managed by a light control system with five programmed settings. Each setting creates a slightly different atmosphere that suits all times of the day (pre-dinner, post-dinner, late night hours), of the opening hours (9:00 p.m. to 3:00 a.m.) and the number of visitors.

Two decades after the initial opening of the Zsa Zsa a new owner and general changes in Barcelona bar culture have left their traces. The dimmest light setting, meant for late hours only, is used all night. Christmas lights have entered the *poché* behind the bar. The more contemporary icon of the DJ has replaced the iconic giant fruit bowl at the bar, as if the presence of louder music needed a visual explanation. Meanwhile, Zsa Zsa is advertised as attracting a 'sophisticated business crowd' who wish to 'enjoy a quiet evening'.[5]

Acknowledgements

The author would like to thank Dani Freixes for kindly providing background information on Zsa Zsa in a conversation on 10 March 2006 and Cecilia Rueda Ruiz for acting as an interpreter.

Udo Garritzmann

Sources:

Wagner, H., 'Schankstätten und Speisewirtschaften; Kaffeehäuser und Restaurants', in J. Durm (ed.), *Handbuch der Architektur*, Part 4 *Anlage und Einrichtung der Gebäude*, IV Vol. *Gebäude für Erholungs-, Beherbergugngs- und Vereinszwecke*, Stuttgart: Kroner, 1904, p. 16

www.barcelona.to/bars.htm (accessed 28 May 2006)

05 View towards the front, with the carpet-clad block containing the staircase and caretaker's office of the apartments above, 1988

MAK Café
Österreichisches Museum für
angewandte Kunst, Stubenring 5,
Vienna, Austria
1993
Architect: Hermann Czech

01 View of the café towards
the front bar

The Viennese architect Hermann Czech contributed a series of
designs for cafés, which have managed to establish themselves as
institutions in the city, despite the fact that none of them could
be described as a nostalgic recreation of the pre-World War I
Kaffeehaus. Rather, these establishments, which include the Kleines
Café (1970–4), the Wunder-Bar (1975–6), the 'Salzamt' restaurant
(1981–3) and the bar and restaurant in the Palais Schwarzenberg
(1982–4) could be described as exercises in reconsidering the café: they
use known patterns of planning and architectural elements, such as
mirrors, upholstered benches or samll, sometimes bent wood chairs, to
create environments that are unmistakeably new and, at the same
time, disappear and become absorbed into their surrounding culture.
'A café does not have to be noticed, one should *remember* it' ('ein Lokal
muss man nicht merken, man muss es *sich* merken'), Czech wrote,
suggesting that a successful design convinces not by being spectacularly

1. vestibule
2. garbage storage
3. café

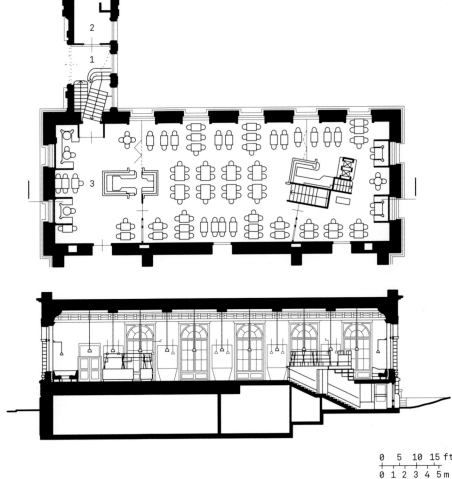

1
Hermann Czech, 'Nur keine
Panik', in *Zur Abwechslung,
Ausgewählte Schriften zur
Architektur*, Vienna: Löcker, 1996,
p. 63

visible but should work at an unconscious level. Czech has summed up his approach in the dictum: 'Architecture is not life. Architecture is *background*. Everything else is *not* architecture.'[1] A design cannot be treated as an isolated event, but must be inscribed into the longer history of cities and the ways in which these have been shaped and used. Every design, whether refurbishing an existing building or a new construction on an 'empty' site is essentially an act of *re*-building (*Umbau*), a modification of an existing situation.

Context: a café in a museum

These concerns for a design approach that allows for appropriation and invites reflections about how history is manifest in architectural conventions and patterns of everyday use, operate productively in a contemporary context and inform the design for a large café on the Ringstrasse, designed in 1990–3. This café, part of the Museum für Angewandte Kunst (MAK, Museum of Applied Arts), was located in what had been an exhibition room. The museum building itself dates

197 MAK Café, Vienna (1993)

04 The entrance on Stubenring

from the 1860s and was designed by Heinrich von Ferstel, who is also the author of the exchange building housing the Café Central (case study on p. 112). Founded as the Austrian response to the 1851 London World Exhibition and the South Kensington museums, the Österreichiches Museum für Kunst und Industrie (as it was then called) had the task of raising the quality of industrial production in the country by presenting exemplary good design to artists and industrials. Von Ferstel's neo-Renaissance building was one of the artistically consistent public buildings on the Ringstrasse.

Functional layout and organization

Czech found a well-proportioned room of about 10 x 30 m with ceilings more than 6 m high, facing both the Ringstrasse and the garden at the back of the museum, lit by large windows on three sides. The main existing architectural feature was a polychrome coffered ceiling and its articulated grid of stuccoed beams and panels. Given the specific character of the room, its dimensions and decorations, the architect decided that the design needed to retain and accentuate the existing, rather than make an attempt to compete with it.

The layout of the MAK Café, consequently, was simple. Two bar units, positioned in the centre line, one placed along this axis, the other turned at an angle, introduced a tripartite division into a space overlooking Ringstrasse, a central part and one facing the garden: the front room as a place for informal encounter and the dining area divisible at the rear bar unit, which contained a pair of service lifts to the kitchen in the basement. The oblique position of the staircase down to the garden exit, optimizing space for kitchen and lavatories, defined the equally oblique position of this bar unit. From both bars, movable partitions could be pulled into the room in order to support the overall division. The two bar units were executed in natural maple with cases for dining glasses and bottles above.

Furniture and fittings

The furniture was chosen to support the proposal of a large monumental room with sections that could be opened up or separated, depending on the time of day or the predominant use as a place for morning coffee and late evening drinks or for dining, also for press conferences and other events. Aluminium lamps, forming a series of anonymous industrial objects and suspended not too high from von Ferstel's ornate ceiling, would establish a sense of neutrality, but also create varied lighting situations below and lend the tall room intimacy at night. In addition to this, the ceiling could be lit by fixtures concealed on top of the bar cases. Custom-designed Thonet chairs, their backs adjusted to allow a reclining position, were used throughout. Dressed in a white coating except for the lower part of the legs, these chairs appeared weightless and, at the same time, revealed the material qualities of the wood. Small tables introduced horizontal

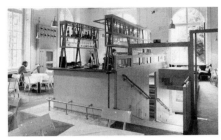
05 The rear bar with on the right the stairs to the garden

mirrors, their black tops reflecting the neo-Renaissance ornament of the ceiling. It was in the careful treatment of the relationships with the outside world, the boulevard and the garden, that particular attention was required. Raised approximately 2 m above street level, the café needed both to be made accessible and visually present to its surroundings.

Czech introduced an entrance by opening up the existing panelling in the rustica of von Ferstel's connecting passage between the museum and the applied arts school building, being a mere symmetrical fake equivalent of a gate into the garden. This door gave access to a vestibule with a free-standing flight of stairs, set at an angle departing from the orthogonal geometry of the building and lit by a large lamp of frosted glass as used on one of Vienna's modern bridges across the Danube. Inside, Czech revived the bench positioned against the niches of the windows on the short sides of the café room, relating to the exterior, the boulevard and the garden in a fashion that is deeply embedded in the tradition of the Viennese *Kaffeehaus*. On the internal wall facing the museum, small round windows allowed a glimpse of the adjacent exhibition spaces, rendering the café into a showcase display of informal sociability and giving a highly controlled, theatrical presence to the museum, as if viewed through a looking glass.

Exploiting these elements which epitomized the qualities of the *Kaffeehaus*, its comfort and festive tranquillity, and reworking them into a contemporary interior full of subtle visual relationships, the MAK café established itself as a social institution. The intelligence of the architectural solutions suggested that Viennese traditions, which only too often are monopolized by the tourist industries, could indeed be reinvented and made productive for contemporary urban culture. Its combination of subtle readjustment and simple, bold planning could, however, hardly be used when a new generation of café owners decided to exploit the space as a flagship restaurant for their chain of franchises selling the image of modern Austrian cuisine and hospitality. The MAK café was gutted in June 2005 to be replaced by a new and spectacular design for a restaurant that makes every effort to be noticed and marketed throughout Europe.

Christoph Grafe

Sources:

Almaas, I.H., *Vienna: Objects and Rituals*, Cologne: Ellipsis/Könemann, 1997

Czech, H., 'Nur keine Panik', in *Zur Abwechslung, Ausgewählte Schriften zur Architektur*, Vienna: Löcker, 1996, p. 63

Gijsberts, P.J., 'Umbau', *Archis*, April 1994: 28–43

06 View towards the rear, with the front bar

Schutzenberger
29, Rue des Grandes Arcades,
Strasbourg, France
1999
Architect: Jean Nouvel

01 The central zone, seen
from the mezzanine

The Schutzenberger Company can be considered typical of the traditional beer industry of Alsace. Founded in Strasbourg in 1740, the brewery until recently remained one of the last two independent family-owned businesses. The Schutzenberger family provided the city with several councillors and the brewery's former head Rina Muller was the president of the Alsace Brewers' Syndicate between 1997 and 2004. This company is well known for innovation and the quality of its beers: it was, for instance, the first to introduce canned beers, or to propose aromatic brews for its female audience. When the factory itself was relocated to Schiltigheim, just north of Strasbourg, in 1866, the family

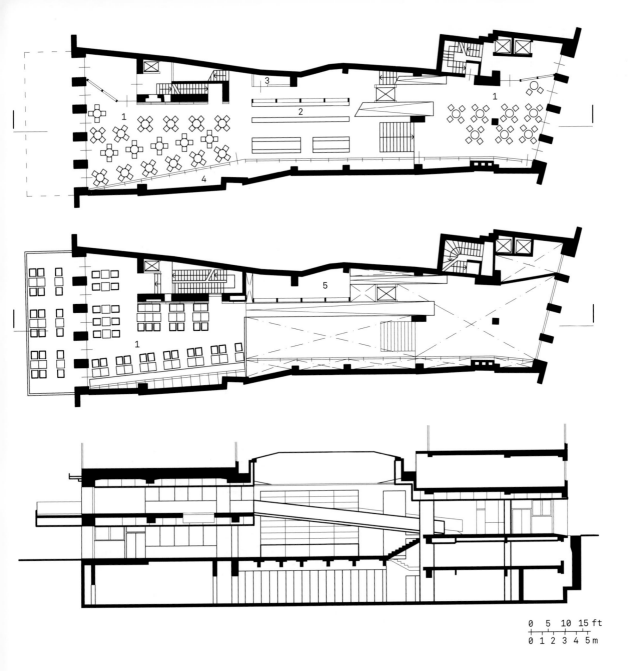

1. pub
2. bar
3. cloakroom
4. projection room
5. control room

opened the *Palais de la Bière* in the city centre, in order to sell the beers produced by the brewery. By the 1930s, the centrally located pub had become a highlight of Strasbourg social life, serving food and remaining open almost 24 hours a day.

When Marie-Loraine Muller became head of the brewery in 2004, large corporate breweries like Kronenbourg had already used their financial power to expand throughout France. Chain restaurants had appeared, both in suburbs and city centres; there, customers were welcomed in reconstituted interiors following the model of the *Bierstube*, and were served traditional dishes and beers from Alsace.

201 Schutzenberger, Strasbourg (1999)

05 The basement storage space
seen through the glass wall

For the refurbishment of the *Palais de la Bière* in 1999, the Schutzenberger Company adopted an alternative strategy. Its history and know-how prevented the owner from turning to folklore, and Marie-Loraine Muller commissioned Jean Nouvel to renovate the interior and to reinterpret the tradition of the *brasserie* (brewery) and the *Bierstube*. The old name *Palais de la Bière* was abandoned, and changed into *Schutzenberger*, in an attempt to label the struggling brewery as an exclusive quality brand. Unfortunately, innovation and daring design proved insufficient to make business better, and the company was declared bankrupt on 19 April 2006. The future of the pub is now uncertain.

Functional organization and layout

The Schutzenberger has a long and narrow footprint, 8 m wide by 40 m long. This footprint is the result of joining together two buildings on opposite sides of a city block by covering the courtyard between them. As a result, the *brasserie* has entrances on both the Place du Temple Neuf and the Rue des Grandes Arcades. The difference in level between the square and the street led to unusual relations between the various floor levels in the building. Because of the lower street level on the side of Rue des Grandes Arches, the first floor here becomes a mezzanine floor in relation to the rest of the pub. This level is connected to the upper ground floor by a long bridge-like ramp that crosses the central space, running above the bar.

Coming in from the Place du Temple Neuf, one descends via a wide staircase down to the former courtyard, where the bar is situated. In this central zone a double or even triple height space allows subdued daylight to enter from above, where the original curved glass brick ceiling has been preserved. Because the ground floor level on the side of the square is higher, it was possible to make an extra floor in the basement here, which houses the kitchen. The large lower basement floor houses the guest toilets, facilities for staff, machine rooms and storage spaces.

Interior decoration and fittings

The Schutzenberger is a large pub, with a usable surface of 900 m². Traditional elements, such as wooden floors and the zinc-topped table appear throughout, while detailed in a contemporary way. In order to provide variety, the pub was subdivided into zones with different furniture, all designed by the Jean Nouvel Design Office. The lower ground floor features traditional small café tables with yellow and orange plastic chairs. In the central zone, directly in front of the bar, a zinc-clad interpretation of a typical long beer table with benches is combined with a large reading table. The upper ground floor is a lounge area with low upholstered armchairs.

To the building structure itself, Nouvel applied methods familiar to his work, such as the application of techniques for the projection of images in order to efface the physical limits of the building.

06 The upper ground floor

This feature dominates the ground floor of the interior: a semi-reflective glass wall was placed along the length of the pub, facing the bar. From the space behind this wall images of old logos and ads of the Schutzenberger brewery are projected onto it. The projections also show what is happening in the pub and on the square and street directly outside the Schutzenberger, and occasionally film fragments. The projections and the reflections of the interior and visitors together blur the boundaries of the space and make it feel less constrained. Large mirrors, suspended from the ceiling at different angles, add to the overall visual confusion. In the basement, the same semi-reflective glass wall was applied differently; here it exposes the storage spaces to the view and in the toilets themselves the space directly behind the wall.

On the mezzanine, which houses the restaurant area of the Schutzenberger, upholstered sofas are placed along the party walls and the rest of the seating is a combination of plastic chairs and upholstered sofas. This space is not just different in function but also in atmosphere. The feature of the reflective glass wall is missing here, replaced by a wall covering of convex mirrors. Artificial lighting is provided by down lights placed above a suspended ceiling of transparent cloth, resulting in a warmer light.

In the rest of the pub, artificial lighting is provided by the glass wall and throughout the pub light boxes with pink, yellow and red neon appear. The central area is also lit from behind the bar, where backlit shelves display bottles and glasses. The result is a rather dark bar, better suited to night use than for a morning cup of coffee, but this was probably to be expected from such a beer-related establishment.

Charlotte van Wijk and David Vernet

Sources:

Boissière, O., *Jean Nouvel*, Basel: Birkhäuser Verlag, 1996

'Brasserie Schutzenberger', *El Croquis*, 4/5(112/113), 2002: 130–7

Hinkfoth, U., 'Abendliches Mirakel', *Archithese*, 34(3), May/June 2004: 64–7

Moldoveanu, M., 'Brasserie Schutzenberger, Strasbourg', *l'Architecture d'Aujourd'hui*, 329, July/August 2000: 24, 26

www.jeannouvel.com (accessed 30 May 2006)

http://forum.touteslesbieres.fr/viewtopic.php?id=111 (accessed 30 May 2006)

http://fr.wikipedia.org/wiki/Schutzenberger_(brasserie) (accessed 30 May 2006)

Select bibliography
Compiled by
Holger Pump-Uhlmann

Albrecht, Peter, *Kaffee. Zur Sozialgeschichte eines Getränkes*, Exhibition catalogue, Braunschweig: Landesmuseum für Geschichte u. Volkstum, 1980.

Albrecht, Peter, 'Coffee-drinking as a symbol of social change in continental Europe in the seventeenth and eighteenth centuries'; *Studies in Eighteenth Century Culture*, 18 (1988): 91–103.

Andreini, Laura (ed.), *Cafés & Restaurants*, Kempen: te Neues, 2000.

Aslan, Carlo and Dru, Line, *Cafés, Restaurants*, Stuttgart: Krämer, 1991.

Ball, Daniela U. (ed.), *Kaffee im Spiegel europäischer Trinksitten*, Zürich: Johann-Jacobs-Museum, 1991.

Bernart Skarek, Brigitta, 'Konglomerat von alten und neuen Wertvorstellungen. Gaststätten in Japan', *Architektur*, 7(4), 2001: 34–7.

Bernier, Georges, 'Paris cafés: their role in the birth of modern art' [exhibition], 13 November–20 December, 1985.

Bersten, Ian, *Coffee Floats, Tea Sinks: Through History and Technology to a Complete Understanding*, Sydney: Helian, 1993.

Beynet, Agricol, *Les Chroniques du Palais-Royal: origine, splendeur et décadence*, Paris 1881.

Binder, Hartmut, *Wo Kafka und seine Freunde zu Gast waren: Prager Kaffeehäuser und Vergnügungsstätten in historischen Bilddokumenten*, Furth im Wald: Vitalis, 2000.

Biziere, Jean Maurice, 'Hot beverages and the enterprising spirit in 18th century Europe', *Journal of Psychohistory*, 7, 1979: 135–45.

Blas Vega, José, *Los cafés cantantes de Sevilla,* Madrid: Cinterco, 1987.

Bödecker, Hans Erich, 'Le café allemand au XVIIIe siècle. Une forme de sociabilité éclairée', *Revue d'histoire moderne et contemporaine*, 37, 1990: 570–88.

Bodor, Ferenc, 'Old coffee houses', *Magyar epitömüveszet*, 4, 1985: 58.

Boettcher, Jürgen, *Coffee Houses of Europe*, London: Thames and Hudson, 1980.

Bologne, Jean Claude, *Histoire des cafés et des cafetiers,* Paris, 1993.

Borrás, Tomás, 'Los cafés literarios', *Villa de Madrid*, 3(12), 1959: 30–5.

Bossio, Jorge Alberto, *Los cafés de Buenos Aires: reportaje a la nostalgía*, Buenos Aires, 1995.

Bramah, Edward and Bramah, Joan, *Coffee Makers,* London: Bramah Coffee Museum, 1989.

Brandstätter, Christian (ed.), *Das Wiener Kaffeehaus*, Munich: Molden, 1978.

Brewster, Pomeroy, *The Coffee Houses and Tea Gardens of Old London*, Rochester, 1888.

Burgert, Helmuth, *Das Wiener Kaffeehaus*, Tirol: Heimat-Verlag, 1937.

Buß, Georg, 'Kaffee und Kaffeehäuser', *Westermanns Monatshefte*, Braunschweig, 1908.

Caradec, François, *Le café-concert*, Paris, 1980.

Christophe, Delphine and Letourny, Georgina (eds), *Paris et ses Cafés*, Paris: Action artistique de la ville de Paris, 2004.

Clayton, Antony, *London's Coffee Houses: A Stimulating Story*, London: Historical Publications, 2003.

Condemi, Concetta, *Les cafés-concerts: histoire d'un divertissement (1849–1914)*, Paris: Quai Voltaire, 1992.

Constantin, Marc, *Histoire des Cafés-Concerts et des Cafés de Paris*, Paris, 1872.

Coste, René, *Les cafetiers et les cafés dans le monde*, 3 vols, Paris, 1955, 1959, 1961.

Courtine, Robert, *La vie parisienne*, vol. 1, *Cafés et restaurants des boulevards: 1814– 1914*, Paris: Perin, 1984.

Cunow, Heinrich, *Politische Kaffeehäuser: Pariser Silhouetten aus der Grossen Französischen Revolution*, Berlin: J.H.W. Dietz, 1925.

Delvau, Alfred, *Histoire anecdotique des cafés et cabarets de Paris*, Paris, 1862.

Depaule, Jean-Charles, 'Conteurs et cafés du Caire', in *Lectures du roman de Baybars*, 2003, pp. 201–8.

Devoto, Alberto, *De los cafés de Buenos Aires*, Buenos Aires, 1995.

Diament, Jacques, *Les cafés de philosophie: une forme inédite de socialisation par la philosophie*, Paris: Harmattan, 2001.

Dias, Marina Tavares, *Os cafés de Lisboa*, Lisbon, 1999.

Díaz, Lorenzo, *Madrid: tabernas, botillerías y cafés (1476–1991)*, Madrid, 1992.

Díaz y de Ovando, Clementina, *Los cafés en México en el siglo XIX*, Mexico: Univ. Nacional Autónoma de México, 2000.

Duis, Perry, *The Saloon: Public Drinking in Chicago and Boston 1880–1920*, Urbana, IL: The University of Illinois Press, 1983.

Dru, Line, *Les Cafés*, Milan, 1988.

Ecker, Ludwig, *250 Jahre Wiener Kaffeehaus. Festschrift des Gremiums der Kaffeehausbesitzer in Wien zur Erinnerung an die Gründung des ersten Wiener Kaffeehauses*, Vienna. 1933.

Eleb, Monique, *La Société des Cafés – Los Angeles*, Paris: Éditions de l'Imprimeur, 2004.

Eleb, Monique and Depaule, Jean-Charles, *Paris – Société des Cafés*, Paris: Éditions de l'Imprimeur, 2005.

Ellis, Ayton, *The Penny Universities*, London: Secker and Warburg, 1956.

Ellis, Markman, *The Coffee House: A Cultural History*, London: Weidenfeld and Nicolson, 2004.

Erki, Edit, *Kávéház-sirató: törzshelyek, írók, mhelyek /válogatta és az összeköt szöveget írta*, Budapest, 1995 [Budapest coffee houses of the past as meeting places for writers, actors and artists].

Espinàs, Josep Maria, *Quinze anys de cafès de Barcelona, 1959 - 1974*, Barcelona, 1975.

Espinàs, Josep Maria, *Obra Completa*: vol. 8: *Escrits sobre Catalunya*, 2, *ciutats de Catalunya: cafés de Barcelona*, Barcelona, 1994.

Excellent Shop Designs, vol. 28: *Cafés, Restaurants, Bars*, Tokyo 1986 (Shten-kenchiku: Bessatsu, 28).

Fitch, Noël Riley, *Die literarischen Cafés von Paris*, Zürich: Artemis, 1993.

Fosca, François, *Histoire des cafés de Paris*, Paris: Firmin-Didot, 1934.

Girouard, Mark, *Victorian Pubs*, New Haven, CT: Yale University Press, 1984.

Girveau, Bruno, *La belle époque des cafés et des restaurants*, Paris: Musée d'Orsay, 1990.

Gomes, Danilo, *Antigos cafés do Rio de Janeiro*, Rio de Janeiro, 1989.

Gorham, Maurice, 'The Pub and the People', *The Architectural Review*, October 1949, p. 213.

Gugitz, Gustav, *Das Wiener Kaffeehaus. Ein Stück Kultur- und Lokalgeschichte*. Vienna: Deutscher Verl. f. Jugend u. Volk, 1940.

Haine, W. Scott, *The World of the Paris Café: Sociability among the French Working Class, 1789–1914*, Baltimore, MD: Johns Hopkins University Press, 1996.

Hattox, Ralph S., *Coffee and Coffee houses: The Origins of a Social Beverage in the Medieval Near East*, Seattle: University of Washington Press, 1996.

Hazeu, Wim, *Literaire Cafés van Antwerpen*, Amsterdam, 1993.

Heering, Kurt-Jürgen (ed.), *Das Wiener Kaffeehaus*, Frankfurt: Insel, 1993.

Heise, Ulla, *Kaffee und Kaffeehaus: eine Kulturgeschichte*, Leipzig: Edition Leipzig, 1987 (English edition: *Coffee and Coffee Houses*, West Chester: Schiffer, 1987).

Heise, Ulla, *Histoire du café et des cafés les plus célèbres*, Paris, 1988.

Hess, Alan, *Googie: Fifties Coffee Shop Architecture*, San Francisco: Chronicle, 1985.

Hoffmann, Paul, 'Aus dem ersten Jahrhundert des Kaffees. Kulturgeschichtliche Streifzüge', *Zeitschrift für Kulturgeschichte*, 8, 1901: 405–41 and 9, 1902: 90–104.

Huddleston, Sisley, *Bohemian Literary and Social Life in Paris: Salons, Cafés, Studios*, London: Harrap, 1928.

Jones, Colin and Spang, Rebecca, 'Sans-culottes, sans café, sans tabac: shifting realms of necessity and luxury in eighteenth-century France', in M. Berg and H. Clifford (eds), *Consumers and Luxury: Consumer Culture in Europe, 1650–1850*, Manchester: Manchester University Press, 1999, pp. 37–62.

Jünger, Wolfgang, *Herr Ober, ein Kaffee! Illustrierte Kulturgeschichte des Kaffeehauses*, Munich: Goldmann, 1955.

Kafe-resutoran: 62 Outstanding Cafés, Tea rooms, Café-bars, Restaurants, Tokyo, 2002.

Kindblom, Maria and Kondisboken, Johan, *Klassiska svenska kaféer och konditorier*, Stockholm, 2003.

Koch, Alexander, *Restaurants, Cafés, Bars*, Stuttgart: Koch, 1959.

Kracauer, Siegfried, 'Caféhaus-Projekte', *Frankfurter Zeitung*, 25 November 1921.

Kracauer, Siegfried, 'Die Frau vor dem Café', *Frankfurter Zeitung*, 13 September 1926.

Kracauer, Siegfried, 'Café im Berliner Westen', *Frankfurter Zeitung*, 17 April 1932.

Kracauer, Siegfried (G. Hellfried), 'Seminar im Café', *Frankfurter Zeitung*, 29 April 1933.

Kraus, Karl, 'Die demolierte Litteratur', Vienna, 1897 (pre-publication *Wiener Rundschau* 15 November, 1 December, 15 December 1896 and 1 January 1897).

Krulic, Brigitte, *Europe, lieux communs: cafés, gares, jardins publics . . .*, Paris: Éditions Autrement, 2004.

Langle, Henry-Melchior de, *Le petit monde des cafés et débits parisiens au XIXe siècle: évolution de la sociabilité citadine*, Paris: PUF, 1990.

Leclaut, Jean, 'Le Café et les cafés à Paris (1644–1693)'. *Annales*, 6 (1951), S. 1–13.

Lemaire, Gerard-Georges, *L'Europe des Cafés*, Paris: Koehler, 1991.

Lemaire, Gérard-Georges, *Theoriés des Cafés*, 2 vols, Paris: IMEC éditions, 1997.

Lepage, Auguste, *Les Cafés politiques et littéraires de Paris*, Paris, 1885.

Lummel, Peter (ed.), *Kaffee – vom Schmuggelgut zum Lifestyle-Klassiker: drei Jahrhunderte Berliner Kaffeekultur*, Berlin: bre bra Verlag, 2002.

Maddox, Adrian, *Classic Cafés*, London: Black Dog, 2003.

Mauro, Frédéric, *Histoire du café*, Paris, 1991.

May, Herbert und Andrea Schulz (eds), *Gasthäuser. Geschichte und Kultur*, Petersberg: Imhof, 2004.

Michelena, Alejandro, *Los cafés montevideanos*, Montevideo, 1986.

Moderne Cafés, Restaurants und Vergnügungsstätten: Aussen- u. Innenarchitektur. Berlin: Polak, 1928.

Nairz, Joerg, 'Das Kaffeehaus. Renaissance einer Institution', *architektur aktuell*, 19(101), 1984: 29–30.

Neumann, Petra (ed.), *Wien und seine Kaffeehäuser: Ein literarischer Streifzug durch die berühmtesten Cafés der Donaumetropole*. Munich: Heyne, 1997.

Oberthür, Mariel, *Cafés and Cabarets of Montmartre*, Salt Lake City, Utah, 1984.

Oldenburg, Ray, *The Great Good Place: Cafés, Coffee Shops, Bookstores, Bars, Hair Salons, and Other Hangouts at the Heart of a Community*, New York: Marlow & Co, 1999.

Pegler, Martin M. (ed.), *Cafés and Coffee Shops*, New York: Retail Reporting Corporation, 1995.

Pegler, Martin M. (ed.), *Cafés and Coffee Shops No. 2*, New York: Visual Reference Publications, 2001.

Peña Muñoz, Manuel, *Los cafés literarios en Chile*. Santiago de Chile, 2001.

Peressut, Luca Basso, *L'architettura del caffè: tradizione e progetto in Europa*, Milan, 1994.

Polgar, Alfred, 'Theorie des Café Central', in Alfred Polgar, *An den Rand geschrieben*, Berlin: Rowohlt, 1927.

Rauers, Friedrich, *Kulturgeschichte der Gaststätten*, Berlin: Metzner, 1941.

Reinders, Pim and Wijsenbeek, Thera, *Koffie in Nederland*, Zutphen: Walburg Pers, 1994.

Roca, Maria Mercè, *La màgia dels cafès*, Barcelona, 1992.

Rocca, Pablo, *Montevideo: altillos, cafés, literatura (1849–1986)*, Montevideo, 1992.

Roden, Claudia, *Coffee*, London: Faber, 1977.

Rössner, Michael (ed.), *Literarische Kaffeehäuser, Kaffeehausliteraten*, Vienna: Böhlau, 1999.

Sampelayo, Juan, 'Noticias y anécdota de los cafés madrileños', *Anales del Istituto de Estudios Madrileños*, 6, 1970: 507–27.

Sapparelli, Bruno, *Des bruits, des cafés, des hommes*, Geneva, 1983.

Scevola, Annamaria, *New Bars, Cafés and Pubs in Italy*, Milan: L'Archivolto, 2001.

Schivelbusch, Wolfgang, 'Der Kaffee als bürgerliche Produktivkraft'. *Ästhetik und Kommunikation. Beiträge zur politischen Erziehung*, 9, 1978: 5–20.

Schivelbusch, Wolfgang, *Das Paradies, der Geschmack und die Vernunft. Eine Geschichte der Genussmittel*. München: Hanser 1980; (English translation, *Tastes of Paradise: A Social History of Spices, Stimulants, and Intoxicants*, New York: Pantheon, 1992).

Schmidt, Karl August, *Geschichte des Pariser Cafégastes*, Berlin, 1909.

Smith, Woodruff D., 'From coffee house to parlour. the consumption of coffee, tea and sugar in north-western Europe in the seventeenth and eighteenth centuries,' in J. Goodman (ed.), *Consuming Habits: Drugs in History and Anthropology*, London: Routledge, 1995, pp. 148–64.

Spiel, Hilde, 'Das Kaffeehaus als Weltanschauung'; *Wien. Spektrum einer Stadt*, Vienna: Biederstein, 1971.

Teply, Karl, *Die Einführung des Kaffees in Wien. Georg Franz Koltschitzky, Johannes Diodato, Isaak de Luca* (Forschungen und Beiträge zur Wiener Stadtgeschichte, vol. 6), Vienna, 1980.

Timbs, John, *Clubs and Club Life. With Anecdotes of its Famous Coffee Houses, Hostelries and Taverns from the Seventeenth Century up to the Present Time*, London: Chatto and Windus, 1898.

Torberg, Friedrich, 'Das Kaffeehaus'; in *Wien. Vorstadt Europas*. Zürich: Artemis, 1963.

Vernes, Michel, 'Cafés de Paris', *Architecture intérieure. C.R.E.E.*, 220, 1987: 88–95.

Wagner, Heinrich, *Handbuch der Architektur* (general ed., Eduard Schmitt), Teil 4: Entwerfen, Anlage und Einrichtung der Gebäude, Halb-Bd. 4: Gebäude für Erholungs-, Beherbergungs- und Vereinszwecke, Teil: H. 1: *Schankstätten und Speisewirtschaften, Kaffeehäuser und Restaurants. Volksküchen und Speiseanstalten für Arbeiter, Volkskaffeehäuser. Öffentliche Vergnügungsstätten. Festhallen. Gasthöfe höheren Ranges. Gasthöfe niederen Ranges, Schlaf- und Herbergshäuser*. Stuttgart, 1904 (3rd edn.).

Welter, Henri, *Essay sur l'histoire du café*, Paris, 1868.

Westerfrölke, Hermann, *Englische Kaffeehäuser als Sammelpunkte der literarischen Welt im Zeitalter von Dryden und Addison*, Jena: Frommann, 1924.

Index